A CHRISTIAN'S GUIDE TO REFUTING
MODERN
ATHEISM

KYLE BUTT

AN EXPANDED STUDY OF THE BUTT/BARKER DEBATE

Printed in China
Cover by Rob Baker
Layout by Moisés Pinedo

All Scripture quotations are from The New King James Version of the Bible, unless otherwise specified. Copyright © 1982, Thomas Nelson, Inc.

Apologetics Press, Inc.

230 Landmark Drive
Montgomery, Alabama 36117

© Copyright 2010
ISBN: 978-1-60063-032-3

Library of Congress Cataloging-in-Publication

Kyle Butt (1976 -)

A Christian's Guide to Refuting Modern Atheism

Includes bibliographic references

ISBN: 978-1-60063-032-3

1. Apologetics & polemics. 2. Religious ethics. 3. Creation. I. Title

212—dc22

ACKNOWLEDGEMENTS

Generally speaking, the list of people that an author acknowledges holds little value for the majority of people reading the book. Many of the readers know very little about the author personally, and they know much less about the people being acknowledged. In reality, acknowledgments are little more than a list of names without faces to most readers. Yet acknowledgements represent an extremely important aspect of a work such as the one you are reading. In the first place, they show the author's reliance on the ideas and resources of others, often much more qualified than himself. In addition, they underscore the human element that is necessarily involved in a book. Books are not lifeless ink on paper, they are interactive ideas that originated from the energetic minds of real people. Finally, acknowledgements help the reader to see that books are labors that require patience, understanding, and effort from a community, not just an individual. In that light, I would like to acknowledge the following people. First and foremost, I express my extreme gratitude to my Creator Whose existence was the focus of the debate, and Who has supplied humanity with copious evidence of His reality. Next I would like to thank my delightful wife Bethany Anne Butt who patiently listened for months to my incessant recapping of the issues involved in the debate. To Thomas Baxley, who repeatedly engaged me in "mock debates" to help me prepare, I owe my gratitude. In addition, I would like to thank the men from Apologetics Press who contributed their works to this book: Dave Miller, Eric Lyons, and Caleb Colley. I would also like to acknowledge Wayne Jackson who contributed to the book, and whose trenchant thoughts have been invaluable to me through the years. His Web site www.ChristianCourier.com contains a wealth of outstanding apologetic material. To my parents, mother and father-in-law, brothers and their families who all attended the debate, thank you for the support. And to the group of men from Montgomery, Alabama who discussed, prayed, and fasted with me, thank you. And to all the others who have helped edit, design, print, and distribute this work, may God bless you all.

ABOUT DAN BARKER

Dan Barker is a former denominational minister and evangelist who became an atheist in 1983. Since that time, he has been one of the most prolific and outspoken atheists in the world. He joined the Freedom From Religion Foundation in 1987 and served as its Public Relations Director until 2004, when he was elected co-president of the Foundation. Currently, the FFRF has approximately 14,000 members and is one of the largest atheistic organizations in existence. Dan has written several books including, *Just Pretend: A Freethought Book for Children*, *Losing Faith in Faith: From Preacher To Atheist*, and *Godless: How An Evangelical Preacher Became One of America's Leading Atheists*. The foreword to *Godless* was written by Richard Dawkins, arguably the most notable atheist of the last two decades. Barker is recognized in the atheistic community as one of its most able debaters. The "Year In Review" section of the FFRF Web site noted that he participated in 13 debates in 2009. Throughout his career, he has participated in approximately 75 debates. In *Godless*, he claims that he has been involved in more timed, moderated debates than any other atheist (2008, p. 68). Some of those debates include:

"Did Jesus Rise from the Dead?" A debate with Michael Horner at the University of Northern Iowa (1996)

"Does God Exist?" A debate with Richard Howe at the University of Florida (1997)

"Does the Triune God Live?" A debate with Douglas Wilson at the University of Delaware (1997)

"Does God Exist?" A debate with Rubel Shelly at the University of Alabama in Birmingham (1998)

"Does God Exist?" A debate with Tom Rode at Ohio State University (1999)

"Does God Exist?" A debate with Phil Fernandes at Bellevue Community College (2000)

"Did Jesus Rise from the Dead?" A debate with Mike Licona at the University of Wisconsin (2003)

"Does Ethics Require God?" A debate with Peter Payne at the University of Wisconsin (2005)

"Does God Exist?" A debate with Todd Friel at the University of Minnesota (2006)

"Evolution and Intelligent Design—What are the Issues?" A debate with John Rankin at the New Testament Church in Plymouth, Massachusetts (2006)

"Christianity versus Atheism," A debate with Dinesh D'Souza at Harvard University (2008)

"The Bible: Fact or Fiction?" A debate with Mark Chavalas at the University of Wisconsin-LaCrosse (2009)

"Can We Be Good Without God?" A debate with Dan Waugh at Indiana University (2009)

"Can We Be Good Without God?" A debate with Dinesh D'Souza at the University of Minnesota (2009)

"Can We Be Good Without God?" A debate with Kevin Cauley Texas State University (2009)

"The Jesus Story is Cut from the Same Cloth as Other Ancient Mythologies." A debate with James White at the Newberg Christian Church in Newberg, Oregon (2009)

"Without God We are Nothing." A debate with George Pell at Macquarie University (2010)

"Is Christianity the One True Faith?" A debate with Greg Clarke at the University of Wollongong (2010)

ABOUT KYLE BUTT

Kyle Butt is a Christian apologist who graduated from Freed-Hardeman University with a B.A. in Bible and Communication and an M.A. in New Testament Studies. He has authored or co-authored more than 20 books, including *Out With Doubt: A Look at the Evidences for Christianity*, *Behold! The Word of God: Exploring the Evidence for the Inspiration of the Bible*, *Truth Be Told: Exposing the Myth of Evolution*, and *The Dinosaur Delusion: Dismantling Evolution's Most Cherished Icon*. For over nine years he has served as the editor of *Discovery* magazine, a monthly periodical about Scripture and science for third through sixth grade children. Kyle has worked in the Bible department at Apologetics Press for more than a decade. Apologetics Press is a tax-exempt, non-profit organization dedicated to the defense of New Testament Christianity. This was Kyle's first formal debate.

ABOUT THE EVENT

The debate was held on the campus of the University of South Carolina in Columbia on February 12, 2009. It was sponsored by the atheistic student organization known as the Pastafarians. The debate was a part of the Darwin Day events that were scheduled to commemorate the 150th anniversary of the publication of *Origin of the Species*, and the 200th anniversary of Darwin's birth. The venue for the debate held approximately 550 people and was filled to capacity. According to various reports from those who attended, between 150-250 people were turned away due to fire code restrictions. The debate was streamed online via a live Internet feed, with an estimated audience of 25,000. Shortly thereafter, it was made available in DVD format, with several thousand distributed. The debate was also posted on Internet video sites such as YouTube.com and Housetohouse.com. At the time of the printing of this book, an estimated 50,000 to 100,000 people have watched the debate.

TABLE OF CONTENTS

PREFACE

The debate format offers a unique perspective on an issue. It combines the personalities of the disputants, with the strengths or weaknesses of each position in a way that encourages interaction between two views. In many cases, publically debating a proposition can help uncover the flaws and inconsistencies of a particular position, while at the same time bringing to light the truth and validity of other beliefs. In some ways, a debate is one of the most valuable ways to analyze the truth of any position.

The debate format, however, does have its weaknesses. One of those is the simple fact that time must be a factor. Public debates cannot go on indefinitely. There is an agreed upon amount of time given to each disputant. The live audience's attention span and ability to sit and listen must factor into the decision about the proper amount of time. Generally speaking, a few hours are about all that an audience can take. Because of this necessary time limitation, there will always be some issues that cannot be addressed fully during the debate.

Written exposition does not have the time limitation of a debate. Although writing lacks the dynamic interaction between live personalities, the reader can put the book down at any time, come back to it at his leisure, skim to important issues, or digest slowly and repeatedly before moving on to the next idea. Thus, it seems necessary to consider both public debate and written discourse as valuable tools to arrive at the truth of any statement.

On February 12, 2009, I was invited by a secular student organization of the University of South Carolina to debate the well-known atheist Dan Barker. Barker is the co-president of the Freedom From Religion Foundation, the largest atheistic organization in North America. The debate took place on the campus of the University of South Carolina in Columbia. The venue for the debate held about 550 people. It was filled to capacity, and several were turned away due to seating limitations. Barker affirmed the proposition: "I know the God of the Bible does not exist." I denied that proposition. The entire debate lasted about two hours with alternating speeches from Dan and myself and an audience question segment that lasted about 30 minutes.

The debate generated great interest in both the Christian and the atheistic communities. After the debate, we at Apologetics Press received hundreds of e-mails, phone calls, and letters asking for copies of the debate, asking questions about certain points, or simply expressing appreciation for our participation. Because of the excitement stirred by the debate, it became apparent that a more complete handling of the issues discussed in the debate would be beneficial. Thus Apologetics Press determined to make the debate available in written format, combined with a complete refutation of various ideas brought forward during the debate in favor of atheism: the resource you are now reading.

In order to get the most out of this resource, you will need to understand the format. Under the section title: "The Debate," we have included the complete transcript of the debate. Under the section title: "The Refutation," we have taken statements or arguments Dan used to support atheism and thoroughly analyzed and refuted them. We have not expounded on every statement made by Barker for two reasons. First, we felt that several of the answers given in response to Barker during the debate were sufficient to refute his comments. Second, we felt some of the statements had little or no bearing on the topic and did not need an answer.

The refutation of Barker's arguments has been a collective effort by those at Apologetics Press. Much of the material was written prior to the debate and slightly adjusted to fit this format. Since some of the material appeared in independent articles, there is some repetition of certain quotes and concepts that are important to multiple aspects of the debate. Several different authors who are associated with Apologetics Press have contributed materials, so that my role in this production has often been one of an editor and not an originator of the materials. Credit to contributing authors will be given when feasible and appropriate.

Dan Barker has been recognized in the atheistic community as one of its most powerful propagators. Richard Dawkins, renowned Oxford atheist, said that Barker "is now one of American secularisms most talented and effective spokespeople." Due to the nature of the atheistic philosophy, most defenders of it use the same basic outline. Because this book is designed, not only to answer Barker's arguments, but also to answer those of the atheistic community in general, some of the refutations will be much more lengthy than would be necessary simply to answer Barker's material. It is our expectation and prayer that the refutation of Dan Barker's material will serve as a valuable guide that can be used to refute most modern atheistic attacks on the God of the Bible.

Kyle Butt

August, 2010

PART 1

BUTT/BARKER DEBATE ON THE EXISTENCE OF GOD

OPENING REMARKS BY ANDREW CEDERDAHL

Good evening. My name is Andrew Cederdahl, and I am president of the Pastafarians at the University of South Carolina. On behalf of our organization, we would like to thank everyone for coming tonight. We have a great discussion ahead. So who am I? What is all this? Where did I come from? Where am I going? What values do I endorse? These are the great questions of which we are all seeking the answers to, or at least should be seeking the answers to. Your answer to the question we present tonight, "Does God exist?" is likely to influence your answers to all other great questions. That is why the question of God's existence is one of the most fundamentally important questions we can ask ourselves.

I would like to congratulate and thank you all for agreeing to join us in this dialogue tonight. I've got to be honest, though. I'm a little disappointed at the current state of our dialogue, especially with regard to religion. It seems as though comfort, convenience, and tradition now prevail over meaningful and critical dialogue, which aspires to challenge us with the uncomfortable, inconvenient and unconventional questions. Religion has become the topic in which questioning is unacceptable. Yet we as human beings must ask these questions in our lifetimes, because the quest for answers enables development and stifles the crude onset of static indifference towards the very questions which make life fulfilling. Socrates said that the unexamined life is not worth living, and I couldn't agree more.

Tonight we recognize that asking the question of God's existence constitutes one of the most integral parts in an examined and, thus, meaningful life. When I was a child, I could be one of those annoying little inquirers. How many people used to be annoying little inquirers when they were children? I know I was. I wanted to know why things were the way they were, and I wanted to see things for myself. So, not surprisingly, Santa Claus was an early target in my young and misguided quest to tackle the questions of the cosmos. I wanted to see the jolly, fat man myself Christmas Eve, so I could ask him a question or two about his methods.

I devised Santa trap after Santa trap year after year, of course, taking his safety and well-being into consideration with some carefully placed pillows by the fireplace. I wanted to ask Santa how a sleigh balanced on our tilted roof and, most important, how his elves got so talented they could produce the very same products under my tree that were sold at the local Walmart. Then I wanted to ask him how companies like Walmart made their money if he simply went around making their products and giving them freely to children, scolding them in the process for the most prolific black market this world has ever seen. Of course, I was exaggerating that last part a little bit. But the moral of the story is, I risked my presence and reputation with Santa, year after year with my traps, all in the name of a few questions. Even in my six-year-old mind, I was more interested in the magic of Santa Claus than I was in a few toys.

I want to restore my childhood inquiry tonight to bigger questions, and I hope you'll join me. In growing up, I realized that my Santa escapades had become a wonderful metaphor for life. Santa represents the big questions which cause excitement and wonderment in our beautiful world. The toys represent the earthly distractions which keep us from living life to its fullest. And the Santa trap represents the free thinker who is willing to risk all reputation and judgment from society in the quest to find the truth.

I want to challenge everyone tonight, everyone from all sides, all persuasions, to temporarily abandon all the internalizations of what society has told us to believe through our lifetime and regain an appreciation for critical thinking. Examine what our debaters have to say tonight. Examine the evidence. Examine the reasons and come to your own conclusions. On this bicentennial celebration of Charles Darwin's birthday—the man who continues to evoke dialogue with the ramifications of his discoveries—let us begin the discussion. Thank you very much.

At this time, I'd like to introduce our moderator tonight. Reverend Dr. Neal Jones is a Minister of the Unitarian Universalist Fellowship of Columbia and the President of the Columbia Chapter of Americans United for the Separation of Church and State. He is one of the plaintiffs in the lawsuit which halted production of the "I believe" license plates. Please welcome to the stage Dr. Reverend Neal Jones.

MODERATOR NEAL JONES: INTRODUCTION OF SPEAKERS AND FORMAT EXPLANATION

Allow me to introduce our speakers this evening. Dan Barker is co-president of Freedom from Religion Foundation. A former minister and evangelist, Mr. Barker became an atheist in 1983. He is the author of the book *Just Pretend: A Freethought Book for Children*, and *Losing Faith in Faith: From Preacher to Atheist*. His latest book is *godless: How an Evangelical Preacher Became One of America's Leading Atheists*. A graduate of Azusa Pacific University with a degree in religion, Mr. Barker now puts his knowledge of Christianity into challenging religious belief.

A professional pianist and composer, he performs freethought concerts and is featured in the foundation's musical cassettes: *My Thoughts Are Free*; *Reasons Greetings*; *Dan Barker Salutes Freethought Then and Now*; a 2-CD album *Friendly Neighborhood Atheist*; and the CD *Beware of Dogma*. He joined the foundation in 1987 and served as the public relations director. He was first elected co-president in 2004.

Recently, the Freedom from Religion Foundation has sponsored "Praise Darwin" billboards in Dayton, Tennessee, and Dover, Pennsylvania, which, as you know, are the locations for the Scopes monkey trial and what is commonly referred to today as Scopes II up in Dover, Pennsylvania—both in order to celebrate the birth of Charles Darwin and promote science.

Our second speaker is Kyle Butt. For the past nine years, Mr. Butt has worked at Apologetics Press, a 30-year-old, nonprofit organization dedicated to the defense of New Testament Christianity. Mr. Butt graduated from Freed-Hardeman University with a B.A. in Bible and communication, and an M.A. in New Testament studies. He's the author or co-author of 20 books dealing with topics such as the existence of God, the inspiration of the Bible, the historicity of Jesus Christ, and creation-evolution debates. He is the editor of *Discovery* magazine, a monthly periodical about Scripture and science for kids. He is also the associate editor of *Reason & Revelation*, a monthly journal of Christian evidences. He frequently presents seminars around the country and has recorded several such seminars that are available on DVD. He and his wife Bethany have been married for nine years and they have three children. Please join me in welcoming our two speakers, Kyle Butt and Dan Barker. [The two speakers enter the room and stand at their respective podiums.]

Good evening, gentlemen, and welcome. Allow me just very briefly to review our format this evening to which both of you have consented. Each of you will be allowed 15 minutes to present your propositions, and then each will be allowed ten minutes apiece for rebuttal. And then, I guess in Perry Mason style, we will allow you five minutes each to cross-examine each other with brief questions and brief answers. And then we will take a very quick break to allow the cameras to change their film and allow questions from the audience. We will allow 20 minutes of that. And we will ask that our audience ask each of you alternating questions so it will be fair and equal. And then after our questions, we will allow each of you five minutes for your concluding remarks.

So we will begin with Mr. Barker. Oh, by the way, I will be strict about the time limits. When you have two minutes left, I will hold up this sheet. When you have one minute left, I will hold up this sheet. And if you persist, I will have to interrupt you, which will be hard for a Southern boy to do because we are so polite, but I will persist, and I will do what I have to do. Okay. We will start with Mr. Barker. And Mr. Barker, the proposition that you are affirming is that the God of the Bible does not exist.

DAN BARKER'S FIFTEEN-MINUTE OPENING SPEECH

Thank you. Does anybody in the house have the gift of faith healing by any chance? I just about lost my voice this week. I almost canceled. But I couldn't miss this for anything. This is really fun. Thank you, Pastafarians. Thank you, Andrew. And I guess, thank you, Charles Darwin. None of us would be here, right, if it weren't for evolution, the fact of evolution. Happy birthday, Charles Darwin. Today is his 200th birthday.

I'm not going to tell you my whole story, but you heard the title of my book. My new book is called *godless: How an Evangelical Preacher Became One of America's Leading Atheists*. I was a true believer. I believed in Jesus. I felt the Holy Spirit. I preached. I saw converts. I was a missionary. I was an evangelist, Christian songwriter. If I was not a true Christian, nobody is a true Christian. It was true within my heart. I changed my mind because I learned that Christianity is not true.

Richard Dawkins wrote a really funny forward to the book in which he says—you can tell me if this is a compliment or not— "Dan Barker is the most eloquent witness of internal delusion that I know." He's got a lot of laughs in here. You can read my story. You can read why I'm an atheist. You can read what's wrong with Christianity. And then life is good at the end. Millions of good people live happy, moral, productive, meaningful lives without believing in a god.

Usually in these debates, we debate the general question: "Does God exist, or a god exist." But tonight we're discussing a specific God. I just want to touch briefly on the general arguments, which are arguments for probability. First of all, there's no evidence for a god. If there were, by now somebody should have won the Nobel Prize for pointing that out to us, the existence of a hitherto unknown force in the cosmos. No one's done that. I used to think there was evidence. There is none.

Second, there's no coherent definition of a god. How can we debate something that we can't even define? God is defined as a spirit. But what is that? Third, there are no good arguments for the existence of a god. And apologists have come up with maybe a dozen or so different types of cosmological, first cause, prime mover and so on, teleological design arguments, ontological, moral arguments, personal experience and so on. They're all bad arguments. Most of them boil down to what we call the "god of the gaps." You find something that we don't understand yet and go, "Aha, how do you explain that? Must be a god, right?"

People who think the design argument is really powerful are kind of like the guy who says, "Look at that. How did they get all those rivers to flow right along the state borders? How do you explain that? Think of the engineering, the cost, you know. It's amazing." Or like Julia Sweeney says in her play, "Look at how a human hand was made to fit so perfectly into a glove. Look at that. Four fingers and a thumb. How do you explain that?" Well, these are bad arguments. They're backward arguments.

Number four, there are no good replies to the arguments against the existence of a god, such as the problem of evil. All you have to do is walk into any children's hospital and you know there is no God. Prayer doesn't make any difference. Those people pray for their beloved children to live, and they die. A few of them, just by chance, a few of them live; and some of their parents say, "Praise God, he answered my prayer." He must have hated those other kids.

Number five, there is no agreement among believers as to the nature or the moral principles of this God that they're arguing for. You name it. They all differ with each other. And number six is an observation. There's no need for a belief in a god. You can live a really happy, joyful, wonderful, meaningful life without that religious baggage. And I think even better.

But all of that doesn't disprove God. That shows that God is unproved. It gives us a very high level of confidence, a very high probability that there is no God. And most of the time, scientists, when they get to 95%, 98%, they round it up. Just like you and I might say, "There are no leprechauns." But can you prove that? You probably agree with me, there's no leprechauns, right? But if backed against the wall, we would have to say, well, they're highly unlikely. They might be hiding somewhere, right? But we round it off in our mind. We say, "Yeah—that's a probabilistic argument." Like the British have on the signs of their busses this month in England, "There probably is no God, stop worrying and enjoy your life," right?

But tonight's debate is not about that. Tonight's debate is about the God who is pictured in this book, the Bible. I hope you brought your Bibles, because we're going to do some Bible study here. And when you discuss a specific God, the job is much easier. We don't—in this case, we don't have to reduce it to a problem of probabilities. We can make it a question of certainty. The God that's depicted in this book certainly, one hundred percent does not exist. I know it, and you can know it as well, because it's a different type of a question. It's a question of certainty.

For example, if I said, "Do you believe in the existence of a married bachelor?" What would you say? You would say, "Well, not only does a married bachelor not exist, it cannot exist, by definition. Or a square circle." If you tell me that the God of the Bible is a married bachelor, I will say, "He does not exist." And that's how we can know that there are mutually incompatible properties and characteristics of the God that's in this book that rule out the possibility of his existence.

For example, in Malachi 3:6, God said, "I am the Lord, I change not." Yet all through the Bible we see God changing his mind. In Ezekiel 32:14, "The Lord repented of the evil which he thought to do unto his people." By the way, I'm giving one or two examples, but there are multiple examples throughout the Bible, which I detail in my book, if you want to go into greater depth. The God of the Bible does not change, and the God of the Bible does change. He does not exist. It's like a married bachelor.

In Exodus 20:5, God said, "I the Lord am a jealous God, visiting the iniquity of the fathers upon the children unto the third or fourth generation." The God of the Bible punishes people for their parents' sin. However, in Ezekiel 18:20, "The Son shall not bear the iniquity of the father." In Deuteronomy 24:16, "Neither shall the children be put to death for the fathers. Every man shall be put to death for his own sin." The God of the Bible punishes children for their parents' sin. The God of the Bible does not punish children for their parents' sin. He does not exist.

In Psalm 145:9, "The Lord is good to all." Deuteronomy 32, "He's a God of truth and without iniquity." However—and you find a lot of God is good verses in the Bible—Isaiah 45:7, God said, "I make peace and create evil." *Bara ra* in Hebrew. "I the Lord do all these things." Lamentations 3: "Out of the mouth of the most high proceedeth not evil and good." Jeremiah 18, "Thus saith the Lord, behold I frame evil against you." Ezekiel 20:25, "I gave them statutes that were not good and judgments whereby they should not live." The God of the Bible is good. The God of the Bible is not good. He does not exist.

Does God tempt people? James 1:13 said, "Let no man say I am tempted of God. God cannot be tempted with evil, neither tempteth he any man." However, Genesis 22:1, "It came to pass after these things that God did tempt Abraham." God does not tempt people. God does tempt people. He does not exist.

In Exodus 20:13 in the Ten Commandments, "Thou shalt not kill." In Leviticus 24:13, a different phrasing of it with a different Hebrew word, "He that killeth any man shall surely be put to death." However, we find in Exodus 32, "Thus saith the Lord God, put every man his sword by his side. Slay every man his brother, his companion and neighbor." First Samuel 6, "The people lamented because the Lord had smitten many of the people with the great slaughter." The Bible is filled with examples of the biblical God committing, commanding and condoning killing. The God of the Bible says, don't kill. The God of the Bible says kill. He does not exist.

Should we own slaves? Leviticus 25 said yes. The Bible is a proslavery book. "Of the children of the strangers that sojourn among you, you shall buy them and they shall be your possession. They shall be your bondsmen forever." You find all sorts of pro-slavery books in the Bible. You can sell your sons and daughters into the hands of the children, and so on. Even Jesus said that some slaves you ought not to beat as hard as other slaves. He was that compassionate. And, "Slaves, obey in all things your masters," it says in Colossians. However, Isaiah says: "Undo the heavy burdens, let the oppressed go free, break every yoke." "Neither be called masters, for one is your master, even Christ." The God of the Bible is pro-slavery. The God of the Bible is anti-slavery. He does not exist.

In Romans 15:33, we find out that he is called the God of peace. Yet, in Exodus 15:3, "The Lord is a man of war." In the Old Testament he's a war God, and you can see his actions. He's a hateful, vicious, tyrannical, brutal, discriminatory war God. The God of the Bible is a God of peace. The God of the Bible is a God of war. He does not exist.

What about his son? Jesus said, "Peace I leave with you, my peace I give unto you." And when he was born, "On earth peace, good will toward men." However, Jesus himself said, "Think not that I have come to send peace on earth. I came not to send peace but a sword." He said to his disciples, "If you don't have a sword, sell your garment and buy one." The God of the Bible is peaceful. The God of the Bible is not peaceful. He does not exist.

Jesus said, "Though I bear record of myself, my record is true." Yet a few verses earlier, he said, "If I bear record of myself, my record is not true." He contradicted himself. The God of the Bible's witness is true. The God of the Bible's witness is not true. He's a married bachelor. He does not exist.

John 1:18 says, "No man has seen God at any time." Can God be seen? No. Exodus 33, "Thou canst not see my face, for no man shall see me and live," and on and on. First John, in the New Testament, "No man has seen God at any time." However, in Genesis 32, "For I have seen God face to face." Exodus 33:11, "And the Lord spake unto Moses face to face as a man speaks unto his friend." The God of the Bible cannot be seen. The God of the Bible can be seen. He does not exist.

Is he powerful? "Behold, I am the Lord, the God of all flesh," in Jeremiah 32. "Is there anything too hard for me?" Jesus said, "With God all things are possible." And, yet, in Judges 1:19, read this: "The Lord was with Judah. He drove out the inhabitants of the mountain, but he could not drive out the inhabitants of the valley." Why? Because they had chariots of iron. God is all powerful. God cannot even fight chariots of iron. God does not exist.

Does God live in light or does God live in darkness? I Timothy 6, "The king of kings, lord of lords, dwelling in the light which no man can approach." James 1:17, "He's the father of lights." And on and on we see God is light, there is no darkness in him at all. However, in 1 Kings 8, "Then spake Solomon, the Lord said that he would dwell in the thick darkness." First Samuel 22, "He made darkness, pavilions round about him dark waters in thick clouds of the sky." Psalm 18:11, "He made darkness his secret place." So, God lives in light. God lives in darkness.

Does he accept human sacrifice? In some verses, "Yes," in some verses, "No." Remember the thing about when Abraham—he asked Abraham to sacrifice his son, Isaac. By the way, Abraham should have said, "No way, I'm better than you, I'm not going to kill my son."

Look what God said after he stopped it. He said, "Lay not thine hand upon the lad, neither do thou anything unto him for I now know that you fear God seeing that you have not withheld your son." I know now? I thought God knew everything. The Bible says God knows the future, but here he is saying I didn't even know. The Bible even says God searches and understands all the imaginations of the heart. The God of the Bible knows the future. The God of the Bible does not know the future.

By the way, if the God of the Bible knows the future, that means he knows all of his own future actions, doesn't it? He knows what he's going to do tomorrow at twelve noon, which means he can't change what he's going to do tomorrow at twelve noon. He's not omnipotent. If he does change what he was going to do, then he was not omniscient. In order to have freewill and be a person with freewill, you have to have options open to you that you can make a decision. If your decisions are predetermined in advance, you are not a free person. If the God of the Bible is defined as a free personal being who knows the future, then the God of the Bible does not exist.

Since we have no good reason to believe in a god, in general, and since the God of the Bible is defined in mutually incompatible terms, we can know as a fact that the God of the Bible does not exist. Maybe the flying spaghetti monster exists. That might be a different debate. But the God of the Bible we know with certainty does not exist.

Moderator Neal Jones: Mr. Butt, you have 15 minutes to present your proposition the God of the Bible does exist.

KYLE BUTT'S FIFTEEN-MINUTE OPENING SPEECH

Thank you. I would like to express my deep appreciation for all of you being here this evening to discuss this question of utmost importance. I would certainly like to thank Andrew and the Pastafarians for making this possible. I would certainly like to thank Dan for allowing us to have this discussion this evening. And most importantly I would like to thank my God, whose existence I am here to defend this evening.

Now, in Dan's book *godless*, Richard Dawkins says that Dan is now "one of America's most effective and talented spokespeople." Dan Barker has been involved in some 67 debates, I think he was telling me, formal moderated debates like this. He is in the upper echelons of the atheistic society. In fact, as I was looking for some things on the Internet just before this debate, I came across the JREF blog site. It looked like they had some things going on there. And they were discussing the debate and mentioning how they thought Dan was going to smash me this evening. And they said, "I think Dan is the best debater in the atheistic community." They talked about Hitchens and Dawkins and said they might have a few little flaws and they thought Dan made up for those in certain areas. And they said, "Yes, I think this debate promises to be very interesting, the way that watching a lion take down a water buffalo is interesting." So I thought that was interesting. At the bottom they said, "At least Kyle's parents weren't cruel enough to name him Seymour." Well, I think they did discuss Harry for a little while, but they decided on Kyle.

Right now in the United States of America—says George Barna in the June 11th, 2000, Barna update—about 9% of the population believe in no religion. That means about 1 out of every 11. The converse of that is that about 85% of the people in the United States of America today say they know there is a God. That means out of the 220 million adults in the United States of America today—about 180 million adults—if you were to walk up to them on the street and say, "Do you believe that there is a God," they would say, "Yes, I absolutely do believe that."

Out of 180 million adults—from what I understand the Barna research telling us—there are about 5 million that claim pure atheism. I'm certainly not suggesting this evening we should take a head count and say there are 180 million that believe in God, there are 5 million that claim pure atheism, about 20 million that would claim no religion whatsoever; thus God has it. Absolutely not. That is not what I'm saying at all. You and I both know you cannot come to truth based on majority rule. But here is what I am saying. I am saying there are some arguments that are pressing, that are powerful and that are persuasive that have convinced 180 million Americans to believe in a God.

Now, these Americans, some of them were like Dan at one time. In fact, I spoke at a small congregation just Wednesday evening, and it just so happened that two of the men in that congregation—one of them was an atheist until he was 19 and converted out of atheism. The other one was an atheist until he was 43. I asked them what caused them to convert to Christianity. And they said, "The truth of the evidence."

Sometimes Christians and those who believe in the God of the Bible are painted as superstitious, as having a faith where they will take a leap in the dark, where they do not have the evidence to prove what they believe, but they just somehow in their heart have a warm feeling and that is what they accept. But let me tell you, friends, that is not what the Bible says about faith.

In fact, the biblical faith—Jesus Christ spoke very explicitly when He said, "You shall know the truth, and the truth shall make you free." No question there. No doubts. No room for, "It is a possibility; there might be a chance; it is a 99% probability." This is a knowledge claim. And it is a knowledge claim that you can know. When Paul was standing before the Romans, Festus said, "Paul, much learning is driving you mad." What did Paul say? "Oh, no, most noble Festus, I speak the words of truth and reason." That is what we are here to debate this night, truth and reason.

Here are two of the very powerful arguments for the existence of God. They do not take a Ph.D. to understand. They do not take a rocket scientist to comprehend. They are very, very simple. But up until this time, no atheist in the history of humanity has had an adequate answer for these two arguments. Number one, here is what you know. When you see design in the material world, it demands a designer. Number two, here is what you know. There are some things that are objectively right and objectively wrong. Some things are right. Some things are wrong. And they are always right and they are always wrong.

Let's look at that first one, the idea of design. Dan said, "Wow, what about the rivers, how did they all just happen to be on the state borders?" Who do you think decided to make sure that the rivers were what divided the states? Humans. Intelligent designers were the ones that labeled those as the state borders. Just like a hand fits into a glove? Who designed the glove? Is that glove an accident of nature? Did you just walk out into the woods and pick up the glove and somehow it automatically, miraculously fit on the hand? Absolutely not. That glove was designed by an intelligent designer.

Suppose you are walking on the beach, you look down, you see something in the sand. You move the sand away. You pick up a laptop computer. You press the on button; it comes on. You see that this laptop computing device will compute information at the rate of hundreds or millions of bits per second. It has all the latest gadgets and gizmos. It is the most advanced technological computing system you have ever seen in laptop form. Now, you have a question to ask yourself. Number one, "Where did this laptop computer originate?" You know there are only two answers to that question? Number one, it originated by purely naturalistic chance processes over millions of years by random chances, working with some type of selection going on. Or, number two, it was constructed and built by an intelligent designer who purposely put the functional complexity into that computing device.

Let me ask you a very serious, very easy question. Have you ever met anybody who said a laptop computer was not designed by an intelligent person? Never. I've never seen it; never met a person that does. Right now we have a capacity crowd of 550 people in this auditorium tonight. From what I understand, several people had to be turned away, some of them flying or driving from several hours away. I'm sorry about that. But I'm glad that you have the opportunity to be here personally. Now, in this room, we've got 550 of the most amazing computing devices that have ever been devised—the human brain. The human brain weighs about three pounds in the average adult person. The human brain computes information the likes of which would make any laptop computer look like a kinder-gartner's toy.

Let me read to you a quote from a man by the name of Richard Lewin. He is a British anthropologist, and here's what he says:

> Ten billion neurons are packed into the brain; each on average has 1,000 links with other neurons, resulting in more than 60,000 miles of wiring. Connectivity on that scale is beyond comprehen-sion. For instance, the fastest computer clocks up a billion or so operations a second, which pales in significance beside the 100 bil-lion operations that occur—in the brain of a fly at rest. To say that the brain is a computer is a truism, because what goes on in there is unquestionably computation. But so far, no man-made computer matches the human brain.

Were you, as a human being, designed? It is an easy question. With an easy answer. It is a question that a 6-year-old understands very well. I was discussing this with one of the gentlemen who was talk-ing to me about the debate. He had a 6-year-old daughter. He was explaining to his daughter the two positions, me standing up for the God of the Bible, brother—Mr. Barker standing up for the idea of atheism. And the 6-year-old, when told about the atheistic idea, asked the simple question. She said, "Well, who does he think made him?" Well, who does he think made him? And I'm certainly not attacking Dan Barker whatsoever. In fact, Dan Barker is as able of a spokesman for atheism as you can possibly find. Therefore, in the course of a discussion like this, if you see that the case for the God of the Bible is stronger, then you have to lay the blame at the athe-istic philosophy, not at the defender of that philosophy.

The second idea—the idea that there are some things that are right and some things that are wrong. Are there some things that are right and some things that are wrong? Because if there are, ob-jective moral standards demand a standard outside of human likes and dislikes. If there are objective moral standards, true right and true wrong, then there must be a God in which those standards are grounded. Now, we understand that completely. In fact, that's been understood for hundreds of years, thousands of years.

When the Nazi Germans after they had brutally massacred some 10 million people, 6 million Jews, they were on trial at Nuremberg. Robert Jackson in his closing comments said that they had committed crimes against humanity and they had violated the law and, he said, a law that rose above the transient and provincial. Where would you get a law that rises above the transient and provincial? Let me tell you where you cannot get it. You cannot get it from evolutionary atheism. It is impossible.

But do not take my word for that. I am not making a statement and then not backing it up with a fact other than just my statement. Listen to William Provine. In 1998, William Provine was invited to speak on the University of Tennessee campus at, none other than, Darwin Day. He just happened to say in that particular speech that he gave, that if there is no God, then there is no ultimate foundation for ethics.

Listen to what Charles Darwin said. He said, if there is a person who does not believe in a personal God, then—and I'm going to quote him for you—he "can have for his rule of life, as far as I can see, only to follow those impulses and instincts which are the strongest to him or which seem the best to him." Darwin said, "Look, if you have a guy that does not believe in God, then the best he can do is whatever feels the best to him, that's what he needs to do." So that means that if the atheistic communists of the Nazi Germans— if they killed 6 million Jews—what Darwin said was, you just do what feels the best to you.

So if a person decided that it felt the best to him to kill, what, 6 million Jews, well, you could not say he ought to do any different. And if a person decided to spend the rest of his life selling everything that he had and feeding the poor, you could not say that he was doing right or wrong. You could simply say he was following the best impulses to him.

Dan understands this perfectly. In fact, let me tell you how well Dan understands this. The world's leading ethicist, according to Dan—I think it is on page 328, 314 of his book, *godless*, is a man by the name of Peter Singer. Peter Singer said this. In essence, he said, there is no moral difference between killing a dog, a pig or a human. Let me read the quote to you. He says:

> If we compare a severely defective human infant with a nonhuman animal—a dog or a pig, for example—we'll often find the nonhuman to have superior capacities. Only the fact that the defective infant is a member of the species *Homo sapiens* leads it to be treated differently than the dog or the pig. Species membership alone, however, is not morally relevant. If we can put aside the obsolete and erroneous notion of the sanctity of all human life, we may start to look at human life as it really is.

Here is how well Dan understands this. In his book *Maybe Right, Maybe Wrong*, he said, "Human beings are part of nature. We are not better than nature," page 26. In his debate with Paul Manata, Dan said this—and I quote—"In the end of the cosmos, it's not going to matter. You and I are like ants or rats or like pieces of broccoli really. There is no value to our species; we are not any better than nature."

What you have heard from Dan Barker is a litany of alleged Bible contradictions. We have an answer for every one of those. Most of those are simple semantic tricks that have been played by someone who approaches the Bible with the idea of skepticism in the first place. If you noticed, if a person goes down a list in a debate of some—I think there were about 20, maybe 25 of those...

Dan Barker [from his side of the podium]: Fourteen.

Kyle Butt: Fourteen. I was counting the first six reasons why he said that there were not good reasons for a God: no legitimate definition, those, etc. So that would make it right at 20. Then you can see that in a 15-minute or 10-minute debate, he is not wanting answers. There is no possible way to answer that many ideas in a ten-minute rebuttal. So what is he wanting to do? I think what he is wanting to do is try to overwhelm you. You did not even really have time to stop and think about the various individual things that he was throwing out there. And you cannot blame Dan for that. It is a very good, very popular debate tactic. But we will get to some of that in my rebuttal.

Moderator Neal Jones: Thank you. Mr. Barker, you will have ten minutes to refute Mr. Butt's arguments.

DAN BARKER'S TEN-MINUTE REBUTTAL

The six-year-old might just as well have asked, "God, who does he think made him?" If the design of the—if functional complexity requires a designer, then the functional complexity of the mind of the designer itself, by definition, by logic, also requires a designer.

If you go from a computer up to a human, you make that leap up to the human and say, "Look how amazing that human brain is who made the computer"—by the way, some computers can outperform humans in many functions. But if you're going to make that leap and say, "Look at that," well, then you look at the mind of the human and say look how amazing that is and you make another leap up to a bigger mind that's even more complex and more organized and more functional. Why are you stopping there?

If the six-year-old is justified in asking me who do I think made me, then we skeptics are justified in asking this creator of yours, who I assume you think has a pretty wonderful brain, wonderful mind that functions—it's orderly, right, pretty amazing? We're justified in asking the same question of that being. We get into an infinite regress, because then we need a creator for the God who made God, right? If you can say, well, we can stop at that level, well, then why don't we stop at this level?

Let's stop at the level of what we do know. We do know in nature complexity arises from simplicity. We do know that. The complexity of a crystal arises from the simplicity of the way molecules mathematically and geometrically can combine. We can see complexity arising around us from simpler origins. There are many examples of that—amino acids.

And we can also show how—and Darwin basically showed us—how natural selection can be the designer. Not an intelligent designer, but the designer by the limited ways that nature functions. The limited ways that molecules can put together. The limited ways arithmetically things can combine and compete—that complexity can arise from simplicity. Creationism can't do that. Creationism has to simply assume the very complexity that you are arguing for. You're saying look at that.

So your design argument falls apart logically. It is not a good answer. In Dawkins' book, he posits the Boeing 747 argument. Obviously, if there's a God, who made him? This basically is an argument from incredulity. It's not an argument from what you know. How do you connect the dots from that? Suppose I agree with you. I don't know; how do you explain this complexity? How do you connect the dots from that question, like when the ancients said who made the thunder? What happened? It must be Thor. It must be Zeus. Yet now that we know more about weather, now that we know more about electricity, that gap has closed. That god has died out. You still think that science is never going to close gaps, because there are unanswered questions about complexity, origin, the original life forms. Who are you to predict that science has reached its dead-end?

There are no objective moral values in the Universe. There are not. We make values in our brain. A value is a function of a brain that's functioning—just like digestion is the function of the stomach. Thought and values is the function of a computing brain—that you admit works, right? But we make values based upon what we need to survive, what we need to enhance our lives, what we need to avoid pain in our lives. And we make comparisons of those values. When the brains die and the values go away, they don't exist. They are not things. A value is relative to an organism.

But most atheists will say—and I don't speak for all atheists—most atheists will say values can be objectively justified. They are not objective values because a value is the function of a brain, of a mind, right? But to be objective means to exist independently of a mind. So how can you have something in the mind that exists independently of the mind? That's an oxymoron. You cannot have an objective value. You can have values that you can objectively justify by looking at your actions. And all of us do this—Christians, Jews, Muslims, humanists, atheists, agnostics. We all do this. We're all basically humanists.

We're all basically situational ethicists in our lives, and so is the Bible if you look at some of the decisions in the Bible. They were situationally justified. Rahab was praiseworthy for the lie that she told. But you have more than one option for your actions. How much harm does this one cause? How much harm does this one cause? And if you have time, you try to weigh those actions and say, "If I'm going to be a moral person, I'm going to pick the path that results in the least amount of harm." That's what morality is. It's not a big objective thing.

We flatter ourselves to think that we are somehow special in the cosmos. It's much more meaningful to accept who we really are. We are not egotistical. We should humble ourselves and realize we are part of nature. Isn't that amazing? Isn't that wonderful that we can function in this way? We are social animals. And by the way, Peter Singer is arguing not against human rights. He's arguing for animal rights. If there's no difference between animals and human beings, then let's treat other animals as if they were special, too. You're misconstruing what he was saying.

And you really stuck your foot in it this time—I'm sorry—by saying that Hitler was an atheistic communist? Did you actually say that? You did say that. He's on the record. Hitler was not a communist. Hitler was a Nazi, a national socialist. Hitler believed in a God. He was not atheistic. He talked about the creator all the time. He was a creationist. He credited Jesus as the inspiration for his exterminating the Jews. They wore "Gott mit uns"—God is with us—on their belt buckles. Those Nazis were Lutherans and Catholics. Hitler was a member of the Catholic church, never excommunicated. He credited Jesus—He was really a lousy Christian, I have to admit. He was a really weird Christian. But he was not an atheist. So correct yourself, Lyle. Hitler was not an atheist, and he was not a communist. Do a little bit of history there.

Kyle Butt: That's true. (From his podium)

Mr. Barker: And I also want to compliment you on correctly pointing out that, of course, truth is not determined by majority rule. Truth is not determined by vote. If it were, we should take the vote away from women, because most of the planet doesn't think women should have rights. In fact, none of our founders of our country thought women should vote. If we want to go back to the tradition, women should not vote, women should stay home, women should not go to college, women don't even own their own property. This all comes out of the Bible, by the way.

But we know there are principles of truth that transcend majority rule. So I'm glad you pointed that out. I'm glad you pointed out that truth can be held by one person, even if the majority of the world disagrees with them.

There are other reasons besides reason and truth that people come to their faith. The most obvious one is geography. Geography is the greatest single predictor of what religion a person will have. If you're born in Baghdad, you can predict pretty much what religion that person will have. If you're born in Tennessee, you can pretty much predict what kind of a person you're going to be with religion, generally. It is the highest predictor.

So, the arguments that you just gave are not arguments for a God. There's no way anybody can know there's a God because there's a question mark in their brain about design. How do you make the leap between that question mark? Then should I just plug in my favorite god? You're arguing for the God of the Bible. And, by the way, those scriptures I quoted were not taken out of context. They were carefully studied. I hear this all the time: If you would study it correctly. I know the Bible. I translated from original languages. I have some Greek knowledge here. I know what it says. I know the Bible contradicts itself. It was written by ignorant human beings who said a few true things. But by and large, the Bible is not a reliable source of truth. It exaggerates. It has historical mistakes and anachronisms in it. It has contradictory advice. It has some really bad advice. It has a Deity whose vanity is so fragile that he gets angry and has to kill off entire people.

In Psalm 137:9, he told us that we should be happy to take the innocent babies and dash them against the stones. That's—even if that God did exist, I might not necessarily want to worship such a monster. I might ask him to confess his sins to me. What a guy— what if I were to treat my kids like this? I created you and I boss you and now you must bow down to me and you must be like slaves and you can't think for yourselves. If that kind of a God does exist, then he has earned my extreme disrespect. And if he wants to prove what a big, macho man he is by sending someone like me to hell, then let him do it. Fine. I go to hell gladly, proudly, knowing that I have resisted somebody like—a dictator like that who would create a hell in the first place.

Think about it. Any system of thought that's based to any extent upon a threat of violence—which is what hell is—it's a threat of eternal torture. Any system of thought that has that thought in it that scares the minds of children, who go to bed at night wondering if they're going to go to hell, is a morally bankrupt system.

You should not be proud to hold that Bible under your arm. It is morally bankrupt and you're better than that. There's a better way. The Bible served its time. It is irrelevant. It is anachronistic. It is immoral. And humanistic morality based upon, to some degree—not completely, but to some degree—on the natural instincts that we evolved through natural selection—even Thomas Jefferson said he thought compassion was a natural instinct.

Scientists are now concluding, especially in the last five, ten years—there's all sorts of scientific explanation for the origin of reciprocal altruism. We can see it in other species. We can see it in ourselves. And most of us fall along that bell curve somewhere. Some of us are saints and some of us are sinners, if I can borrow some words. Most of us fall somewhere in the middle as human beings.

We know what it means to be moral without consulting some ten commandments that came from some mountain on high, only three of which are relevant to modern American law. The other seven are totally irrelevant. The first four have nothing to do with ethics. It is a bad system of law, and we can think for ourselves and rise above. We can know. Not only can we know by looking at the Bible that the God of the Bible does not exist, we can know that the atheistic way is actually a superior intellectual and moral way of thinking.

Moderator Neal Jones: Mr. Butt, you have ten minutes to refute the arguments of Mr. Barker.

KYLE BUTT'S TEN-MINUTE REBUTTAL

Dan just said that there are naturalistic explanations for the altruism that is in humans. One of the books that he often refers to is the book by Matt Ridley. It is called *The Origins of Virtue*. He used this in the John Rankin debate. I just wanted to read to you a statement from Matt Ridley.

After writing this book, he put this in the prologue. He said this—this man is one of the most respected in the scientific community for writing on this particular topic—he said, "I can't even be confident that many of the ideas I discuss in this book are right." Well, that is the kind of thinking that is going to prove that altruism can be naturalistically explained; it certainly, absolutely, positively cannot.

Dan was right. I did mess up there and say a false statement about Hitler, that he was a Nazi communist. That certainly is not the truth. But Dan said that Hitler was a Christian. Let me read to you a statement from Hitler, *Table Talks*, October 19th, 1941: "The reason why the ancient world was so pure, light and serene was that it knew nothing of the two great scourges, the pox and Christianity."

He said in *Table Talks*, December 13th, 1941: "When all is said and done, we have no reason to wish that the Italians and Spaniards should free themselves from the drug of Christianity. Let's be the only people who are immunized against the disease."

You can see that he certainly was no Christian. In fact, if you look at what he did and why he did it, you see that his idea that nature is the ultimate standard is the reason that he decided he would breed the ultimate Aryan race. If you look at Charles Darwin's subtitle to "*The Origin of Species…On the Preservation of Favored Races*—and that's exactly what Hitler was following.

Dan says I'm misunderstanding Peter Singer; he's arguing for animal rights, not against human rights. Let me give you a statement by Singer. This is a quote. He was talking about abortion. And he said this: "Yet, in discussing abortion, we say that birth does not mark a morally significant dividing line. I can't see how one could defend a view that a fetus could be replaced before birth but newborn infants may not."

You see, what Singer was saying is, "We should be able to kill our children two weeks or a month after they are born, because sometimes we do not know what diseases they will have until they are born, so I do not see that birth is a morally dividing line." What is the difference between a baby that is in its mother's womb not yet born and when it is born one day old? He says, there is no difference. Does that sound like he is arguing for animal rights there? No, it certainly sounds like he is devaluing human rights. And that is exactly what he is doing.

Now, Dan said, "I have studied this material on the alleged Bible contradictions and I know this material for sure." Let me give you an example of what Dan knows, at least—let me take that back. I am not attacking Dan at all. These are standard run-of-the-mill—and when I say run-of-the-mill, I am not degrading them. I am saying they are used very often.

Let me give you an example. Here in John chapter 5, this one is used very, very often. John chapter 5, verse 31, Jesus Christ said: "If I bear witness of myself, my witness is not true." Is Jesus saying that if He makes a statement and it is Himself making the statement, then he is making a false statement? No, he is certainly not.

What we see when we go over to John 8:17, if you had your Bibles—which I didn't expect you to bring them. But if you did have them, in John 8:17, it says: "It is also written in your law that the testimony of two men is true." So there was some understanding in the first century of the word "true" that somehow we are missing.

What was the understanding? It is very easy to understand. The Old Testament said that if a person is on trial, the testimony of two or three witnesses would count against that person as adequate testimony. The testimony of one witness, although it may be true, was not valid testimony to condemn a person. Suppose Jesus stood up and said: "I'm the son of God." Is that a true statement? Is it false? It's not false. But in a court of Jewish law, would it have stood up to verify the fact of the statement? No.

Now suppose Jesus stands up and says, "I am the son of God and the works that I do from the Father testify of Him." He has two witnesses that are saying the exact same thing. Does that mean one of them is false and the other is true? No, it means they are both saying the same thing. They are both true, but in the way that this is using the word "true," it means that it is valid testimony in a court of law.

We could go through several of those and show one after another. Let me give you one more example of that. In Psalm 137:9, I believe it was there. If you wanted to, you could turn over there. I think I have this one marked. Psalm 137:9, "Happy shall he be who takes and dashes your little ones against the stone." Whoa! That sounds bad, doesn't it? That sounds like God is saying you need to go out and take the babies of these people and dash them against the stone. That is not what it is saying. In fact, this is a predictive statement. He is talking about Babylon. And He says that the Persians are going to come in and take your children and dash them against the stone.

The way He uses that word happy is the same way that Jeremiah uses it in Jeremiah chapter 12 verse one. Jeremiah says: "Lord, why does the way of the wicked prosper and why is he happy who deals treacherously?" Is he really happy who deals treacherously? No. Is God condoning a person who deals treacherously? No. He is using the word "happy" for a transient, fleeting happiness that eventually will end in that person's destruction if he or she does not repent and turn to God.

Dan has said: "Well, this entire idea of design, you are saying that if there is something functionally complex and you have to posit something more functionally complex." It has two fallacies.

Fallacy number one, have you ever come across a laptop on the beach, looked at it and realized that it had functional complexity and then thought to yourself: "You know what, if I say an intelligent human being designed it, then I have to have an explanation for the human. And I have not seen any humans on this beach, so I am just going to say that no intelligent person designed it so I do not have to explain the human." Would you do that? You would not.

Here is the thrust of the argument. The thrust is that whatever the material world exhibits, then God has to exhibit those same qualities. What he is saying is, if you see design in the material world, then whatever you say happens in the material world has to happen with God. But that is false. In fact, God has always been supernatural, outside of nature. God is the first, uncaused eternal, all-powerful, all-knowing, non-natural Being.

The atheist says, "Well, no, you cannot do that. You cannot say that there is something that does not obey natural law." But, then, do you know if you ask an honest atheist—honest about certain things. If you ask a person who is really, really going to tell you what they know about the current ideas of cosmology. At the singularity of the Big Bang—which I certainly do not adhere to—at the singularity of the Big Bang that you say exploded and caused everything that we see—were the natural laws that are in place now in place at the Big Bang?

If you study the cosmological literature, you will see in Hawking's book, *A Brief History of Time*, he says that at the singularity of the Big Bang—now, he is projecting it as a fact, I am certainly not.

But he says, "All natural law would break down at the Big Bang." So what you see, then, is the atheistic community endowing nature with the ability to behave supernaturally. Certainly.

Here is, in essence, what is being said. In essence, what we are saying, along those lines, is this—and I have got a couple little— okay, here we go.

We are saying: "It is ignorant and superstitious to believe that God made everything out of nothing. It is logical and scientific to believe that nothing made everything out of nothing."

We are saying: "God is an effect, and must have a cause. Matter is the uncaused first cause."

We are saying: "If God made everything, then who made God? Matter made everything and nothing made matter."[1]

Now, I am honestly and sincerely not belittling the people who hold these beliefs. In fact, I have looked into the eyes of compassionate, kind, good people who are atheists. There are people like that out there. In fact, I believe that there are several million of them. But they are not kind and considerate and compassionate because of their atheism. They are kind and compassionate and considerate in spite of the atheistic philosophy. Thank you.

CROSS EXAMINATION

DAN BARKER QUESTIONS KYLE BUTT

Dr. Jones: Thank you. We will now have what the format calls a cross-examination. Each of you will be allowed five minutes to ask each other questions directly. So Mr. Barker, we'll begin with you. You have five minutes to ask Mr. Butt questions directly.

---

[1] Special thanks to Mariano at Atheismisdead.blogspot.com for his permission to use these quotes.

Mr. Barker: Thank you Kyle. It's a pleasure to know you. And you're a very adequate speaker and a very good debater. It's really nice. The Bible says God is a spirit. Can you tell us what is a spirit? What is spirit?

Mr. Butt: It is a nonphysical, incorporeal, ultimate mind.

Mr. Barker: But that doesn't answer the question. What is it? What is—you said—you told us what it is not. You said it is non-corporeal, nonphysical. But, positively, what is spirit? God is a spirit. Obviously, God is made of something, right, that we can define what God is. What, positively, what is spirit?

Mr. Butt: That would be like asking what is darkness? Well, it is the absence of light. What is cold? Well, it is the absence of heat. So in order to nail down exactly what God is—in fact, earlier you said, the people who are talking about design argue for a God of the gaps. We are supposedly saying that we do not know this piece of information, so we are inserting God. Here is what is happening in this—and this is a common question among atheists. We are inserting atheism in a gap of human knowledge. We do not know exactly what a spirit is. We know what it is not and we know how to define it. But because we do not know exactly what it is, the atheistic community has often inserted—atheists say: "Ah, we do not know what a spirit is, thus atheism must be true."

Mr. Barker: But you have not defined it.

Mr. Butt: Certainly.

Mr. Barker: No, you have not defined it. You have not told me what it is. And if it's just the absence of something, then it's nothing. Because cold is the absence of heat. Cold is nothing. Darkness is the absence of light. Darkness is nothing. So if God is a spirit and a spirit is the absence of something, then God is nothing. I have never heard anyone define what a spirit is. It seems like circular thinking. You're assuming—aren't you assuming the very thing you're trying to prove? You're trying to prove there is a transcendent realm, and you're pulling yourself up by your bootstraps and using a word that has no definition. Why don't you just say God is pffflttt? Without defining it, right? What is spirit? Well, let's move on here.

Mr. Butt: Was that a question?

Mr. Barker: Well, yeah. But you didn't—twice you failed to define spirit or even explain what spirit is. So if you can't define it, how can we even discuss whether this thing exists? The second question I have is whether or not you adhere to Popperian falsifiability. I think you agree that in order for a statement to be true, there must be other statements which, if true, would make your original statement false. In other words, what would prove you wrong. What would prove me wrong? If I found a black polar bear, that would falsify the statement that all polar bears are white, right? So would you give me an example of something that would falsify in principle your hypothesis of this God that you say you know exists; or, in simple terms, what would prove you wrong?

Mr. Butt: Okay. Let me just take a quick step back and look at that falsifiability principle. Much of that was propounded by A.J. Ayer's, *Language, Truth and Logic.* In his second edition of that, he came forward and said, "Oh, by the way, the falsifiability principle, it can't be falsified." So there is not a way that you can positively use that all the time. It is good for certain scientific experiments, certain ways that you want to interact with nature. Do you need a falsifiability statement for certain things? Absolutely. But it is certainly not something that is always there. And then you have to—let me answer your question, though.

If Jesus Christ did not come to this Earth, if He did not walk the streets of Palestine, if He did not die on a cross, if He was not buried in a tomb and did not rise on the third day, then everything that I am believing means absolutely nothing.

Mr. Barker: There might be another god.

Mr. Butt: No, because Jesus said, "I am the way, the truth and the life."

Mr. Barker: But he might have been wrong. There might be another god. He might have been wrong. If he didn't exist or he didn't tell the truth, there might be another god besides the God you believe in. By the way, Jesus Christ did not walk this earth, he did not rise from the dead; he's a complete fabrication. And in my book, I demonstrate beyond a shadow of a doubt that the Jesus you believe in is not historical. He's a legend and he's a myth. Finally, let me ask you this. Do you think Eve was perfect?

Mr. Butt: I think my wife is perfect. After God created everything, He said, "Behold it is very good." There were no flaws in the creation of Eve.

Mr. Barker: So why did she sin?

Mr. Butt: That would be like saying: "Did Chrysler create a car that could be driven, and a person get behind the wheel and drive it off a cliff. What was wrong with the car?" Nothing would be wrong with the car. God endowed Eve with the ability to choose between right and wrong. Now, that capacity is perfect.

Mr. Barker: But why did she choose wrong? Why did she blow it? If she was perfect, why did she blow it?

Mr. Butt: She had the perfect capacity to choose right and wrong. That would be like saying…

Mr. Barker: But why did she choose wrong? Why? What was in her that made her choose wrong instead of right? Where did that come from, that flaw of perdition?

Mr. Butt: This is—with all due respect—but I would say: "What is in you that would make you choose the wrong idea and adhere to atheism?"

Mr. Barker: Then if God created me, then God created imperfection, didn't he?

Mr. Butt: No.

Mr. Barker: Don't you see the trap you're in? If God created Eve, who committed a sin, that impulse to sin came from somewhere. She didn't create it herself. It was in her. If I have made a wrong choice, that nature within me was created by this perfect being who created imperfection. He's a married bachelor. A perfect being created imperfection. He does not exist.

KYLE BUTT QUESTIONS DAN BARKER

Dr. Jones: Okay, thank you. Mr. Butt, you have five minutes to cross-examine Mr. Barker.

Mr. Butt: Great. Thank you. Most of these are very simple questions, and just short answers I think will do for most of these. In your debate with Peter Payne, you said—and you made the statement—I have the quote here: "All actions are situational. There is not an action that is right or wrong. I can think of an exception in any case." Do you believe that?

Mr. Barker: Yeah. But the probability of some of those exceptions actually happening are so small that we can rule them out.

Mr. Butt: Sure. Absolutely.

Mr. Barker: We can think of it, yes.

Mr. Butt: So in that, you said—a person came up to the microphone and said: "When would rape be acceptable?" And you said that exact statement. You said: "Most of them you can almost rule them out, but hypothetically, if a bunch of aliens came down and said, 'We're going to destroy all of humanity if you don't rape a girl, would you do that?'" And you said in that debate, "Yes, it would be morally acceptable to rape that girl to save all of humanity." Do you still believe that?

Mr. Barker: It would be horrible. It would be regrettable. I would hate myself. I would probably kill myself after doing it. But I would have the courage, if that was the only option—if that were the only option, then I would go through with it. I would pity that woman. I would pity myself. But morality would require me to take the course of action that results in the least amount of harm. And those of you whose lives that I saved by doing that, you might be disgusted at what I did, but you would be alive rather than dead. So in that weird situation—which is hypothetical and extreme and would never happen—there are cases where what we think are right and wrong could be flipped around.

Mr. Butt: Now, let me ask you this next question. Could you rape two girls to save all of human kind?

Mr. Barker: Well, we're getting into computational.

Mr. Butt: Sure.

Mr. Barker: Yeah.

Mr. Butt: Two thousand?

Mr. Barker: I don't know if I'm up to it. I don't know if you are?

Mr. Butt: I am certainly not. And, if you did notice, that is pretty appalling to make a joke about something that is the most brutal crime that humanity can think of. So continue. Two million? There are six billion people. Would it be permissible to rape two million girls?

Mr. Barker: To save six billion? Yes. Yes, it would be. Because otherwise you've got six billion deaths. Are you telling me we should not do what is morally necessary to do to minimize harm? You can't get through life without some harm.

Mr. Butt: Okay. Let me go to the next question, if you do not mind.

Mr. Barker: Well, I didn't finish answering, actually.

Mr. Butt: I'm sorry.

Mr. Barker: I think we all agree that it is wrong to stick a needle into a baby. That's horrible. But if that baby needs a life-saving injection, we will cause that harm. We will do that. The baby won't understand it, but we will do that because there's a greater good. So humanistic reality understands within situations there is harm and there's a tradeoff of values. And sometimes in—we don't live our lives in emergency mode. But there might be an emergency situation where we might have to do something horrible and regrettable that's against our nature.

Mr. Butt: Okay. Appreciate that. Now, you just said that it might be okay to cause some harm. And your definition of moral—in the Rankin debate and most of your writing—"any person can be called ethical or moral who intends to act in ways that minimize harm." Let me ask you a question. One doctor in Nazi Germany was asked how he could reconcile the death of so many Jews with his Hippocratic oath. And here is what he said. He said, "When you find a diseased appendix, you remove it"—referring to the killing of the Jews as being a diseased appendix, him helping the body of humanity. He was intending to minimize harm in his mind. Was he moral?

Mr. Barker: No, because the rest of us can see—fortunately there are enough of us in humanity who love our species enough, we make laws to protect ourselves from brutal people like that, and you judge a person's morality by their intended action. So he was wrong to do that because—you know, if he wanted to think he was right, he could. But the rest of us know better.

Mr. Butt: Okay. So let's say a person, after raping two million girls, you came to them and you said, "How could you rape two million girls?" And you said, "Well, I was doing it to save humanity"—exactly what the Nazi doctor said he was doing. And you just said he would not be moral. Well, let me go on.

Mr. Barker: But I bet you would thank me if I saved your life.

Mr. Butt: Not at the expense of doing something wrong, because I know that after this life I've got somewhere much better to go.

Mr. Barker: Well, no, you don't know that, Kyle. You don't know that.

Mr. Butt: I do.

Dr. Jones: Let's give both of our speakers a hand.

QUESTIONS FROM THE AUDIENCE

Audience Member: I guess I'll ask Mr. Butt this. I've been debating over several different questions. And so—I'm a biologist, and I'll start by asking—I guess I'll only ask, for design. Which, by the way, is a very tired and run-of-the-mill argument. The overwhelming question for design is why is it so bad? Because when you look at biology, the only thing I could possibly infer from the creator, if I wish, about the creator, if I looked at the design, and I looked at designs over and other and over again that, (A) the creator is incompetent. And certainly these are not—from that design, we can infer nothing that one would argue from a God of the Bible should be properties of that God, from having looked at the design. So I think this is a—I think this is a terrible line of argument because it's so self evident that it leads to the incompetence.

Mr. Butt: Okay. I am going to take that as a question of, "Is design really a good argument?", and the statement: "Design is sloppy." Now, let me give you a reason for some things that could be better. When God created the world, Genesis 1:31, there he said, "Everything was very good." Eve and Adam sinned. What happened because of that sin? Human death came into the world, and since then we have had all kinds of problems that were ushered in because of sin.

When you look at something that is not working properly, well, that is certainly because of the sin that came into the world. Suppose that you turn on a computer and it is not working properly. What do you do? "Oh, this computer must not have been designed by anybody, it is not working properly?" It still has an "on" button. Still has the keys. Still has everything. Let's say it just does not do one particular piece of software correctly.

But let me give you one quote about the design of the eye. Listen to this. "To say that the human eye is definite proof of lack of thoughtful design is a bit presumptuous, I would think." This is from Sean Pitman, M.D. "This seems to be especially true when one considers the fact that the best of modern human science and engineering has not produced even a fraction of the computing and imaging capability of the human eye. Should someone who cannot even come close to understanding or creating the object that they are observing think to critique, not to mention disparage, the work that lies before them, this would be like a six-year-old trying to tell an engineer how to design a skyscraper." I certainly think that is right.

I was writing an article just recently—actually it was not recently, about two years ago, about a bionic arm. It had six motors, cost $10 million. On our Web site, www.apologeticspress.org, this article is there. The article is titled, "A $4 Million Piece of Evidence for Design." This particular arm was attached to the shoulder of a marine. They took nerves out of her body and attached it to the arm so that she could, by thinking, move the fingers. Dr. Kuiken, the head of this particular project, said this is a wonder in human engineering. But he said it is still clumsy compared to the human hand.

We have done the best we can to make an artificial limb that processes and does what a human hand can do. And I dare say—I have had some takers on this proposition—but if I said, "Would you take $4 million for your arm?," most people would certainly say, "No, not and replace it with what we have got, because we do not have anything that is close to as good."

Mr. Barker: Do we have the chance…

Mr. Butt: Yeah, he gets a minute rebuttal, I think.

Mr. Barker: If it's optional—it's an optional rebuttal. The human eye is not one of the better designed eyes on the planet. The retina are facing backwards, unlike squid and octopus, that face forward. We basically have this blind spot. No engineer would design something that clumsy and that bad. We have this blind spot that we basically have to hallucinate to fill in. And by the way, the person you quoted is wrong. The human eye does not compute anything. It's the brain that computes. So if God created the human eye—and I think the questioner was asking why is there so much sloppy sort of gerrymandering type of creation that we would expect from natural selection—then God must love squids better than he loves human beings. Because they're—the hawk eye—the human eyes fall apart. The human eyes, they're adequate, but they're not a very good design. The questioner is pointing out that an intelligent designer would have done a much better job, not just with the eye but with all sorts of other biological adaptations.

Dr. Jones: Next question for Mr. Barker.

Audience Member: Mr. Barker, from one of your comments, I gather that you must believe that there is a hell.

Mr. Barker: No, I don't.

Audience Member: Well, I thought I understood you to say—and I could be wrong...

Mr. Barker: I was speaking counterfactually.

Audience Member:...that you would be willing to go to hell with all the other atheists, for whatever reason it was. Would you agree with the statement that there will be no atheists in hell?

Mr. Barker: If there is a hell and if the atheists get to the end of their life and discover, "Yep, I was wrong, there is a God"—this is counterfactual; this is not that I actually believe it—then, you are right, I would then believe and know that there's a God.

But that does not mean that I would respect or admire a God who would create something like a hell to send someone like me to, and my beloved mother, Patsy Barker, who died as an atheist, with a smile on her face, happy that she lived a good life raising three good boys. That Deity is torturing her in hell, her and Mark Twain and George Gershwin, and Elizabeth Cady Stanton and Aaron Copeland and Johannes Brahms and Prokofiev, Margaret Sanger, Bertrand Russell, Carl Sagan, wonderful people who lived their life.

You're telling me the God that you love and admire has consigned us to eternal torture? Then I would say to that God, you created hell, you go to hell. If you want to torture me forever, fine, you've proved what a big, macho man you are. You do not have my respect. Of course, he doesn't exist. This is all hypothetical.

Audience Member: Well, you—can I retort to that one thing? Huh? I think—I don't think there will be any atheists in hell either, because the Bible says when Jesus returns, every knee will bow and know him and believe in him. So every knee tells me everybody everywhere.

Mr. Butt: Just very quickly. There is something called an argument from outrage. It is not based on any type of logical circumstances. Not based on syllogism or anything like that. Basically, it is an argument that says, you would never want that to happen, would you? And because you do not want it to happen, then it certainly could not happen. Let me read to you a quote from Dan Barker, *godless* on page 347. He says, "Truth is truth. It shouldn't matter what any of us wants to believe." Do I want to believe that Dan Barker's mother will be lost eternally? It's not what I want to believe. Is it the truth? Well, now, that is a completely different statement.

Mr. Barker: Thank you very much.

Dr. Jones: Next question.

Audience Member: Okay. The comment that you made about your relatives going—your good relatives. Nobody gets to go to heaven because they're good. We get to go to heaven because God's good. Only by God's grace.

Mr. Barker: Is that a question? By the way, let me point out something here. That question and the one before. You're both making a false assumption. You're both assuming that the words of the Bible are reliable and dependable. They are not. You have built your house on the sand. Those words are not a source of truth. The Bible is unhistorical and contradictory. If you have to base truth on a book that somebody wrote, then you don't even have a concept of how to find truth. Truth is not handed to us. We use reason. We use logic. We use investigation. We use—so don't quote the Bible to me and think that it makes any difference. If the Bible says something is true, that probably means that it's false.

Mr. Butt: Just very briefly, I had a book out front. We had several hundred books. All of those have been taken. We were giving those away for free. I have written a book called *Behold, the Word of God*. It makes the overwhelmingly powerful, positive case that the Bible is truth. Jesus said, "You shall know the truth and the truth shall make you free." He then said, "My word is truth." And that is the ultimate truth.

Dr. Jones: Question for Mr. Barker.

Mr. Barker: We just had one, I think.

Dr. Jones: That wasn't a question.

Mr. Barker: Well, it was close enough.

Audience Member: You argued earlier about we can't do certain things because of morality, but yet you don't believe in any morality. So there's no justification for your claim that we do things that arc moral.

Mr. Barker: I do believe in morality. I didn't say I don't believe in morality. I said there are no such things as objective moral values. That doesn't mean, though, that relative to our species and the environment that we live in, we cannot say that certain values are not objectively justified.

For example, should I give you a glass of water or a glass of arsenic? We can see in this environment, in the way you evolved, that one of these things would be conducive and good for you; the other would not be. Therefore, if I want to be a moral person, I will pick the course of action that results in the least amount of harm. We can be moral. In fact, that's the only way you can be moral. Absolutistic commandment morality is a toddler morality.

The only way to be truly moral—and I think most Christians agree with this—is you've got to think through each situation and find out what causes harm and where's the least amount of harm. It's not always easy. Sometimes we act by instinct. Thomas Jefferson thought that we just jump in the river to save people by instinct. Maybe some of you do. Maybe some of you don't. But morality is a very precious part of the human experience. But it's not something with a capital "M," an objective cosmic thing out there that we have to seek and find. It is something that we figure out as we get through this life with the minimum amount of harm possible.

Mr. Butt: Water is good for the human, arsenic is not. I would not give you a bottle of arsenic, unless it would save the four people beside you.

Audience Member: What makes your God of the Bible more legitimate than any other God in any other myth?

Mr. Butt: That is a phenomenal question. It is an outstanding question. In fact, I believe ultimately that that is the question that in the 21st-century American society we have to answer. Here is what makes the God of the Bible the true God. God has demonstrated to humanity for the last, you're looking at 6,000 years or so, that He can do things that no other God can do.

In fact, the culmination of Jesus Christ being predicted for 1,000 years, coming and fulfilling all of the 300 and some odd Messianic prophecies to the detail, dying and coming back from the dead exactly as had been predicted in the Psalms verifies the truth that the God of the Bible is the true God. You see, you could have come up with a philosophy that is unfalsifiable, like Dan has mentioned. You could have said: "Well, there is a God out there somehow that does this."

But God closed that door. God says, if Jesus Christ did not come, if He was not a historic person who really died and really rose from the grave, then I am not the true God. Well, God's statements have always stood. The Messianic prophecy has always stood. The predictive prophecy has always stood. Dan will say and has said in many places, that is not true; the Messianic prophecy did not come to pass and all the predictive prophecy. That was in my book. *Behold the Word of God*. I nailed that down. And we have several articles on our site that nail that down. And the God of the Bible has opened Himself up for falsifiability in the historicity of Jesus Christ.

Mr. Barker: There are not 300-plus Messianic prophecies of Jesus. Many of those are Christian reinterpretations of Old Testament versions that they thought were prophecies, especially Matthew. Matthew is fond of digging through the Old Testament saying, "Oh, there's a child mentioned here, let's connect that with the child of Jesus." He was a very sloppy scholar. In fact, he was working from a bad translation, as well you know. The Septuagint is not a very good translation of the Hebrew scriptures. And that word virgin actually was just a young maiden. You know that. You know there's a lot of sloppiness in there.

So—and if you look back, none of them say—if a prophecy in Isaiah had said on December the 25th in the year 1, a man named Jesus—not Immanuel but a man named Jesus—will be born to a mother named Mary at 666 Savior Street in Bethlehem at 12:13 p.m., now, that would be a prophecy.

But what we have are these vague things that were referring to the time they were in; New Testament writers digging back saying, ah, that was a prophecy—when they were not even prophecies in the first place. Most of them were even in the past tense.

Audience Member: Yes, Mr. Barker, in your opening monologue, I believe you threw out 14 statements that said God doesn't exist because…

Mr. Barker: God of the Bible.

Audience Member: No. God doesn't exist because. In one of the statements you said, "God gave us freewill, therefore, God doesn't exist."

Mr. Barker: I didn't say that.

Audience Member: You didn't say that? You made the statement that God gave us freewill…

Mr. Barker: No, I didn't say that.

Audience Member: You made something close to that.

Mr. Barker: I talked about freewill; but, no, I didn't say that. But go ahead. What's your question?

Audience Member: My question is, if I understood what you said, freewill—God can have freewill and we can make a decision. And God should know and God does know what are the consequences of our decision. You're saying that God is not as smart as human beings to know. If I tell my child, "Don't touch the stove," he touches the stove, he's going to burn his hands. You're saying God doesn't exist, He's not smart enough to do that but human beings are. I say that God—freewill does exist. God gave it to us as a gift to learn and to grow. God does exist.

Mr. Barker: What I actually said had nothing to do with human freewill. I wasn't talking about that. That's a debate even among theologians. It's a debate among atheists—are you a determinist or a libertarian freewill or a compatibilist, whatever. What my comment was directed at, whether or not we think humans have freewill, at least most believers in God think God has freewill, God himself is a personal being with freewill, and that God has the ability to make decisions. And if God knows the future, if he knows what his future decisions are going to be, then there is no period of uncertainty between now and then. There's no time for him to change his mind. It's already set if God knows the future.

In fact, I think that's one of the reasons that, as a compatibilist, I think human beings can be argued to have freewill, properly defined, because we don't know the future. If we did know the future, we would throw out the whole concept of freewill. So that's an incompatibility not with humans but with God himself. If God is a free personal being who can make decisions and God knows the future, then God does not have the period of indeterminacy during which he can make his decisions. He might be some kind of a robot or something, which would not merit our adoration. But he cannot be both, at the same time, a personal free being and an omniscient being that knows the future. That was my point. Had nothing to do with freewill.

Mr. Butt: Dan is on record as saying a personal being must have freewill in order to be defined as a personal being. Yet, in his debate with Peter Payne—and I'm quoting this—he says, "I happen to think that we have the illusion of freewill. I'm a strict determinist. We are natural creatures. The material world is all that there is. We actually don't have what we would call libertarian freewill."

He says that you as a person have the illusion of freewill, because you do not know what is going to happen in the future, but really because you are a bag of naturalistic substance, then your actions are already predetermined. By that definition, would you be a personal being? No.

Audience Member: (To Kyle Butt) Yes, I was hoping if you could please expand on your definition of morality a second ago. We provided the examples of arsenic and rape and Hitler. But I think a lot of people were confused because you presuppose that morality is objective. And if that's true, then it's impossible for one action to be moral and immoral. Explain what I mean by that. That would mean when he raped the two million girls, in our minds that would be immoral, but in his mind that would be moral because he had a bigger picture than us. So if there is no objective morality, then actions can be simultaneously moral and immoral. But because you presuppose there is an objective morality, that seemed like a contradiction. But to atheists and humanists, it would not be a contradiction. So could you please redefine that for us?

Mr. Butt: Sure, absolutely. Morality is the way to behave that streams from the essence of God. Now, he said this. He said an action could be moral and immoral at the same time; thus, there cannot be objective moral values or moral standards. Could you shoot a gun into that wall and that be a moral action? Certainly. What you did was pull the trigger. That was your action. Now suppose that there was a two-year-old standing in front of that wall. And even though it might save all of humanity, would you, could you pull the trigger and that very same action be something totally different than it was before? Yes.

Is the action of pulling the trigger the moral or immoral idea or action? Certainly not. What is moral or immoral is how that relates to the standard that God has given, and that comes from the essence of God.

Mr. Barker: And I say we just have two different standards. You're using a dictator for your standard, whose brain I don't know if I should trust. And I'm using a principle of harm as my standard. Not a rule, not commandments, but harm. If the Bible does give us these absolute moral values, then why is it that believers in God don't agree what they are? You name it. Name any moral issue we're struggling with right now. Abortion rights, gay marriage, what else? Stem-cell research, doctor-assisted suicide, the war, what, birth control.

From the Audience: Atheism.

Mr. Barker: Capital punishment. The point here is that you name all of these issues; you will find really good Christians who are devout. They go to church. They pray. They have loving families. They read the Bible. They ask God for guidance on both sides of those issues. Paul wrote in the Bible, "God is not the author of confusion." But can you think of a single book that's caused more confusion than the Bible? You talk about absolute morals, but you don't have them. Those are just words. Real value comes from humanistic, situational ethics in the real world.

Audience Member: I've got a question for both of you. For millennium, religion has been defining God for us. I'm going to create a hypothetical situation. You don't like them, so I thought I'd throw one out there. Suppose science had found a God or an entity or a spirit that actually promoted the first cause, that was the creator of the Universe.

However, science was able to characterize this entity as not being all-powerful, as not being able to think, as having no qualities of man, of not knowing even if man was here, and having no direction for us. Would either one of you gentlemen be willing to call that entity "God" in a new definition?

Mr. Barker: You want to answer it? No. What you just defined is very close to what we might call deism. Deism is not theism. Theism is the belief in a personal God. Kyle is a theist. He believes in a personal God. But deists with a "D" are people—Thomas Jefferson was a deist. Thomas Paine was a deist. Many of the pre-Darwinian enlightenment thinkers were deists. They thought pretty much like that. There is no personal being who writes books and who does miracles and who talks to us. But there might have been some force that started it all. Thomas Paine said there's no Bibles except when you look at nature. That's the Bible of this deistic God.

So if by the word God you mean the capital "G" God of theism, then, no, I would not call that God. But if by the word God you mean the lower case "g" god of deism, well, then, yeah; but it's not anything what any of us in this room were thinking of as a God. We might call it the force. Or we might call it the great tentacles of the spaghetti monster. I don't know.

Mr. Butt: Let me address your question. The fact of the matter is that science has come to the overwhelming conclusion that there is a God. In fact, the scientists of the last century—the scientists who started much of the scientific endeavor—said that they were thinking God's thoughts after Him.

Every single legitimate scientific law that we know for a fact points overwhelmingly to the fact that there has to be an intelligent personal Designer. Life spontaneously generating? We have done 150 years of experiments on trying to get life from nonliving chemicals, and every single one of those has verified the fact that life comes only from previously existing life of its own kind. That is a scientific fact.

It is not a pie in the sky, some fringe, radical, rabid person out there that has come up with the idea and projected it on human society. That has been the foundation of science from the very beginning, finding the truth. And that truth happens to correspond perfectly with what the Bible describes as God.

Audience Member: Yes. I was thinking about the analogy you had with the laptop. And that's not really valid because it doesn't have a way to produce offspring that inherit its traits and stuff. But as human organisms, we do. And so—and you say that we can't—the human body itself can't just randomly happen. That's not what science says. It says it happened gradually. So over billions of years why could the human body not be produced by natural selection and gene mutation?

Mr. Butt: There are several reasons why it cannot. He made a statement. He said that that is not a valid analogy. That is an assertion. No offense. He has got nothing to back that up. He is just saying that. The truth is, it is a valid analogy. In fact, the things that he gave for reasons why—he said, "Because humans can reproduce, humans can…"—he gave us more complexity. So he said it is not a valid analogy because humans can do more than the laptop computer.

Maybe it is an insufficient analogy. Maybe I need to find something else that humans have designed that would come closer to the complexity of a brain, but we do not have anything. That was the best that I have. The second statement was, "What if we had billions of years to come up with the human body." Suppose right now that—well, forget that hypothetical. Let me say this. Number one—and understand this—you do not have billions of years. There are no legitimate, valid, factual studies that will give you billions of years.

Number two—and probably the strongest—you cannot get off the ground. You have to have, ultimately, life come from nonlife. Now, often the creationist is berated for saying, "You believe things that you have not seen." Have you ever met anybody who said, "I have seen life come from nonlife?" Never seen a person do it. But it is presented in every one of your first grade, second grade, third grade, fourth grade, fifth grade books as a scientific fact; and it is nothing of the sort. One of the reasons that you cannot get the human body is because you cannot even get the first cell from nonlife.

Mr. Barker: The questioner is right. The laptop computer is a bad analogy because computers are not self-replicating. In fact, a computer, in a sense—have you ever interacted with a computer and you talk to it and you yell at it and that program seems—it's not a living thing, but you're having relationship with that thing. That computer is made out of nonlife, and yet it is functioning. It is not the stuff it's made of that makes it alive. It's its organization. There is nothing in your body or my body that doesn't come from nonlife. We are made out of the basic elements that are out there, and it's the arrangement of it that matters. So the beauty of Darwinism is the self-replication and of course the variation between the self—replication. What you just said completely misrepresents science. The fact of evolution is the strongest fact in biology ever. It has been repeatedly tested through multiple lines, multiple lines. Natural selection, evolution through natural selection is the only thing that makes sense of who we are as a species. You and I are related to each other genetically in some way. We have a common ancestor somewhere back there. Maybe it's closer than we think.

Mr. Butt: Eve.

Mr. Barker: No, we have a common ancestor closer than that, and I bet it's three or four or five generations ago. I bet we could come back to that point. But when you go back, evolution is not a ladder. It's not a chain. You're obviously misinformed about what evolution is. It's wonderful if you will study it and read it. It is mind-expanding in what it teaches us about who we really are as human beings. Evolution is a bush. You and I are somehow long distant cousins from each other based on a simple ancestor, and we're not the same. You and I are different from each other. Speciation happens at that level over billions of years. That is a fact of science.

Dr. Jones: Question for Mr. Barker?

Audience Member: Mr. Barker, first of all, I'd like to thank you for your patience. And I'd like to—I really appreciate the viewpoints you've brought here today. They've really challenged me and made me think. One thing you asked Mr. Butt earlier was what's one thing that if true would falsify your belief. And I just want to know for you, what's that one falsifying fact?

Mr. Barker: Yeah. Good. So you get the question, right? Falsifiability is important, if for nothing else than to point out the honesty of saying, "Here is what would prove me wrong, go for it." How many people are honest? I will give you one example or maybe two. But there are thousands that I could think of. If Kyle were to pray and ask God—because the Bible says all things whatsoever you shall ask in prayer believing, you shall receive, right?

If Kyle were to pray and ask God to predict something, and Kyle were to turn to me and say, "God told me, Dan, tomorrow at 12:14 p.m., a meteorite from the southwest at 85 degrees would strike your house—not my house—go through the Navajo rug on the second floor, go down into the basement and end up 17 inches below the basement floor composed of 72% iron, 1% iridium, 3% nickel" and so on. And then if that happens exactly as you told me that God told you or predicted, I would say, "Oops, my atheism is falsified," right?

So I could—if Jesus were to materialize on this stage—he did it before, according to your belief system; he materialized through solid door and he floated into the sky. If he were to materialize here and speak to us and tell us the exact geographical coordinates where the ark of the covenant is buried in Jerusalem, in the Holy Land, and if we were to go over there to that point and dig it up and find it, I would say, "Oops, atheism is wrong." I could come up with a lot of stuff like that. What can you come up with that would falsify your hypothesis? Specifically. What would prove you wrong?

Mr. Butt: Absolutely, great. Number one, there are several things that could prove the Christian wrong. If you could prove that Jesus Christ did not exist, that would prove the Christian wrong. If you could prove Jesus Christ did not come back from the dead on the third day as he predicted exactly, that would prove the Christian wrong. Paul said—he opened it for falsifiability—he said, "If the resurrection is not true, then what I'm preaching to you is simply not the case." But you can't do that.

Mr. Barker: Yes, you can.

Mr. Butt: Let me tell you this. Here has historically been what has always happened. The person who has chosen not to believe always says, "If I had just a little more evidence, then I would believe." In John chapter 11, after Jesus raised Lazarus from the dead, the Jewish community looked at that miracle and said: "Now we believe in Jesus"? No. They said: "Now people are believing in Jesus, so we have got to kill Lazarus."

When Jesus Christ was on the cross, do you remember what they said? They said, "If you will come down from there, we will believe." They had not believed when He made blind Bartimaeus see. They had not believed when the things that had been predicted about His life came true—born in Bethlehem of a virgin, going into the city of Jerusalem on—all of those things. Just a little bit more.

You know, I noticed in his previous falsifiability, he [Dan Barker] said, "If you said that this meteorite was going to take place at 7:17, etc." What if we gave him all the information except that 7:17? Well, what would he say? Would he then say, "You didn't tell me 7:17?" Always more information.

Mr. Cederdahl: I've got to give the person responsible for this event a chance to ask a question. I hope you don't mind me asking you a question, Mr. Butt. Two parts. One, do you believe in miracles? And, two, why won't God heal amputees?

Mr. Butt: Great question. Absolutely, positively, yes, I do believe that miracles at one time were commonplace, especially when Jesus Christ was on this Earth. The point of a miracle has always been to confirm that the speaker was speaking for God. Confirmation. Also, there were subsequent points to those. They showed the compassion of Jesus Christ. They showed that God had the power over anything that you could name—over nature, over death, over—you name it, God had the power to control it.

But the real question that he is asking—and it is a very valid one—what about miracles today? I will tell you that I believe that the age of miracles has ceased. Why is that? Because I believe that the Bible has been confirmed. Paul said in Galatians chapter 1: "Though I or an angel of heaven preach any Gospel to you than that which has been preached, let him be accursed."

You see, what God has done for us is given us every single thing that we need to know to live lives in accordance with His will to go to heaven. We do not need any more confirmation of the Word. The Bible says that all things for life and godliness have been given to us. And, so, yeah, I believe in miracles, but I do not believe they are still happening today.

Now, do I believe that God acts in the world? Certainly. I believe that God acts providentially through natural ways that you could not put your finger on and say, "God did that, exactly." Often you see that in hindsight. Do I believe God can still act in this world? Certainly. Do I believe that He acts miraculously like He did in the first century? No.

Mr. Barker: Kyle, you seem to be suggesting that Christians should not pray for miracles now. Christians should not pray for their sick children to get better when the doctors told them that they're going to die of cancer. In the Bible, Jesus very clearly said, "All things whatsoever you shall ask for in prayer believing, you shall receive." "The prayer of faith will save the sick." Now you're telling us, well, that only applied back then. We're in a different, I suppose, dispensation now. He was only talking to them back then, so we should basically throw out those verses, and those promises he made to his disciples do not apply to today? Do Christians in this audience believe that kind of talk? Do you—don't you pray when your child is sick? Don't you pray for the laws of—for God to intervene in some way? Kyle is telling you, you should not, there are no more miracles. Well, I guess we're on the same page on that one.

Audience Member: This question is for Dan Barker. Dan, if the smartest—the thousand smartest scientists in the world today said we needed to reduce the human population immediately because future generations will not be able to live on earth, if they said that and they say we need to go to Columbia, South Carolina, tonight and do that. And they say we need to kill everyone in this audience, would you say that would be right or that would be wrong?

Mr. Barker: Well, I would fight that, obviously. And I'm sure you would, too. I would question their judgment and say that there would probably be better ways to do that; for example, birth control. Let's use birth control. Let's tell the Pope that the Pope is wrong about birth control. Let's limit our family size and let's try to have more respect for the environment. And I—if those scientists said that, I would want to know their reasoning. They would have to convince me. It's hard for me to imagine that the smartest scientists in the world would advocate a genocide, because if they would, they should get in line first, right? I mean, if that was important.

So I would not presume to tell them that they are acting immorally. But I love life enough and I love the people here in this town enough to protect—unlike the God of the Bible, which exterminated entire villages because they offended his vanity, right? I think I love the world enough to see if there's a better way to do it than that.

Mr. Butt: Okay. I want you to notice what Dan just said in answer to that question. He said, there are better ways to take care of overpopulation than coming and killing the 550 people in this audience: birth control. What is often lumped in with birth control? Abortion. So what he is saying there is, "There are better ways to save your life if it happens to be an overpopulation problem. Just kill the unborn child in the mother's womb."

CLOSING STATEMENTS

Mr. Butt: In the concluding remarks, sometimes you need to wrap up some things that were said during the debate. Just one real quick one. When he [Dan Barker] mentioned the idea that the eye of the human is inverted and it is bad design and an intelligent designer would have done better than that, it just so happens that the most acute eye on the planet, the bird eye, happens to be inverted.

I have a quote here from New York, Frank Gill, *Ornithology*, Freeman, 1995. Birds have—this is not an actual quote, it comes from the book—birds have an inverted eye, yet they produce the sharpest images of all animals.

Now, he did get into more of a core of the question. He did say: "If the Bible is the ultimate guide for morality, why is it that you can take any moral issue and you can see Bible-believing people come down on both sides of those issues? And I believe that is a very valid question. But it is one that Dan has answered for us.

In fact, I have a quote from his University of Minnesota speech, October 19th, 2006, "How to be Moral Without Religion." And this is the quote: "A tendency that we all have, we look through our documents to try to find what supports our already-prejudiced views about what we think morality should be like." Yes, that is exactly what happens—the reason we come down on both sides of the moral question when we approach the Bible. If you give this Bible that I am holding in my hand to five different people, they might come up with five different answers. But has the Bible changed every time you gave it to one of the people? No. What did change? The prejudices that a person brought to the text. And that is out of Dan's own mouth.

Let me bring to point one of what I think is one of the most powerful statements that was made in this discussion. Dan—and I have the quote from his book about hell—he said basically the same thing that he said tonight: "If I meet a God and that God created hell, then I'll tell him to go there." And that frightens me even to repeat. I believe that is one of the most blasphemous statements there ever was. I do believe that a person that would believe as Dan does could make a statement like that.

But let's analyze the idea of hell just for a minute. The Bible says that God is a God of love. But do you know what else the Bible says? The Bible says that love allows the freedom to choose. In fact, in the Old Testament, in the book of Deuteronomy—Deuteronomy 30:19, I believe—Moses said to the children of Israel. He said, "Today I put before you the way of blessing and cursing, the way of life and death. Choose life."

You see, God loves you so much that He created you and designed you to have the ability, the freedom, to choose and break His heart. What has God done to persuade you not to choose hell? I will tell you what He has done. He has sent His Son, Jesus Christ, and stripped Jesus of the glory He had in heaven, sent Him as a human being, and allowed sinful humans to nail Him to a cross.

Do you know what the Bible says in the book of Hebrews? The Bible says that every person who chooses hell will trample the blood of Jesus Christ under their feet. That means God says you will go to hell over my dead body. And He put His dead body there. Let me tell you why, if a person goes to hell, they will go to hell. And I am going to give you the quote from Dan Barker himself. He says this, page 70 of *godless:* "Speaking for myself, if the biblical heaven and hell exists, I would choose hell." Do you know what God will allow every one of you to do? Choose. Thank you very much.

Mr. Barker: Thank you, Kyle. You are a very cordial, very civil person. Your Web site is not the one that calls me Dan Barfer, is it?

Mr. Butt: No, I was informed of that tonight, and I was appalled at that.

Mr. Barker: Yeah, I didn't think it was. I think it's some other loving Christian that did that. You quoted from *Table Talk*. You're using a bad version of *Table Talk*. Scholars have found out that since that English translation came out, that was an English translation from a very bad French translation from the German. There's now better translations that actually show what you claim Hitler said, he did not say those things. I was surprised to learn that as well. So that version of *Table Talk* that's available out there, it's worthless. Richard Carrier has done some good work on that with a more direct translation from the actual German.

When Darwin talked about favored races, in those days the word "race" did not mean human race, like Hitler might have used it. In his day the word "race" was just a synonym for animal species. He wasn't talking about favored races like whites over blacks or something.

And falsifiability, the resurrection of Jesus has—the bodily resurrection of Jesus has been summarily disproved. Jesus did not bodily rise from the dead. I have an entire chapter in my book showing that. The early Christians didn't even believe that. They believed that when Jesus died, he went to heaven just kind of like grandma died and went to heaven. The bodily resurrection of Jesus is a myth. And by your own admission of falsifiability, you should reject your faith in Christianity.

What Kyle did tonight was he talked a lot, but he didn't connect any dots. Did you notice that? Our debate is, does the God of the Bible exist? He didn't give us any evidence for that God. You quoted a bunch of Bible verses. But the point of the Bible itself being reliable is a very important point. The book that you believe in is that house built on the sand. That book is not a reliable source of truth. Why do you hitch your wagon to that? Why not hitch it to the Vedas or to the Quran? They all say they have had changed lives as well. I don't think Jesus existed. Maybe there was a self-proclaimed—there were many self-proclaimed Messiahs in the first century. Maybe there was a Yeshua the Christ. There was a Theodis the Christ, there was a Judas the Christ. There was an Egyptian Jew Messiah. There were many other self-proclaimed Messiahs that Josephus writes about. By the way, he did not write about Jesus. That was a later interpolation. But maybe there was this self-proclaimed Messiah named Yeshua. But the things that he said were put into his mouth many, many, many, many years later.

But one thing he said, if he said it, that I think actually is worthwhile, he said, they who are whole—those who are healthy don't go to the doctor. It's only they who are sick. Christians have a pessimistic view of human nature. You think human beings are sick and need a doctor to be fixed up. You think there's something wrong with us and we need to be saved. You think that if we would submit to the doctor, that he would heal us. But we atheists and agnostics don't view ourselves as sick. We don't view ourselves as sinners. We don't feel a conviction of wrong. We make mistakes. We don't buy into this supernatural, mythological lie that you people are promoting that there's something actually spiritually wrong with humanity.

Suppose you were convicted of a horrible crime. You were in prison, and then you learned that you were being released. Wow! You'd feel free. "Wow, I'm being saved! This is wonderful!" And I would feel great, too. But what would make you feel better? Knowing that you had been released because of the good graces of the governor who decided to bestow mercy upon you and pardon you and let you free? Which would be pretty neat if that happened. Or knowing that the reason you were being released was because you were found to be innocent of the crime in the first place? What would give you more dignity? What would make you feel better? For the world to know, "Hey, I didn't even do that crime!" That's how we atheists and agnostics are.

We don't buy into this ancient primitive book of contradictory and unhistorical and unscientific words. These are just words on a page. This book was written by human beings. Human beings make mistakes. What, were they exempt? Were they superhumans or something? Did they never misinterpret? Did they never goof? Why are you conferring some supernatural authority to these human beings that—it's in all religions as well. If you look at the Bible with not a bias of faith and loyalty, you can see very easily that this is not a reliable book to base our life on. But most of your arguments are based on quoting the scripture as if it was some kind of a magic talisman. Oh, quote the Bible, that will make everything important. Well, it doesn't.

If you don't buy into that myth in the first place, if you don't see yourself as sick, if you don't see yourself as needing a Savior, if you rise above that toddler mentality of putting yourself down, of denigrating your rationality, of denigrating your—whatever urges you have to sin within you—and we all have them—but view yourself neutrally as a natural creature in a natural environment doing the best we can to truly figure out how to be moral human beings with reason and compassion, then you could be a better person. I'm not saying you're a bad person. But get rid of the baggage. Get the monkey off your back and take some advice of Jesus. Don't be one of the sick people that has to go to the doctor. Clap your hands and say, "I did not commit the crime!"

From the Audience: Amen!

Mr. Barker: Who said that? Most Christians are afraid that people are going to start thinking for themselves. The Bible says very clearly—Paul says, "Bring into captivity every thought unto the obedience of Christ." Captivity is not freedom. And in Proverbs, you know, "Lean not on your own understanding." Most Christians are afraid that people will think for themselves. Most atheists are afraid that they won't. Thank you. [Directed to Kyle Butt] Shake again? Good job, man.

Dr. Jones: Let's thank both of our speakers, Dan Barker and Kyle Butt.

PART 2

A BRIEF INTRODUCTION
TO PART 2

In the refutation segment of this book, many of the sections will refer back to comments that Barker made during the debate. These sections will note the page number from the first part of this book that contains the statement. The notation will appear in parenthesis. For instance, if Dan alleged that there is no coherent definition of God, and his allegation is found on page six of the first part of this book, then the section answering that statement will contain the following reference: (Part 1, p. 6). As was mentioned in the preface, some arguments are not answered in the refutation section, either because the answer does not focus on the central issue, or because my responses during the debate adequately answered the assertions. For instance, on page six, Barker stated that his first argument against God's existence is that there is no evidence for it. In my opening statement, I included the arguments that design demands an intelligent designer, and that for objective moral standards to exist, there must be a God. There are many more arguments for God's existence, but these two stand as adequate evidence refuting Barker's assertion that none exists. Furthermore, since various authors contributed to the responses to Barker's assertion, their names will be included in the sections that they wrote. Sections that do not have an author's name were written by me. In addition, at the end of this section there is list of articles, books, and resources that address issues that were briefly touched upon in the debate and merit additional consideration.

DAN OPENLY ADMITS HE WILL LIE

According to Dan Barker, there are some instances in which lies are "considered virtuous." He stated, "But **we all know** that it is sometimes necessary to tell a lie in order to protect someone from harm" (1992a, p. 345, emp. added). In his book, *Losing Faith in Faith*, Barker gave a scenario about a woman who is being hunted by her abusive husband, and he concluded: "I would consider it a moral act to lie to the man."

Barker, then, finds it a moral practice to lie if he thinks that such a lie will keep a person from harm. What is one of the things that Barker thinks is most harmful? Listen to his statement:

> Religion is a powerful thing. Few can resist its charms and few can truly break its embrace. It is a siren who entices the wandering traveler with songs of love and desire and, once successful, turns a mind into stone. It is a Venus fly trap. Its attraction is like that of drugs to an addict who, wishing to be free and happy, becomes trapped and miserable (1992a, p. 51).

From this statement, one can see that Dan Barker places religion at the top of his "most harmful" list. On page 233 of his book he declared: "Religious morality is dangerous." On page 286 he said that certain religious people are "abusing their children" by teaching them things like "evolution is a Satanic lie." And on page 214, Barker explicitly stated: "Dear Believer: You ask me to consider Christianity as the answer for my life. I have done that. I consider it untrue, repugnant and **harmful**" (emp. added).

Putting Mr. Barker's statements together in logical form: (1) he considers it moral to lie in order to "protect someone from harm;" (2) he considers religion to be harmful; (3) then it follows that Mr. Barker would lie in order to dissuade a person from believing in God or religion.

Therefore, in the course of the debate, or any of Barker's debates or writings for that matter, you cannot assume that he is telling the truth. In fact, if it will help the cause of atheism, then by his own admission, there is a good chance that he will lie in order to keep the listener or reader from "harm." This idea is crucial if a person wants to accurately assess Barker's position. If Dan will lie, then the only way to know if he is telling the truth is if he provides legitimate documentation of the validity of a statement. Yet Dan rarely ever documents anything that he says during a debate. One of the most apparent characteristics of his debating style is the lack of documentation. Since Dan admits he will lie, the first question that a person should ask of every statement Barker makes is: "How do we know Dan is not lying?" As we go through this debate, we will continually be asking that question.

Also, please notice that I am not attacking motives. This is not an *ad hominem* argument attempting to slander Dan's character. I am simply pointing out that Dan has openly admitted that he will lie. By highlighting Barker's mode of operation in this area, I'm doing nothing more than informing you, as the reader or listener, of a tactic that Barker himself admits he will use.

A COHERENT DEFINITION OF A GOD

D uring the debate, Dan stated: "There's no coherent definition of a God. How can we debate something that we can't even define? God is defined as a spirit, but what is that?" (Part 1, p. 6). He admitted that this argument does not disprove God, but he claimed that it makes the idea of God so unlikely and improbable that we should simply "round up" and disbelieve in God" (Part 1, p. 7).

As with many of Barker's other statements, his "no coherent definition" idea is simply an assertion that seems plausible only until it is critically analyzed in light of sound reasoning. First, God can be defined in such a way that brilliant men and women for thousands of years have been able to intelligently discuss God's attributes, existence, and qualities. In fact, the vast majority of standard dictionaries give a working definition that most third-graders understand. For instance, the *Merriam-Webster Online Dictionary* gives the following definition for "God": "1. the supreme or ultimate reality: as a: the Being perfect in power, wisdom, and goodness who is worshipped as creator and ruler of the universe" (2009). *The American Heritage Dictionary's* primary definition of "God" is: "1. God a. A being conceived as the perfect, omnipotent, omniscient originator and ruler of the universe, the principal object of faith and worship in monotheistic religions" (2000, p. 753). *Webster's Third New International Dictionary*, a massive volume of almost 3,000 pages, defines "God" as: "the supreme or ultimate reality: the Deity variously conceived in theology, philosophy, and popular religion: as **a** (1): the holy, infinite, and eternal spiritual reality presented in the

Bible as the creator, sustainer, judge, righteous sovereign, and re-deemer of the universe who acts with power in history carrying out his purpose…" (1993, p. 973).

So coherent, in fact, is the definition of God that it is absent from books such as *The New York Times' Everyday Reader's Dictionary of Misunderstood, Misused, Mispronounced Words* (1972). The term "God" is defined in every major dictionary, it is absent from the books that compile words that are difficult to understand, and the term has been used in meaningful conversation for thou-sands of years since the dawn of humanity. In order for a person to say that God cannot be coherently defined, he would need to change the meanings of the words "coherent" or "defined." The fact that the term "God" is included in this book, and the read-er can differentiate it from all the other concepts and terms be-ing discussed, goes a long way to proving that the term can be meaningfully defined.

But let us dig deeper into Barker's assertion and deal with an-other idea he presents. Barker has a problem with the term "spirit," and he claims that no one knows exactly what a spirit is (Part 1, pp. 29-31). Thus, he suggests, it is impossible for God to be something that no one can explain. In answer to Barker's assertion, we could simply give another list of dictionary definitions of the word "spir-it." *The Merriam-Webster's Online Dictionary* gives several meanings of the word, including: "1: an animating or vital principle held to give life to physical organisms" or "4: the immaterial intelligent or sentient part of a person" (2009). A lengthy list of dictionary defi-nitions would most likely bore the reader, but it would show that the term "spirit" is used in common parlance, easily understood, and discussed.

The idea that Barker seems to be presenting, then, is not that people have a difficult time defining or discussing terms like "God" or "spirit." Barker seems to be indicating that since everybody's definition of a "spirit" is not identical, and since we do not know everything about a "spirit," then the concept must be useless. Of course, if we eliminate all the concepts that we do not unanimously agree upon or that we do not completely understand, our discussions would be extremely limited. For instance, in Richard Dawkins' book *The Selfish Gene*, Dawkins attempted to define the word "gene," but he noted: "My definition will not be to everyone's taste, but **there is no universally agreed definition of gene**" (2006b, p. 28, emp. added). Charles Darwin himself, when discussing the term "species" (which term was in the title of his most famous book), wrote: "Nor shall I here discuss the various definitions which have been given of the term species. **No one definition has satisfied all naturalists**; yet every naturalist knows vaguely what he means when he speaks of a species" (1860, p. 38, emp. added). Quotes like these two could be multiplied and are sufficient to show that there need not be unanimous agreement about a term in order for it to have meaning.

Furthermore, it would be impossible to limit our vocabulary to concepts that are completely and fully understood. Can we use words that describe things that we do not totally understand? Indeed, not only is it permissible, but it is commonly practiced by all. For instance, in his book, *The Blind Watchmaker*, Dawkins stated: "Nobody has yet invented the mathematics **for describing the total structure** and behaviour of such an object as a physicist, or even **of one of his cells.** What we can do is understand **some of the general principles** of how living things work, and why they exist at all" (1996, p. 3, emp. added). Notice that Dawkins admits that we cannot fully understand and describe a single cell, but that does not stop us from defining its generalities and using them to discuss the concept of a "cell." In his series, *Origins of Life,* Robert Hazen has an entire lecture titled "What is Life?" In that lecture, he attempted to define the term "life," but noted that he had seen at least 48 definitions: "Yet, remarkably, no two definitions are the same" (2005, p. 49). He further stated: "As you can imagine, scientists crave an unambiguous definition of life. Such a definition remains elusive" (p. 50). Hazen quipped that many scientists are "loath to draw too narrow a definition [of life—KB] in our present **state of ignorance**" (p. 51, emp. added); "I would argue that scientists in the early 21st century are in the same boat [as those in the 18th century—KB]— no position to define life.... To summarize this lecture, there is no simple answer to the question, 'What is life?'" (p. 58). Using Barker's line of reasoning in light of Dr. Hazen's lecture on life, there must be no such thing as life, since we do not have a definition upon which all scientists agree. As you can see, such a conclusion is irrational. Furthermore, Barker and the scientific community have no qualms discussing ideas such as dark matter, dark energy, and black holes, even though these concepts cannot be accurately defined.

DEFINING "SPIRIT" POSITIVELY

In the cross-examination section of our debate, Barker asked me what a spirit is. I stated that a spirit is a "non-physical, incorporeal mind." He responded by saying, "But that doesn't answer the question. You told us what it is not. You said it is non-corporeal, non-physical. But positively, what is a spirit?" (Part 1, pp. 29-31). Notice that my definition included the positive concept of a spirit being a mind. Barker conveniently focused on the words "non-physical" and "incorporeal," but intentionally ignored the definition of spirit as a mind. Barker refuses to deal with the concept of an immaterial mind because he is a materialist. In his debate with Peter Payne, Barker stated: "We are natural creatures. The natural world is all there is" (2005). What Barker means by the term "natural" is: "composed of physical matter." His atheistic philosophy will not allow him to admit that there is anything other than matter. This false, materialistic assumption is his fundamental problem with the term "spirit." It has been shown extensively and definitely, however, that humans possess an immaterial, rational mind that cannot be relegated to mere physical matter (see Harrub and Thompson,

2004; Thompson and Harrub, 2004). The mere fact that you can read, comprehend, analyze, and assess Barker's assertion proves that something immaterial is at play.

Incidentally, Barker's assertion that negative terms cannot be used to give positive meaning to something is vacuous. In his book *godless* (a negative term in itself), Barker gives a lengthy definition of what he believes the term "atheism" means. He stated: "It turns out that *atheism* means much less than I had thought. It is merely the lack of theism. It is not a philosophy of life and it offers no value.... [T]o be an atheist, you don't need any positive philosophy at all.... Basic atheism **is not a belief**" (p. 98, emp. added, italics in orig.). According to Barker, atheism can be defined in purely negative terms without offering a single positive concept, the very thing he accuses those who define "spirit" of doing.

Furthermore, in answering his question during the cross-examination, I mentioned two words, darkness and cold, that are often understood in negative terms. *Merriam-Webster Online Dictionary* defines darkness as: "1 a: **devoid** or partially **devoid** of light: **not** receiving, reflecting, transmitting, or radiating light" (2009, emp. added). Even though "darkness" is defined in negative terms as the absence of light, there is no doubt that darkness exists.

CONCLUSION

God is the uncaused, all-powerful, all-knowing, merciful, gracious, eternal Spirit whose personality and attributes are manifested in the pages of the Bible. Virtually every dictionary gives an understandable and reasonable definition of God, books that deal with difficult words omit God, and God has been the main subject of discussion and study of the vast majority of the most brilliant thinkers for millennia. The rhetorical tactic suggesting that God cannot be defined is nothing more than an assertion based on a materialistic philosophy that is unfounded. In truth, God can be clearly defined and delineated from all other entities to such an extent that Dan Barker and I can be involved in a formal debate and both know exactly what (or rather Who) we are discussing—God, the God of the Bible.

THE PROBLEM OF EVIL

Kyle Butt & Dave Miller

Three minutes and 15 seconds into his opening speech, Dan stated that one reason he believes God does not exist is because "there are no good replies to the arguments against the existence of God, such as the problem of evil. All you have to do is walk into any children's hospital and you know there is no God. Prayer doesn't make any difference. Those people pray for their beloved children to live, and they die" (Part 1, p. 7). Barker suggested that "the problem of evil" is one of the strongest positive arguments against the existence of God.

What, precisely, is the so-called "problem of evil"? Atheists like Barker note that the Bible depicts God as all-loving as well as all-powerful. This observation is certainly correct (e.g., 1 John 4:8; Genesis 17:1; Job 42:2; Matthew 19:26). Yet everyone admits that evil exists in the world. For God to allow evil and suffering supposedly implies that He is not all-loving, or if He is all-loving, He lacks the power to eliminate them. In either case, the God of the Bible would not exist. To phrase the "problem of evil" more precisely, the atheist contends that the biblical theist cannot consistently affirm all three of the following propositions:

God is omnipotent.

God is perfect in goodness.

Evil exists.

Again, the atheist insists that if God is omnipotent (as the Bible affirms), He is not perfect in goodness since He permits evil and suffering to run rampant in the world. If, on the other hand, He is perfect in goodness, He lacks omnipotence since His goodness would move Him to exercise His power to eliminate evil on the Earth. Since the Christian affirms all three of the propositions, the atheist claims that Christians are guilty of affirming a logical contradiction, making their position false. Supposedly, the "problem of evil" presents an insurmountable problem for the Christian theist.

In truth, however, the "problem of evil" is a problem for the atheist—not the Christian theist. First, atheistic philosophy cannot provide a coherent definition of "evil." There is no rational way that atheism can accurately label anything as "evil" or "good." On February 12, 1998, William Provine, a professor in the Department of Ecology and Evolutionary Biology at the distinguished Cornell University, delivered the keynote address at the second annual Darwin Day. In an abstract of that speech on the Darwin Day Web site, Dr. Provine asserted: "Naturalistic evolution has clear consequences that Charles Darwin understood perfectly. 1) No gods worth having exist; 2) no life after death exists; 3) **no ultimate foundation for ethics exists**; 4) no ultimate meaning in life exists; and 5) human free will is nonexistent" (Provine, 1998, emp. added). Provine's ensuing message centered on his fifth statement regarding human free will. Prior to delving into the "meat" of his message, however, he noted: "The first 4 implications are so obvious to modern naturalistic evolutionists that I will spend little time defending them" (1998, emp. added). If there is no foundation upon which to base any ethical conclusions, then how could an atheist label any action or occurrence as "evil," "bad," or "wrong"?

Frederick Nietzsche understood atheistic philosophy so well that he suggested that the bulk of humanity has misunderstood concepts such as "evil" and "good." In his work *Beyond Good and*

Evil, Nietzsche wrote: "We believe that severity, violence, slavery, danger in the street and in the heart, secrecy, stoicism, tempter's art and devilry of every kind—that everything wicked, terrible, tyrannical, predatory, and serpentine in man, **serves as well for the elevation of the human species as its opposite**" (2007, p. 35, emp. added). Nietzsche's point simply was that what we might call morally "evil" actually helps humans evolve higher thinking capacities, quicker reflexes, or greater problem-solving skills. Thus, if an "evil" occurrence helps humanity "evolve," then there can be no legitimate grounds for labeling that occurrence as "evil." In fact, according to atheistic evolution, anything that furthers the human species should be deemed as "good."

As C.S. Lewis made his journey from atheism to theism, he realized that the "problem of evil" presented more of a problem for atheism than it did for theism. He stated:

> My argument against God was that the universe seemed so cruel and unjust. But how had I got this idea of *just* and *unjust*? A man does not call a line crooked unless he has some idea of a straight line. What was I comparing this universe with when I called it unjust...? Of course, I could have given up my idea of justice by saying it was nothing but a private idea of my own. But if I did that, then my argument against God collapsed too—for the argument depended on saying that the world was really unjust, not simply that it did not happen to please my private fancies. Thus in the very act of trying to prove that God did not exist—in other words, that the whole of reality was senseless—I found I was forced to assume that one part of reality—namely my idea of justice—was full of sense. Consequently, atheism turns out to be too simple (Lewis, 1952, pp. 45-46, italics in orig.).

Theistic apologist, William Lane Craig, has summarized the issue quite well:

> I think that evil, paradoxically, actually proves the existence of God. My argument would go like this: If God does not exist then objective moral values do not exist. (2) Evil exists, (3) therefore objective

moral values exist, that is to say, some things are really evil. There-fore, God exists. Thus, although evil and suffering at one level seem to call into question God's existence, on a deeper more fundamental level, they actually prove God's existence (n.d.).

Craig and Lewis are correct. If objective evil actually exists in the world, and some things are not the way they "should" be, then there must be a standard outside of the natural world that would give meaning to the terms "evil" and "good"—and the atheistic assumption proves false.

AN EMOTIONAL APPEAL

In addition to the fact that "evil" cannot even be discussed without reference to God, Barker rested the force of his statement on an emotional appeal. He said: "All you have to do is walk into any children's hospital and you know there is no God" (Part 1, p. 7). Is it really the case that anyone who walks into a children's hospital is immediately struck by the overwhelming force of atheism? No, it is not true. In fact, it is the farthest thing from the truth. Anticipating Barker's tactics, I [KB] visited the children's hospital in Columbia, South Carolina and met a lady who volunteered there. When asked why she volunteered, she pointed to a bullet hole in her skull. She said that it was a blessing she was still alive and she wanted to give something back, since God had allowed her to live. When asked if many of the volunteers in the hospital were religious, she responded that many of them were from churches in the area, i.e., churches that believe in the God of the Bible.

According to Barker's "line of reasoning," the lady with whom I talked should not believe in a loving God, the volunteers that gave their time to the hospital should not believe in a loving God, I should no longer believe in a loving God (since I walked through the hospital), nor should any other person who has visited that facility. The falsity of such reasoning is apparent. Seeing the suffering in a children's hospital does not necessarily drive a person to atheism. Truth be told, most people who visit a children's hospital, and even have children who are patients there, believe in the God of the Bible. Barker's assertion does not stand up to rational criticism.

Furthermore, Barker's emotional appeal can easily be turned on its head: Walk through any children's hospital and observe the love, care, and concern that the parents, doctors, and volunteers show the children, and you know atheistic evolution cannot be true. After all, evolution is about the survival of the fittest, in which the strong struggle against the weak to survive in a never-ending contest to pass on their genes. If evolution were true, parents and doctors would not waste their valuable resources on children who will not pass on their genes. Only theism can account for the selfless devotion and care that you see in children's hospitals.

SOME SUFFERING IS ACCEPTABLE

When the "problem of evil" is presented, it quickly becomes apparent that the term "evil" cannot be used in any meaningful way by an atheist. The tactic, therefore, is to swap the terms "suffering," "pain," or "harm" for the word "evil," and contend that the world is filled with too much pain, harm, and suffering. Since it is evident that countless people suffer physical, emotional, and psychological harm, the atheist contends that, even though there is no real "evil," a loving God would not allow such suffering. [NOTE: The atheist's argument has not really changed. He is still contending that suffering is "bad" or "evil" and would not be present in a "good" world. In truth, he remains in the same dilemma of proving that evil exists and that suffering is objectively evil.]

At first glance, it seems that the atheist is claiming that a loving, moral God would not allow His creatures, the objects of His love, to suffer **at all**. Again, the atheist reasons that humans are supposed to be the objects of God's love, yet they suffer. Thus, God does not love or does not have the power to stop the suffering—and therefore does not exist.

The thoughtful observer soon sees the problem with this line of reasoning, which even the skeptic is forced to admit: it is morally right to allow some suffering in order to bring about greater good. On numerous occasions, Dan Barker and his fellow atheists have admitted the validity of this truth. During the cross-examination period of our debate, Barker stated:

> You can't get through life without some harm.... I think we all agree that it is wrong to stick a needle into a baby. That's horrible. But, if that baby needs a life-saving injection, we will cause that harm, we will do that. The baby won't understand it, but we will do that **because there is a greater good**. So, humanistic morality understands that within certain situations, there is harm, and there's a trade off of values (Part 1, pp. 34-35).

In his debate with Peter Payne, Barker stated: "Often ethics involves creating harm. **Sometimes harm is good**" (Barker and Payne, 2005, emp. added). In his book, *Maybe Right, Maybe Wrong: A Guide for Young Thinkers*, Barker wrote: "When possible, you should try to stop the pain of others. **If you have to hurt someone**, then hurt them as little as possible.... If you do have to hurt someone, then try to stop as soon as possible. A good person does not enjoy causing pain" (1992b, p. 33, emp. added).

It becomes evident that the atheist cannot argue against the concept of God based on the mere existence of suffering, because atheists are forced to admit that there can be morally justifiable reasons for suffering. Once again, the argument has been altered. No longer are we dealing with the "problem of evil," since without the concept of God, the term "evil" means nothing. Furthermore, no longer are we dealing with a "problem of suffering," since the atheist must admit that **some** suffering could be morally justifiable in order to produce a greater good. The atheist must add an additional term to qualify suffering: "pointless."

POINTLESS OR UNNECESSARY SUFFERING

Since the skeptic knows that some suffering could be morally justified, he is forced to argue against the biblical concept of God by claiming that at least some of the suffering in this world is **pointless** or unnecessary. The skeptic then maintains that any being that allows pointless suffering cannot be loving or moral. In his book *The Miracle of Theism*, J.L. Mackie noted that if the theist could legitimately show that the suffering in the world is in some way useful, then the concept of the God of the Bible "is formally possible, and its principle involves no real abandonment of our ordinary view of the opposition between good and evil" (1982, p. 154). In light of this fact, Mackie admitted: "[W]e can concede that the problem of evil does not, after all, show that the central doctrines of theism are logically inconsistent with one another" (p. 154).

Did Mackie throw in the proverbial towel and admit that the "problem" of evil and suffering does not militate against God? On the contrary, he contended that even though some suffering or evil might be necessary or useful, there is far too much pointless evil (he terms it "unabsorbed evil") in the world for the traditional God of the Bible to exist. He then concluded: "The problem, therefore, now recurs as the problem of **unabsorbed evils**, and we have as yet no way of reconciling their existence with that of a god of the traditional sort" (p. 155, emp. added). Notice how Mackie was forced to change the "problem of evil" to the "problem of **unabsorbed** evil."

Dan Barker understands this alteration in the "problem of evil" and has used it himself. In a debate with Rubel Shelly, Dan used his standard argument that the suffering in a children's hospital is enough to show God does not exist. Shelly responded with a lengthy rebuttal, bringing to light the idea that suffering in this world can be consistently reconciled with God's **purposes** for mankind. In concluding his comments, Shelly stated: "The kind of world, apparently, that unbelief wants is a world where no wrong action could have bad effects or where we just couldn't make wrong actions" (Barker and Shelly, 1999). Barker responded to Shelly's comments, saying:

> I'm not asking for a world that's free of pain.... No atheist is asking that the world be changed or requiring that if there is a God, He be able to change it. I'm not asking for a world that's free of consequences. I think pain and consequences are important to a rational education.... What I am asking for is for human beings to strive as much as possible for a world that is free of **unnecessary harm** (1999, emp. added).

Barker went on to describe a scenario in which a forest fire forces a baby fawn to flee its home. In the process, the fawn catches its leg in a snare and is consumed by the flames. Barker then stated that he believed no one's soul or character was edified by the fawn's suffering, thus it would be an example of unnecessary or useless suffering. Barker further admitted that even though some suffering is acceptable, there simply is far too much to be reconciled with a loving God. Here again, it is important to notice that Barker's entire argument has been altered. It is no longer a "problem of evil (harm)," but now he has amended it to the "problem of **unnecessary** evil (harm)."

The next question that must be asked is: What would classify as "pointless," "unnecessary," or "unabsorbed" suffering? The simple answer that the atheistic position must suggest is that any suffering that **the atheist** does not deem necessary is pointless. As Timothy Keller points out, the fact is that Mackie and others use the term "pointless" to mean that they, themselves cannot see the point of it. Keller stated: "Tucked away within the assertion that the world is filled with pointless evil is a hidden premise, namely that if evil appears pointless to me, then it must *be* pointless" (2008, p. 23, italics in orig.). Keller further noted:

> This reasoning is, of course, fallacious. Just because you can't see or imagine a good reason why God might allow something to hap-

pen doesn't mean there can't be one. Again we see lurking within supposedly hard-nosed skepticism an enormous faith in one's own cognitive faculties. If our minds can't plumb the depths of the universe for good answers to suffering, well, then, there can't be any! This is blind faith of a high order (p. 23).

Indeed, it is the atheist who lives by the blind faith that he mistakenly attributes to the theist.

THE PURPOSE OF HUMAN EXISTENCE

In his monumental volume, *Have Atheists Proved There Is No God?*, philosopher Thomas B. Warren completely undercut the atheist's use of the problem of evil. He insightfully demonstrated that the Bible teaches that "God has a morally justifiable reason for having created the world...in which evil can (and does) occur" (1972, p. 16). What is that reason? God created the planet to be "the ideal environment for soul-making" (p. 16). God specifically created humans to be immortal, free moral agents, responsible for their own actions, with this earthly life being their one and only probationary period in which their eternal fate is determined by their response to God's will during earthly life (p. 19). Hence, the world "is as good (for the purpose God had in creating it) as any possible world" since it was designed to function as man's "vale of soul-making" (p. 19). The physical environment in which humans were to reside was specifically created with the necessary characteristics for achieving that central purpose. This environment would have to be so arranged that it would allow humans to be free moral agents, provide them with their basic physical needs, allow them to be challenged, and enable them to learn those things they most need to learn (p. 47).

Whereas the atheist typically defines "evil" as physical pain and suffering, the Bible, quite logically, defines evil as violation of God's law (1 John 3:4). Observe, therefore, that **the only intrinsic evil is sin**, i.e., disobeying or transgressing the laws of God. Hence, pain and suffering are not intrinsically evil. ("[I]ntrinsic evil on the purely physical level does not exist" [p. 93]). In fact, animal pain, natural calamities, and human suffering are all necessary constituent variables in the overall environment designed for spiritual development. Such variables, for example, impress upon humans the very critical realizations that life on Earth is uncertain, precarious, and temporary. They also demonstrate that life on Earth is brief—that it will soon end (p. 58). Such realizations not only propel people to consider their spiritual condition, and the necessity of using this life to prepare for the afterlife, they prod people to contemplate God! Suffering, pain, and hardship encourage people to cultivate their spirits and to grow in moral character—acquiring virtuous attributes such as courage, patience, humility, and fortitude. Suffering can serve as discipline and motivation to spur spiritual growth and strength. It literally stimulates people to develop compassion, sympathy, love, and empathy for their fellowman (p. 81).

WHO IS IN THE BEST POSITION TO KNOW?

Since atheists cannot say that real, moral evil exists, they must adjust their objection and say that a loving God would not allow suffering. This position quickly becomes indefensible, so again the position is altered to posit that **some** suffering is morally permissible, but not pointless or unnecessary suffering. Who, then, is to determine if there truly exists unnecessary suffering that would negate the concept of God? Some atheists, such as Barker, are quick to set themselves up as the final judges who alone can set the proper limits of suffering. Yet, when those limits are analyzed, it again becomes apparent that the "problem of evil" is a legitimate problem only for the atheist.

In his book *godless*, Dan Barker stated: "There is no big mystery to morality. Morality is simply acting with the intention to minimize harm" (2008, p. 214). In his explanation about how to minimize harm, Barker wrote: "And the way to avoid making a mistake is to try to be as informed as possible about the likely consequences of the actions being considered" (p. 214). Reasoning from Barker's comments about morality, if there truly is an omniscient God Who knows every consequence of every action that ever has been or ever will be taken, then that Being, and only that Being, would be in a position to speak with absolute authority about the amount and kind of suffering that is "necessary." Barker and his fellow atheists may object to God's tolerance for suffering, but were God to condescend to speak directly to them, He could simply respond by saying: "What you do not know is...," and He could fill in the blank with a thousand reasons about future consequences that would legitimize the suffering He allows.

Indeed, this is precisely the tact God employed with Job, when He challenged Job's knowledge and comprehension of the mysteries of the Universe:

> Who is this who darkens counsel by words without knowledge? Now prepare yourself like a man; I will question you, and you shall answer Me. Where were you when I laid the foundations of the earth? Tell Me, if you have understanding. Have you comprehended the breadth of the earth? Tell Me, if you know all this. Do you know it, because you were born then, or because the number of your days is great? Shall the one who contends with the Almighty correct Him? He who rebukes God, let him answer it. Would you indeed annul My judgment? Would you condemn Me that you may be justified? (Job 38:2-4,18,21; 40:2,8).

God's interrogation of Job elucidated the fact of humanity's limited knowledge, especially as it relates to suffering. In contrast to this, Barker wrote:

> Why should the mind of a deity—an outsider—be better able to judge human actions than the minds of humans themselves? Which mind is in a better position to make judgments about human actions and feelings? Which mind has more credibility? Which has more experience in the real world? Which mind has more of a right? (2008, p. 211).

Of course, Barker's rhetorical questions were supposed to force the reader to respond that **humans** are in a better position to understand what actions are moral, or how much suffering is permissible. In light of his comments about knowing the consequences of actions, however, Barker's position falls flat. Whose mind knows more about the consequences of all actions? Whose mind is in a better position to know what will happen if this action is permitted? Whose mind has the ability to see the bigger picture? And Who alone is in the position to know how much suffering is permissible to bring about the ultimate good for humankind? That would be the infinite, eternal, omniscient Creator—the God of the Bible.

DOES GOD'S EXISTENCE REST UPON HUMAN CONSENSUS?

In Dan's list of "probability" arguments, he included as his fifth argument against God's existence the following comments: "There is no agreement among believers as to the nature or the moral principles of this God that they are arguing for. They all differ with each other" (Part 1, p. 7). According to Dan, since those professing Christianity come down on both sides of moral issues such as abortion, divorce, and the death penalty, then the God Who wrote the Bible "in all probability" does not exist, and the Bible must not be a sufficient guide for human morality.

Is Dan correct in his assessment that disagreement among professed believers nullifies the existence of God? Certainly not. Barker is incorrect for a number of reasons, the majority of which are quite clear after the briefest consideration of the argument. First, we could simply say that Dan's argument, used against his own brand of atheism, refutes itself, since he admits that atheists do not agree on moral issues. In his book *godless*, Barker stated: "**Most** atheists think that values, though not objective things in themselves, can be objectively justified by reference to the real world…. Although **most** atheists accept the importance of morality, this is not conceding that morality exists in the universe" (2008, pp. 213-214, emp. added). Notice that Barker qualifies his statement with the word "most," implying that some atheists do not see morality as he does. In his discussion of human free will, Barker wrote: "By the way, this contributes to my compatibilist position on human free will. (**Not that all atheists agree with me**.) I am an determinist, which means that I don't think complete libertarian free will exists.... **I admit that my definition of free will is subject to debate**" (2008, p. 128, emp. added). If Barker's statement about disagreement of professed believers is true, we could, with equal force, use it on atheism and say that since there is no agreement among atheists on moral issues, then atheism "in all probability" is false.

Of course, Barker does not want to extend his "truth" criterion to atheism. And his statement is inherently flawed in the first place. If two or more people disagreed on whether the holocaust happened, but they all professed to be honest historians, would their disagreement prove that there never was a holocaust? If two people, who both claim to be honest geographers, disagree on the fact that the continent of North America exists, would that negate its reality? Or if two or more people adamantly disagreed on the idea that Dan Barker exists, would his existence be jeopardized based on their disagreement? No, on every count. Agreement among people cannot be used as evidence of the truth or falsity of any proposition.

Barker's atheistic colleague, Sam Harris, has eloquently written on this truth. He disagrees with many atheists about ethical questions. In spite of his atheism, he contends that objective right and wrong do exist (an impossible proposition for a true atheist to maintain, by the way). He wrote:

> The fact that people of different times and cultures disagree about ethical questions should not trouble us. **It suggests nothing at all about the status of moral truth**. Imagine what it would be like to consult the finest thinkers of antiquity on questions of basic science: "What," we might ask, "is fire? And how do living systems reproduce themselves? And what are the various lights we see in the night sky?" We would surely encounter a bewildering lack of consensus on these matters. Even though there was no shortage of brilliant minds in the ancient world, they simply lacked the physical and conceptual tools to answer questions of this sort. **Their lack of consensus signified their ignorance of certain physical truths, not that no such truths exist** (2004, p. 171, emp. added).

The irony of this quote from Harris is that it manifests the atheistic community's lack of consensus on ethical issues, which should disprove atheism according to Barker's line of reasoning. Furthermore, it hammers home the self-evident truth that consensus among professed followers of any concept or entity has no bearing on its existence or its claim to truth. Harris further remarked: "It is quite conceivable that everyone might agree and yet be wrong about the way the world is. It is also conceivable that a **single person might be right in the face of unanimous opposition**" (2004, pp. 181-182, emp. added).

While it is true that the lack of consensus on moral issues by those who profess Christianity does nothing to discount the existence of God, it is appropriate to ask why such disparity exists. Again, it is ironic that Dan Barker has answered his own question in this regard. In his speech, "How to be Moral Without Religion," given at the University of Minnesota on October 19, 2006, Barker stated: "A tendency that we all have, we look through our documents to try to find what supports **our already prejudice views** about what **we think morality should be like**." In one succinct sentence, Barker explained why there is a lack of consensus among professed believers on moral issues. It is not because God does not exist. It is not because the Bible is hopelessly confusing and cannot be understood. It is not because there is no objective moral truth. It is simply because humans bring **their already prejudiced views** to the text of the Bible and try to force it to say what they "think" it should say.

IS THERE A NEED FOR A BELIEF IN GOD?

Dan Barker certainly is no stranger to the debate arena. He has been involved in over 70 moderated debates, many of which have dealt with the concept of God's existence. One of his favorite ideas to present in his debates and writings against God's existence is his opinion that a person does not need a belief in God to be happy or satisfied in life. In our debate, three minutes into his opening statement, Barker said: "There's no need for a belief in a god. You can live a really happy, joyful, wonderful, meaningful life without that religious baggage" (Part 1, p. 7). Is it true that nothing of value is lost when a person jettisons belief in God? Absolutely not. In fact, there are devastating emotional, societal, and psychological consequences of atheism.

THE BITTER FRUITS OF ATHEISM

As was noted previously (p. 72), William Provine, a professor in the Department of Ecology and Evolutionary Biology at the distinguished Cornell University, stated: "Naturalistic evolution has clear consequences that Charles Darwin understood perfectly. 1) No gods worth having exist; 2) no life after death exists; 3) no ultimate foundation for ethics exists; 4) no ultimate meaning in life exists; and 5) human free will is nonexistent" (Provine, 1998). Oxford professor Richard Dawkins concurred with Provine by saying: "Absolutist moral discrimination is devastatingly undermined by the fact of evolution" (2006a, p. 301).

Comments from such high-profile evolutionists provide an excellent springboard from which to examine the logical consequences of belief in naturalistic evolution. If it is true that humans evolved from non-living, primordial slime, then any sense of moral obligation must simply be a subjective outworking of the physical neurons firing in the brain. Theoretically, atheistic scientists and philosophers admit this truth. Charles Darwin understood it perfectly. He wrote: "A man who has no assured and ever present belief in the existence of a personal God or of a future existence with retribution and reward, can have for his rule of life, as far as I can see, **only to follow those impulses and instincts which are the strongest or which seem to him the best ones**" (1958, p. 94, emp. added). On a pragmatic level, however, when a person or group of people actually allow the theoretical idea to influence their actions, the brutality of evolution's immorality is brought to light, and its absurdity is manifested.

DEVALUING OF HUMAN LIFE

It is an easily ascertainable fact that belief in atheistic evolution devalues human life, demoting it to the base level of animal status. Such thinking logically leads to the adoption of measures that destroy innocent human life, but are still viewed by atheistic thinkers as "moral." For instance, in 1983, Peter Singer published an article in the prestigious magazine *Pediatrics* titled "Sanctity of Life or Quality of Life?" In the article, he contended that there is no moral burden to keep alive human infants who are born with mental retardation or other developmental problems such as Down's syndrome. The entire article presents a case against the sanctity of human life, and suggests that the lives of some animals would be much more valuable than the lives of mentally retarded children. In fact, he alluded to the fact that modern, evolutionary teaching has destroyed the idea of the sanctity of human life:

We can no longer base our ethics on the idea that human beings are a special form of creation.... Our better understanding of our own nature has bridged the gulf that was once thought to lie between ourselves and other species, so why should we believe that the mere fact that a being is a member of the species *Homo sapiens* endows its life with some unique, almost infinite, value?... If we compare a severely defective human infant with a nonhuman animal, **a dog or a pig**, for example, **we will often find the nonhuman to have superior capacities, both actual and potential, for rationality, self-consciousness, communication, and anything else that can plausibly be considered morally significant**. Only the fact that the defective infant is a member of the species *Homo sapiens* leads it to be treated differently from the dog or pig. **Species membership alone, however, is not morally relevant**.... If we can put aside the obsolete and erroneous notion of **the sanctity of all human life**, we may start to look at human life as it really is: at the quality of life that each human being has or can achieve" (Singer, 72[1]:128-129 emp. added).

In his book *The God Delusion*, Richard Dawkins expressed the same idea when he wrote: "Notice now that 'pro-life' doesn't exactly mean pro-*life* at all. It means pro-*human*-life. The granting of uniquely special rights to cells of the species *Homo sapiens* is hard to reconcile **with the fact of evolution**.... The *humanness* of an embryo's cells **cannot confer upon it any absolutely discontinuous moral status**" (2006a, p. 300, italics in orig., emp. added).

In his book *Created from Animals: The Moral Implications of Darwinism*, self-proclaimed Darwinian James Rachels stated that when the true moral implications of evolution are understood,

human life will no longer be regarded with the kind of superstitious awe which it is accorded in traditional thought, and the lives of non-humans will no longer be a matter of indifference. This means that **human life will, in a sense, be devalued**, while the value granted to non-human life will be increased. A revised view of such matters as suicide and euthanasia, as well as a revised view of how we should treat animals, will result (1990, p. 5, emp. added).

He further noted: "The big issue in all this is the value of human life.... The difficulty is that **Darwinism** leaves us with fewer resources from which to construct an account of the value of life" (p. 197, emp. added).

According to atheistic evolution, whether a human child lives or dies should depend on the level of potential suffering, intelligence or lack thereof, mental retardation, or physical handicap. If resources are so limited that an intelligent chimpanzee and a human child cannot both be kept alive, then the child's intelligence or threshold of suffering should be compared to the chimpanzee's. If the chimp happens to be more "intelligent" or more capable of suffering, then the "simple" fact that the child is a human should not confer any special moral status. Thus, according to this line of thinking, it would be morally right to eliminate the human child in favor of the chimpanzee. Rachels presented this idea quite clearly:

> An infant with severe brain damage, even if it survives for many years, may never learn to speak, and its mental powers may never rise above a primitive level. In fact, its psychological capacities may be markedly inferior to those of a typical rhesus monkey. In that case, moral individualism [of which Rachels is a proponent—KB] would see no reason to prefer its life over the monkey's (1990, pp. 189-190).

The absurdity of such thinking flies in the face of everything that humans have understood to be moral. The framers of *The Declaration of Independence* understood the special place that humans hold. They penned the famous words: "We hold these truths to be self-evident, that all men are created equal, that they are endowed by their Creator with certain unalienable rights, that among these are life, liberty, and the pursuit of happiness" (1776). Notice that the *Declaration* framers believed that **humans** had certain rights that were "self-evident." In fact, the framers simply recorded this idea that had been understood by humanity for millennia.

What happens when individuals, who believe that humans should not be given any special moral status, put their belief into action? James Rachels shed a sickening light on that question when he concluded:

> Some unfortunate humans—perhaps because they have suffered brain damage—are not rational agents. What are we to say about them? The natural conclusion, according to the doctrine we are considering, would be that their status is that of mere animals. And perhaps we should go on to conclude that they may be used as non-human animals are used—perhaps as laboratory subjects, **or as food** (1990, p. 186).

Population Elimination

Forrest Mims III is the Chairman of the Environmental Science Section of the Texas Academy of Science. He edits a publication titled *The Citizen Scientists*. On March 3-5, 2006, Mims attended the 109th meeting of the Texas Academy of Science, which was held at Lamar University in Beaumont, Texas. Mims related the events that occurred during that meeting in an article titled *Meeting Doctor Doom* (2006). [Unless otherwise noted, the following quotes and facts are derived from that article.]

At the meeting, Dr. Eric R. Pianka, "the University of Texas evolutionary ecologist and lizard expert who the Academy named the 2006 Distinguished Texas Scientist," delivered a speech to about 400 attendees. Just before Pianka spoke, Mims noted that an official of the Academy was involved in a conversation with the cameraman who was recording the meeting. The conversation resulted in the cameraman pointing "the lens of his big camera to the ceiling and slowly walking away." Mims started taking notes on the speech when Pianka began by warning the audience that most people are not ready to hear what he had to say to the assembly.

Mims noted that one of Pianka's main points was that humans should not be given special status among other animals. "Pianka hammered his point home by exclaiming, 'We're no better than bacteria!'" In his speech, Pianka suggested that the Earth cannot survive the current human population increase, and that something needs to be done "to reduce the population to 10 percent of the present number." Pianka then mentioned several ways this might occur. "His favorite candidate for eliminating 90 percent of the world's population is airborne Ebola (Ebola Reston), because it is both highly lethal and it kills in days instead of years." The speech ended with a question-and-answer period. Mims noted: "Immediately almost every scientist, professor and college student present stood to their feet and vigorously applauded the man who had enthusiastically endorsed the elimination of 90 percent of the human population. Some even cheered."

Of course, many within the evolutionary community did not want to connect themselves closely with the idea that an evolutionary ecologist seems to think that his evolutionary ideas need to lead to the mass destruction of five billion humans. They quickly accused Mims of misrepresentation. On April 6, 2006, Nick Matzke wrote:

> The wingnut echo chamber has recently gone insane over the idea that Eric Pianka, a distinguished and much-loved ecologist at UT, advocates mass genocide by ebola in order to bring down world population. The allegation was leveled by disgruntled creationist Forrest Mims, and rapidly spread to the blogosphere via places like Dembski's blog (three posts!) and Telic Thoughts, and then went to the Drudge Report and caused a national media firestorm appearing in my local paper by Monday morning. I smelled a rat from the beginning, and now I have been proved right. KXAN News36 in Austin, TX, **has just debunked the whole thing** (2006, emp. added).

Matzke's statement that the information from News36 debunked "the whole thing" was far from the truth. In fact, in a letter dated April 10, 2006, Assistant Professor Dr. Kenneth R. Summy, the Vice-Chairman of the Environmental Science Section of the Texas Academy of Science, wrote:

> My overall impression of Dr. Pianka's presentation was a 'doomsday' message that life on earth is about to end, and the sooner the

human population crashes the better. I hope he was joking or being sarcastic when he stated that a pandemic of ebola virus would be great for the earth? [sic] no sane person would really believe that (2006).

Dr. Summy further noted:

Forrest Mims did not misrepresent anything regarding the presentation. I heard these statements myself, and would be willing to bet that most of the audience attending the presentation got the same impression that I did. In my opinion, the message contained in the keynote address detracted from what was otherwise an excellent meeting (2006).

The following statements by a student "defending" Dr. Pianka add further credence to Mims' record: "Dr. Pianka's talk at the TAS meeting was mostly of the problems humans are causing as we rapidly proliferate around the globe.... He's a radical thinker, that one! I mean, he's basically advocating for the death of all but 10% of the current population! And at the risk of sounding just as radical, I think he's right" ("Dr. Eric R. Pianka...," 2006; see also "Revisiting...," 2006).

Additionally, Dr. Pianka personally posted several student evaluations of his teaching. One student commented: "I don't root for ebola [sic], but maybe a ban on having more than one child. I agree...too many people [are] ruining this planet" ("Excerpts from Student Evaluations," 1999). Another wrote: "Though I agree that convervation [sic] biology is of utmost importance to the world, I do not think that preaching that 90% of the human population should die of ebola [sic] is the most effective means of encouraging conservation awareness" ("Excerpts from Student Evaluations").

The fact is, Dr. Pianka's evolutionary concepts of ecology push him to conclude that humans are no better than bacteria and that the human population needs to be dramatically reduced. As much as many of his fellow evolutionists would like to distance themselves from such radical thinking, they cannot logically do so.

Atheistic evolution implies that humans are no better than bacteria. They may have more capacity to suffer, they may have more complex brains and body structures, but in the end, one living organism is only as valuable as another. If you have the moral right to destroy millions of bacteria because they are hindering the "progress" of humanity, you have the same moral right to destroy billions of humans because they are causing ecological problems for other, equally valuable, organisms on the planet.

Abortion

The *Merriam-Webster Dictionary* defines abortion as: "the termination of a pregnancy after, accompanied by, resulting in, or closely followed by the **death** of the **embryo or fetus**" ("Abortion," 2008, emp. added). In the United States, this murderous practice has been legal since January 22, 1973, and has resulted in the deaths of more than 48 million innocent human lives in this country alone. If the abortions performed in Europe and Asia during the same time period were added to this figure, the death toll would easily reach into the hundreds of millions. Is it immoral to terminate the lives of unborn human children?

According to the atheistic evolutionary community, abortion is not an immoral practice. In fact, it is often viewed as something moral and right. One line of reasoning used to justify the practice is the idea that humans should not be treated differently than animals, since humans are nothing more than animals themselves. The fact that an embryo is "human" is no reason to give it special status. Dawkins wrote: "An early embryo has the sentience, as well as the semblance, of a tadpole.... One school of thought cares about whether embryos can suffer. The other cares about whether they are human.... Secular moralists are more likely to ask, 'Never mind whether it is *human* (what does that even *mean* for a little cluster of cells?); at what ages does a developing embryo, of any specie become capable of *suffering*?'" (2006a, pp. 297-298, italics and parenthetical items in orig.). Dawkins identifies himself as a "secular moralist" who would not factor into the moral equation the idea of "humanness." How would he and other "secular moralists" decide if a human embryo should live? He noted:

> A consequentialist or utilitarian is likely to approach the abortion question in a very different way, by trying to **weigh up suffering**. **Does the embryo suffer?** (Presumably not if it is aborted before it has a nervous system; and even if it is old enough to have a nervous system it surely suffers less than, say, an adult cow in a slaughterhouse.) (2006a, p. 293, parenthetical item in orig., emp. added).

The modern atheistic moralist simply "weighs up suffering." If the human embryo has not yet reached the stage at which a nervous system develops, then it is less valuable than an animal that does have a nervous system. And even if it does have a nervous system, it probably does not suffer as much as a cow in a slaughterhouse. Thus, it would be more moral to stop killing cows in a slaughterhouse than to stop allowing humans to abort their children. As atheistic writer Sam Harris noted: "If you are concerned about suffering in this universe, killing a fly should present you with greater moral difficulties than killing a human blastocyst [three-day-old human embryo—KB]" (2006a, p. 30). He further stated: "If you are worried about human suffering, abortion should rank very low on your list of concerns" (p. 37).

The moral bankruptcy of such thinking is brutally obvious. Since when is the amount of suffering the criterion by which moral decisions of human life and death are made? Yet that is exactly what Dawkins, Barker, and their fellow atheistic moralists contend. Dawkins wrote: "Of course, it could be argued that humans are more capable of, for example, suffering than other species. This could well be true, and we might legitimately give humans special status by virtue of it" (2006a, p. 301). According to Dawkins, it would be logically permissible to kill any person as long as they do not suffer, or others (like parents or siblings) do not suffer because of their deaths. Suppose, then, a society decides that five-year-old orphans with no siblings are less than ideal and need to be eliminated. In keeping with Dawkins' morality, if policemen sneak up behind the children and deliver an immediately lethal bullet to their brains so that they never feel any pain, then such actions could be as morally viable as killing adult cows in a slaughterhouse. Dawkins and his fellow atheistic thinkers have absolutely no grounds on which to assert that killing five-year-olds in this fashion is "wrong."

Peter Singer admits the reality of this logical implication of atheistic evolution. In his chapter titled: "Justifying Infanticide," Singer concluded that human infants are "replaceable." What does Singer mean by "replaceable"? He points out that if a mother has decided that she will have two children, and the second child is born with hemophilia, then that infant can be disposed of and replaced by another child without violating any moral code of ethics. He explained: "Therefore, if killing the hemophiliac infant has no adverse effect on others, it would, according to the total view, be right to kill him. The total view treats infants as replaceable" (2000, p. 190).

He went on to argue that many in society would be aghast at killing an infant with a disability like hemophilia, but without good reason. He argued that such is done regularly before birth, when a mother aborts a child in utero after prenatal diagnosis reveals a disorder. He stated:

> When death occurs before birth, replaceability does not conflict with generally accepted moral convictions. That a fetus is known to be disabled is widely accepted as a ground for abortion. Yet in discussing abortion, we say that birth does not mark a morally significant dividing line. I cannot see how one could defend the view that fetuses may be "replaced" before birth, but newborn infants may not (2000, p. 191).

Singer further proposed that parents should be given a certain amount of time after a child is born to decide whether or not they would like to kill the child. He wrote: "If disabled newborn infants were not regarded as having a right to life until, say, a week or a month after birth it would allow parents, in consultation with their doctors, to choose on the basis of far greater knowledge of the infant's condition than is possible before birth" (2000, p. 193). One has to wonder why Singer would stop at one week or one month. Why not simply say that it is morally right for parents to kill their infants at one year or five years? Singer concluded his chapter on infanticide with these words: "Nevertheless the main point is clear: **killing a disabled infant is not morally equivalent to killing a person**. Very often it is **not wrong at all**" (p. 193, emp. added). When the logical consequences of atheistic evolution are so clearly spelled out by its adherents, the prospects are grisly indeed.

Animals Kill Their Offspring

Another line of reasoning used to justify abortion (and various other immoral practices) is the idea that since humans are animals, it is right for them to behave like animals. Charles Darwin himself proposed in a chapter of *The Descent of Man*: "My object in this chapter is to shew that there is no fundamental difference between man and the higher mammals in their mental faculties" (1871, p. 446). Thus, it is suggested that if we can find an example of animals engaging in an activity, such would provide enough moral justification needed for humans to practice the same. Applying this idea to abortion, Barbara Burke wrote: "Among some animal species, infant killing appears to be a natural practice. Could it be natural for humans too, a trait inherited from our primate ancestors? Charles Darwin noted in *The Descent of Man* that infanticide has been 'probably the most important of all checks on population growth throughout most of human history'" (1974, 185:653).

Notice that Burke recognizes the fact that humans kill their offspring, and justifies the practice by referring to "analogous" activities in the animal kingdom. Maybe, she reasons, humans kill their infants or unborn children because they inherited the murderous practice from their animal ancestors. By reasoning in this fashion, she attempts, not only to suggest that killing human infants is not morally neutral, but that it could be morally right if the practice is used to check population growth. In this regard, James Rachels wrote:

> Finally, if one is nevertheless tempted to believe that humans are psychologically unique, it is useful to remember that the whole enterprise of experimental psychology, as it is practiced today, assumes otherwise. **Animal behaviour is routinely studied with an eye to acquiring information that can then be applied to humans.** Psychologists who want to investigate maternal behaviour, for example...might study the behaviour of rhesus monkey mothers and infants, assuming that whatever is true of them will be true of humans—because, after all, **they are so much like us** (1990, p. 166, emp. added).

In response to such thinking, several points need to be considered. Humans are not animals. There is no documented evidence verifying the false idea that humans evolved from lower organisms (see Harrub and Thompson, 2002). In fact, all observable evidence verifies that humans maintain a completely unique status in regard to their mental, emotional, and cognitive components (see "In the Image...," 2001; Lyons and Thompson, 2002). To justify human behavior based on behavior observed in the animal world exhibits a grotesque ignorance of everything humans understand about morality. Ten percent of the diet of an adult Komodo dragon often consists of its cannibalizing young Komodo dragons. Would anyone be so irrationally disturbed as to suggest that, because we see infant cannibalism in Komodo dragons, it would be natural for humans to eat their young as well? Apparently so. James Rachels wrote: "The whole idea of using animals as psychological models for humans is a **consequence of Darwinism. Before Darwin, no one could have taken seriously the thought** that we might learn something about the human mind by studying mere animals" (1990, p. 221, emp. added).

If all conceivable human behavior can be justified based on the idea that it mimics animal behavior, then why not abolish all laws, allow stronger humans to kill the weaker ones, allow mothers to eat their babies, allow men to murder sexual rivals, allow women to murder and cannibalize their lovers after intercourse, and simply chalk up such a deplorable situation to "nature"? The logical consequences of such philosophical justification are as obvious as they are ridiculous. The ploy to justify abortion (and other equally reprehensible immoralities) by suggesting that it is "natural" is little more than an attempt to cast aside all moral constraints and debase society to the point of mindless bestiality. Yet such is the logical result of atheism.

DEATH IN THE NAME OF ATHEISM

Not all atheists are grotesquely immoral people. In fact, many of them would be viewed as moral individuals who do not steal, murder, abuse their children, or violate laws. The point to be made is not that all atheistic thinkers are living out the logical implications of their beliefs. The point is that the philosophy of atheism logically implies that immorality is acceptable or non-existent. It is true that most atheists do not put the implications of their belief into practice, but it is also true that some do, and that their actions cannot be construed to be anything other than what they are—the logical consequences of atheistic, evolutionary thinking.

Of course, "respectable" atheists deny that people commit heinously immoral crimes at the instigation of atheism. As Dawkins has stated: "Individual atheists may do evil things but they don't do evil things **in the name of atheism**" (Dawkins, 2006a, p. 278, emp. added). His assertion is patently false. People often do evil things in the name of atheism. These people understand their evolutionary atheism to be a primary contributing factor to their evil actions, and the full weight of atheism's logical conclusions justifies their behavior.

Columbine

April 20, 1999 will go down in U.S. history as the date of one of the most nefarious, murderous criminal acts in modern times. Two teenage boys, Eric Harris and Dylan Klebold, after months of elaborate planning, opened fire on their schoolmates, killing 12 of their peers and one teacher, injuring 23 others, and then committing suicide. Evidence posted on the Web and in written documents showed that the two teens had concocted detailed plans to kill hundreds of students with homemade explosives, but most of their macabre plans went awry.

Hundreds of police investigators, educators, political leaders, and other professionals delved into the reasons why Harris and Klebold snapped as they did. One eye-opening aspect of the research has been the very clear connection between the evolutionary idea of natural selection and Harris' desire to kill his fellow humans. On the day of the shooting, Harris wore a white T-shirt with the words "Natural Selection" emblazoned on it ("Columbine," 2008). This was not coincidental, but was designed to make a statement. According to the Jefferson County Sheriff's Office Report, in a document found in his room, Harris wrote: "I would love to see all you f-------ds die. NBK. I love it! sometime [sic] in April me and V will get revenge and will **kick natural selection up a few notches**" (as quoted in "Columbine," 2008, emp. added). His diary also stated: "I will sooner die than betray my own thoughts. but [sic] before I leave this worthless place, I will kill whoever I deem **unfit** for, anything at all, especially life" (as quoted in "Columbine," 2008, emp. added).

In his article titled "Kill Mankind. No One Should Survive," Dave Cullen reported extensively on the investigation surrounding the Columbine massacre. He wrote:

> "They do consider the human race beneath them," one investigator said. Harris "talks a lot about **natural selection** and that kind of leads into his admiration of Hitler and Nazism and their 'final solution'—that we, the human race have interrupted or disrupted **natural selection** by inventing vaccines and stuff like that. In one of his writings, he talks about that: 'It would be great if there were no vaccines, because people who should have died would have died, and we wouldn't be perpetuating this kind of stuff'" (1999, emp. added).

The Columbine killers' evolutionary beliefs cannot be disconnected from their brutal slayings.

Finland Massacre

Another example of this type of relationship between atheism and immoral behavior comes from Finland. An 18-year-old man named Pekka Eric Auvinen marched into his school and shot and killed seven of his schoolmates as well as the headmistress. He then turned the gun on himself and committed suicide. When such gruesome carnage occurs, we naturally ask, "Why?" What would drive a young man like Auvinen to commit such horrific atrocities? In Auvinen's case, the answer is clear.

Auvinen explained the philosophy that led him to commit this dastardly mass murder. On a Web site message board post from before the slaying, he explained that he was a self-avowed "cynical existentialist, anti-human humanist, anti-social social-Darwinist, realistic idealist and god-like **atheist**" ("Teen Dead...," 2007, emp. added). He went on to state: "I, as a **natural selector**, will eliminate all who I see **unfit**, disgraces of human race and failures of **natural selection**" (2007, emp. added). There you have it. The reason he murdered eight innocent people is because he was an atheistic evolutionist who devalued human life and believed that he had the right to destroy any living being who he considered to be less fit than himself.

As much as evolutionists insist on separating themselves from such disgusting displays of immorality, the logical implications of their godlessness tie them indubitably to Auvinen's actions. The only thing that separates Auvinen from other atheists is that he acted out the logical implications of his atheistic belief. It is high time atheism's immorality is recognized, repudiated, and exposed for the reprehensible fruit it bears.

Jeffrey Dahmer

Jeffrey Dahmer was one of the most notorious serial killers in modern history. He murdered 17 men and boys, dismembered them, stored human body parts in his apartment, practiced homo-sexual necrophilia and cannibalized his victims (Dahmer, 1994, p. 10). He was convicted of 15 counts of murder and sentenced to serve over 900 years in prison. During his incarceration, he was murdered by another inmate.

When a person perpetrates such brutal and deranged crimes against his fellow man, natural questions that arise in the minds of those who hear the details include: Why would a person commit such heinous crimes? What would cause a person to become such a murderer? In Jeffrey Dahmer's case, he supplied the world with the answer.

In 1994, Stone Phillips interviewed Jeffrey Dahmer and his father Lionel Dahmer for NBC's *Dateline*. In that interview, Stone Phillips asked Jeffrey Dahmer several questions regarding the possible causes of Dahmer's behavior. In one portion of the interview, Jeffrey explained that he took complete and personal responsibility for his actions, and his crimes could not be blamed on his parents, school, or other external circumstances. Following those remarks, Jeffrey said: "There comes a point where a person has to be accountable for what he's done." His father, Lionel, then asked him: "Let me ask. When did you first feel that everyone is accountable for their actions?" Jeffrey responded:

> Well, thanks to you for sending that creation science material. Because **I always believed the lie that evolution is truth**, the theory of evolution is truth. That we all just came from the slime, and when we died, you know, that was it. There was nothing. **So the whole theory cheapens life**.... And I've since come to believe that the Lord Jesus Christ is the true Creator of the Earth. It didn't just happen (Phillips, 1994, emp. added).

Lionel Dahmer then began to discuss the period of time during Jeffrey's upbringing that he thought most influenced Jeffrey's murderous behavior. Lionel said: "At that period of time I had drifted away from a belief in a Supreme Being. And I never, as a result, passed along the feeling that we are all accountable. In the end, He owns us. And that basic concept is very fundamental to all of us."

Stone Phillips then asked Lionel: "You feel that the absence, at least for a while, of a strong religious faith and belief may have prevented you from instilling some of that in Jeff?" Lionel responded: "That's right." Phillips then turned to Jeffrey and asked: "Is that how you feel?" Jeffrey responded to Phillips' question: "Yes, I think that had a big part to do with it. If a person doesn't think that there is a God to be accountable to, then what's the point of trying to modify your behavior to keep it within acceptable ranges? That's how I thought, anyway" (Phillips, 1994).

To what, then, did Dahmer attribute his gruesome, horrifying crimes? He simply said he believed that evolution is true, that humans arose from primordial slime, and that there is no personal accountability inherent in the theory. Dahmer understood the logical implications of atheistic evolution perfectly. Dahmer's behavior appalls society because he had the brains and drive to put the theoretical implications into practice in real life. When he did, society was justifiably outraged at his behavior. But such outrage is justifiable only in the context of a God to Whom all people are accountable. Without such accountability, Dahmer was right to conclude: "What's the point of trying to modify your behavior to keep it within acceptable ranges?" Dahmer is yet another example of a person who committed heinously evil crimes in the name of atheism.

SEXUAL DEVIANCE AND PERVERSION

Not only does atheistic evolution devalue human life, it also taints many of the most important areas of human interaction. Sexuality is one area of human behavior that has been completely disrupted by the erroneous concepts of evolution and atheism. In a work he titled *Ends and Means*, atheist Aldous Huxley wrote:

> I had motives for not wanting the world to have meaning; consequently, assumed it had none, and was able without any difficulty to find reasons for this assumption.... For myself, as no doubt for most of my contemporaries, the philosophy of meaninglessness was essentially an instrument of liberation. The liberation we desired was simultaneously liberation from a certain political and economic system and liberation from a certain system of morality. **We objected to the morality because it interfered with our sexual freedom** (1937, pp. 270, 273, emp. added).

Following Huxley's argument, if we assume that the world was not created by God, and that there is ultimately no real meaning to human existence, then we can have sex with whomever, whenever, and in whatever way we choose. Evolutionary atheism offers sexual deviance a blank check to be filled out in whatever way each "naked ape" chooses. Numerous examples can be shown in which atheistic evolution is used to explain and defend sordid sexual perversions.

Rape and Evolution

Working under the assumption of naturalistic evolution, and knowing the ethical implications of such, Randy Thornhill and Craig T. Palmer co-authored a book titled *A Natural History of*

Rape, published by the MIT Press in 2000. In their preface they stated that they "would like to see rape eradicated from human life" (p. xi). A noble thought—to eradicate such a detestable practice. Their self-professed purpose is to educate their readers as to the causes of rape. They feel this education will help their readers understand rape better, and be more fully equipped to initiate programs that will prevent rape more efficiently than the current programs.

Yet, as noble as their suggested aim may be, Thornhill and Palmer embarked on an impossible task. Since they apply naturalistic, evolutionary thinking to rape, they are forced to say, in essence, that there is really nothing ultimately wrong with the practice (although they do not like it and want to see it eradicated). In the third chapter, titled "Why Do Men Rape?," the authors note: "The males of most species—including humans—are usually more eager to mate than the females, and this enables females to choose among males who are competing with one another for access to them. But getting chosen is not the only way to gain sexual access to females. In rape, the male circumvents the female's choice" (2000, p. 53).

Comparing humans with animal species, the authors view rape as a natural way for males to circumvent the selection process. In fact, they claim: "Human rape arises from men's **evolved machinery** for obtaining a high number of mates in an environment where females choose mates" (p. 190, emp. added). They further state that "[e]volutionary theory applies to rape, as it does to other areas of human affairs, on both logical and evidentiary grounds. There is no legitimate scientific reason not to apply evolutionary or ultimate hypotheses to rape" (p. 55).

In their proposed "scientific" reasons why men rape women, Thornhill and Palmer suggest that in some cases heavy metals such as lead "disrupt psychological adaptations of impulse control," which may lead to a "higher rate of criminality" (p. 58). They stated: "Lead may account for certain cases of rape, just **as mutations may**"

(p. 58, emp. added). Thus, rape may simply be caused when a male of a species is exposed to an excess of some type of heavy metal like lead or by mutations. Sam Harris added: "There is, after all, nothing more natural than rape. But no one would argue that rape is good, or compatible with a civil society, because it may have had evolutionary advantages for our ancestors" (2006, pp. 90-91). Joann Rodgers quipped: "Rape or at least rape-like acts clearly exist in many species, giving additional weight to both rape's 'natural' roots and its 'value' in our biological and psychological legacy" (2001, p. 412). She further commented: "Even rape, fetishes, bondage, and other so-called aberrant sexual behaviors are almost certainly biologically predisposed, if not adaptive, and may therefore be what biologists call 'conserved' traits, attributes or properties **useful or essential** to life across all cultures and genomes" (p. 11, emp. added).

The fallacy with this line of thinking is that it flies in the face of everything humans know about moral decisions. Furthermore, it transforms a vicious, morally reprehensible activity into something that may allegedly be caused by mutations or other phenomena that exempt the rapist from taking responsibility for his actions. Such "scientific" explanations for an immoral action like rape are absolutely appalling. When boiled down to its essence, as Thornhill, Palmer, Harris, and Rodgers, have so well illustrated, proponents of naturalistic evolution can never claim that any activity is wrong in an ultimate sense. This being the case, any action that a person chooses to do would be considered just as morally right as any other action, since all human behavior would be the by-product of evolution. As Darwin himself said, "A man who has no assured and ever present belief in the existence of a personal God or of a future existence with retribution and reward, can have for his rule of life, as far as I can see, only **to follow those impulses and instincts which are the strongest or which seem to him the best ones**" (1958, p. 94, emp. added). If a man follows his impulse to rape a woman, atheists cannot say, and more and more will not say, it is wrong.

Homosexuality

In the section dealing with abortion, we noted how evolutionists often appeal to nature to justify immoral behavior. They claim that if animals can be found to exhibit a certain behavior, it is then moral for humans to engage in that behavior as well. Evolutionists have followed this line of reasoning in their defense of homosexuality. For example, the Oslo Natural History Museum opened the world's first exhibit documenting cases of "homosexual" behavior in nature. One of the statements in the exhibit reads: "We may have opinions on a lot of things, but one thing is clear—homosexuality is found throughout the animal kingdom, it is not against nature" (Doyle, 2006).

In a *Live Science* article titled, "Animal Sex: No Stinking Rules," the author wrote:

> Animals flout established rules when it comes to the game of love and sex. In fact, the animal kingdom is full of swingers. Bonobos are highly promiscuous, engaging in sexual interactions more frequently than any other primate, and in just about every combination from heterosexual to homosexual unions. Mothers even mate with their mature sons.... Bonobo societies 'make love, not war,' and their frequent sex is thought to strengthen social bonds and resolve conflict. This idea could explain why bonobo societies are relatively peaceful and their relatives, chimpanzees, which practice sex strictly for reproduction, are prone to violence (n.d.).

Of course, the fallacy of such thinking has already been exposed. Immoral behavior cannot be justified by referring to animal behavior. Furthermore, homosexuality is certainly "against nature," that is, the natural way that God designed **humans** to function. The inspired apostle Paul condemned homosexuality:

> For this reason God gave them up to vile passions. For even their women exchanged the **natural use** for what is **against nature**. Likewise also the men, leaving the **natural** use of the woman, burned in their lust for one another, men with men committing

what is shameful, and receiving in themselves the penalty of their error which was due (Romans 1:26-27, emp. added).

Homosexuality controverts **human nature** in at least two fundamental ways. First, on a basic physical, anatomical level, homosexuality disregards the natural use of the sexual organs of men and women. Males and females were **designed** to be sexually compatible in order to reproduce and bear offspring (see Genesis 1:28). If homosexuality was a natural, genetic occurrence (which it is not—see Harrub and Miller, 2004), the genes responsible for it would quickly disappear due to the inability of same sex couples to reproduce. Second, God designed men and women to be capable of a relationship, in marriage, unlike any other human relationship. When a man and a woman are joined together, they become "one-flesh," a biblical phrase that describes the epitome of intimacy and compatibility (Genesis 2:23). God specifically designed Eve, and all future women, to be perfect helpers suitable for Adam and subsequent men. And, while it is true that sinful humans often fail to achieve the intimacy and oneness designed by God, it is not because of faulty design, but of people's sinful decisions. God designed men and women to be **naturally** compatible both physically and emotionally. Homosexuality circumvents that inherent compatibility.

Sex Behind the Bike Sheds

In the United States of America, one would be hard pressed to find a person who does not understand that teenage pregnancy among unwed mothers is a colossal problem in this country (as well as many others). Contributors to the official Web site of The National Campaign to Prevent Teen and Unplanned Pregnancy, explain: "Despite hitting the lowest level in 30 years, 31% of teenage girls get pregnant at least once before they reach age 20" ("The National Day...," 2008). The site further informs its readers that 750,000 teens per year get pregnant. In order to curb this destructive trend, the government sanctioned a day designated as "The National Day to Prevent Teen Pregnancy," the ninth annual of which occurred on May 5, 2010. Organizations that partnered in this effort included The American Academy of Pediatrics, The American Medical Association, Big Brothers Big Sisters of America, Centers for Disease Control and Prevention, the March of Dimes, the National 4-H Council, and a host of other well-known groups.

In the official *Teen Discussion Guide* of "The National Day to Prevent Teen Pregnancy," the authors noted: "Sex has consequences—both physical and emotional." They further stated: "Not having sex is the best and safest choice to prevent pregnancy..." ("Teen Discussion Guide," 2008). In a section of the guide titled "Fact or Fiction," the authors wrote: "Fact: Abstinence is the only 100% effective way to prevent pregnancy" (2008). It is abundantly clear that the general population of approximately 300 million people in the U.S. recognize teen pregnancy as a problem and would like to see it stopped.

The only sure solution to teen pregnancy is equally clear—total sexual abstinence among unmarried teenagers. When thinking about ideas or philosophical frameworks that would encourage such abstinence, where would one turn? The obvious answer is to the New Testament. The Bible repeatedly stresses the need for sexual purity, and condemns sexual activity outside of the marriage bond. Hebrews 13:4 makes that point abundantly clear: "Marriage is honorable among all, and the bed undefiled; but fornicators and adulterers God will judge." The apostle Paul admonished his readers to "put to death your members which are on the earth: **fornication**, uncleanness, passion, evil desire, and covetousness, which is idolatry" (Colossians 3:5, emp. added; cf. 1 Corinthians 6:18). The New Testament clearly and consistently presents sexual guidelines that, if followed, would prevent 100% of out-of-wedlock teen pregnancy.

When attention is turned to the philosophy of atheistic evolution, the situation is much different. Not only do the logical implications of evolution not prohibit teen pregnancy, they actually encourage and justify it. In June 2006, Dr. Lawrence Shaw, deputy medical director at the Bridge Centre in London, spoke at the 22nd annual conference of the European Society of Human Reproduction and Embryology ("Teenage and 60-Year-Old...," 2006). In his speech, he explored the alleged evolutionary history of humans, and how that heritage affects present human behavior. Speaking directly to the issue of teen pregnancy, Shaw stated:

> Therefore, before we condemn our teenagers for having sex behind the bike sheds and becoming pregnant, we should remember that this is a natural response by these girls to their rising fertility levels. Society may "tut, tut" about them, **but their actions are part of an evolutionary process that goes back nearly two million years;** whilst their behaviour may not fit with Western society's expectations, it is perhaps useful to consider it in the wider context (as quoted in "Teenage and 60-Year-Old...," 2006, emp. added).

Shaw's rationale is in complete harmony with the implications of evolution, while at the same time completely at odds with what is morally justified. In *Sex: A Natural History*, Joann Rodgers wrote about a high school sophomore who was longing to entice the local football star into a "few stolen kisses" or a sexual "backseat tumble." Concerning this teen, Rodgers wrote:

> Her physiological need, her reproductive status, and her strategies are not altogether removed from that of the Florida black beetle, Lara the bonobo, or the castle-bound Guinevere longing for Lancelot. Athleticism and body building, one-night stands, romantic love, and jealousy, along with infidelity, monogamy, and homosexuality, are so universally demonstrable across species and cultures that they have long been presumed in large measure to have been drawn through the filter of sexual evolution and biology" (2001, p. 11).

According to evolution, promiscuous teenagers are not morally responsible for negative sexual behavior. They simply are programmed to pass on their genes to the next generation. Teenagers who are getting pregnant might not fit into "Western society's expectations," but they are not doing anything immoral or wrong—according to the theory. They are simply acting on their evolutionary impulses that span back some two million years, just like black beetles and bonobos.

Evolution and Adultery

Why would a person make a solemn vow to be sexually faithful to his spouse in a committed marriage relationship, but then break that vow and commit adultery with another person? Is there anything morally wrong with adultery? As with other deviant sexual practices, evolutionary theory explains adultery in purely naturalistic terms, absolving adulterous perpetrators of any moral delinquency. In her article titled "Are Humans Meant to be Monogamous?," Jeanna Bryner said: "Evolutionary psychologists have suggested that men are more likely to have extramarital sex, partially due to the male urge to 'spread genes' by broadcasting sperm. Both males and females, these scientists say, try to up their evolutionary progress by seeking out high-quality mates, albeit in different ways" (n.d.). Bryner quoted Daniel Kruger, an evolutionary psychologist at the University of Michigan's School of Public Health, who said: "We're special in this regard [the tendency to be monogamous— KB], but at the same time **like most mammals**, we are a polygynous species." Bryner then explained: "Kruger said humans are considered 'mildly polygynous,' in which a male mates with more than one female" (n.d.). According to atheistic evolution, adultery is not a morally debased breach of a marriage contract, but rather simply the outworking of the "evolutionary urge" to pass on one's genes to the next generation in the most effective way possible.

Joann Rodgers noted: "Indeed, lifelong monogamy appears to be as rare in us as in the animal world, at least among the so-called alpha or most powerful males and females" (2001, p. 341). Rodgers further stated: "Other evidence for a natural tendency to *infidelity* emerges from how easily and simply our behavior and our biochemistry can be subverted to the game" (p. 341, italics in orig.). She paralleled human sexual behavior with studies done on birds, such as the reed warbler, bluebirds, and the pied flycatcher, as well as other animals, such as primates and prairie voles. Concerning these studies, she said that "evidence for the prevalence and reward of promiscuity in females is considerable" (p. 342). Rodgers concluded:

> And in humans and most animals, adultery and infidelity—what Fisher calls "nature's Peyton Place"—are widespread, common, tolerated, and in fact reinforced by our biology. Only if promiscuity really maximizes a woman's reproductive edge is it worth both the risk and her having evolved those subtle deceits such as hidden ovulation and the capacity to hide or fake orgasm (p. 343).

Notice that Rodgers takes it to be a matter of fact that humans naturally commit adultery. She reasons that such is the case because adulterous females maximize their reproductive "edge." In fact, she is so bold as to state that if adultery were not evolutionarily productive, it would not exist, and the fact that it occurs so often, both in humans and in animals, is evidence that it is beneficial as far as evolution is concerned.

What does Rodgers have to say about the feelings of guilt and shame that often accompany adulterous relationships? She admitted that "[g]uilt and shame always seem to be part and parcel of sexual cheating" (p. 341). But she suggested that "shame, guilt, and concepts of sexual morality *evolved* just as surely as our tendency to stray" (p. 379, italics in orig.). Analyzing adultery, then, from an evolutionary standpoint, it is simply a natural, inherited behavior, that is often accompanied by the evolved emotions of shame and guilt, but it has several practical, reproductive advantages and that is why it persists. According to such evolutionary thinking, humans should hardly even attempt to regulate sexual activity or apply moral constraints to it. Rodgers quipped: "What seems to be the case is that human societies do best when they **live and let live**, up to a point, in order to keep our social responsibilities and our biological drives in some balance" (p. 353, emp. added).

Such thinking is debased and illogical. Sexual misconduct is not a product of evolution, it is the product of selfish decisions made by the parties involved. Society cannot clear its bespattered conscience with a single swipe of the evolutionary eraser. We must face the fact that we as a society are acting immorally, and we must resolve to teach the one philosophy that can remedy the situation: there is a God in heaven and we must live according to His Word.

Pedophilia

Since sexual behavior such as promiscuity before marriage, adultery, and homosexuality are generally viewed by atheistic evolutionists as "mainstream" and harmless when involving consenting adults, most evolutionists have no problem openly declaring them to be products of evolution. Yet it is difficult, though not impossible, to find an "honest" evolutionist that will extend the logical implications of atheistic evolution to fringe, grotesque sexual behaviors such as pedophilia. In truth, if adultery and promiscuity are nothing more than the outworking of evolutionary urges, are not **all** sexual behaviors? Who is to say which behaviors are "moral" and should be maintained, or which ones are "immoral" and wrong? Such is the quagmire into which evolutionists have plunged themselves.

In a chapter titled "Bad Sex," Joann Rodgers wrote: "In addition, even the criminal justice system is coming to recognize that while pedophilia and other forms of exploitive sex must be punished in order to protect victims, the perpetrators may also be victims—not necessarily of any abuse **but of their biological predispositions**" (2001, p. 429, emp. added). She then quoted psychiatrist Fred Berlin, who said: "Nothing in the research suggests that perversions **are 'volitional'** or that their expression is a **failure of self-control**" (p. 429, emp. added).

Notice the implications involved in these statements. Pedophiles allegedly are victims of their biological predispositions. Furthermore, their actions are not "volitional" (based on their own choices or freewill), nor are their actions a failure to control their urges. One has to wonder why, then, such behavior should be punished. If it is not volitional, or controlled by a person's will, we cannot expect punishment to alter the behavior. Furthermore, if pedophilia is not a lack of self-control, why would we expect punishment to hinder those contemplating committing such acts in the future? If pedophiles are biologically predisposed to sexual perversion, cannot will themselves in any other direction, and are not suffering from a lack of self-control, punishment can neither change their behavior nor discourage them (or others) from future involvement in it. If evolution is true, then **all** sexual behaviors, including pedophilia, homosexuality, necrophilia, bestiality, polygamy, and promiscuity are equally "moral" options. As Rodgers wrote:

> In the origin and development of species, no surviving component of sex, can be considered *unnatural* or unnecessary. *All* aspects of sex observable in animals today, no less than sexual reproduction itself, are what biologists and psychologists call "highly conserved." All aspects of sex are the evolutionary winners across the eons of natural selection, of trial and error. They persist in us and every other creature precisely because of their importance in survival (2001, pp. 4-5, italics in orig.).

ATHEISTS' SEXUAL AGENDA

Not only is sexual perversion and promiscuity a direct and logical implication of atheistic evolution, but such sexual laxity is one of the primary **aims** of the atheistic community. In 2007, atheistic writer Christopher Hitchens wrote a book titled *god is not Great: How Religion Poisons Everything*. Hitchens has been critically acclaimed as "one of the most prolific, as well as brilliant, journalists of our time," according to the *London Observer*. The *Los Angeles Times* stated that he is a "political and literary journalist extraordinaire." In *god is not Great*, Hitchens repeatedly argues that biblical sexual purity and monogamous sexual fidelity are not only undesirable, but actually destructive. In his list of four irreducible objections to religious faith, he included that faith "is both the result and cause of dangerous sexual repression" (2007, p. 4). Just six pages later, he wrote that it is absurd to think that someone could know that there is a God and "to know what 'he' demands of us—from our diet to our observances to our sexual morality" (p. 10). Later in the book, Hitchens wrote:

> The relationship between physical health and mental health is now well understood to have a strong connection to the sexual function, or dysfunction. Can it be a coincidence, then, that all religions claim the right to legislate in matters of sex? The principle way in which believers inflict on themselves, on each other, and on nonbelievers, has always been their claim to monopoly in this sphere (p. 53).

In opposition to the "sexual repression" that Hitchens assigns to all religions, he stated: "Clearly, the human species is designed to experiment with sex" (p. 54). He also stated: "Sexual innocence, which can be charming in the young if it is not needlessly protracted, is positively corrosive and repulsive in the mature adult" (p. 227).

In his final chapter titled "The Need for a New Enlightenment," Hitchens concluded his book with a plea to banish all religions. He wrote:

> Above all, we are in need of a renewed Enlightenment, which will base itself on the proposition that the proper study of mankind is man, and woman.... **Very importantly**, the divorce between **sexual life** and fear, and the **sexual life** and disease, and **the sexual life** and tyranny, can now at last be attempted, on the sole condition that we banish all religions from the discourse (p. 283, emp. added).

From Hitchens' writings, it is abundantly clear that one of his primary purposes for getting rid of God is so he, and those who adopt his atheistic propositions, can "experiment" sexually as evolved animals without any fetters of conscience. [NOTE: Many of the religions that Hitchens discusses are guilty of approving unbiblical injunctions regarding sex that deserve denunciation, such as forbidding to marry. Hitchens' point, however, is clear: all religions, including New Testament Christianity, should be abolished so that no sexual restrictions hinder unregulated sexual experimentation.]

Hitchens is certainly not alone in his desire to see atheism propel human sexuality into an unregulated realm of experimental promiscuity. Militant atheist Sam Harris, in his *Letter to a Christian Nation*, attempted to explain to Christians that sexuality has nothing to do with morality. He wrote:

> You [Christians—KB] believe that your religious concerns about sex, in all their tiresome immensity, have something to do with morality.... Your principle concern appears to be that the creator of the universe will take offence at something people do while naked. This prudery of yours contributes daily to the surplus of human misery (2006, p. 26).

Harris further commented that "any God who could concern Himself with something as trivial as gay marriage...is not as inscrutable as all that" (p. 55).

Other atheists have advanced the banner of sexual anarchy into realms such as pornography. David Mills, in *Atheist Universe*, titled chapter nine "Christian Fundamentalists and the 'Danger' of Internet Porn" (2006, p. 190). In that chapter, Mills extrapolates from his atheistic philosophy that pornography is harmless and morally neutral. He stated: "When viewed in historical perspective, it is difficult to believe that teenage males are genuinely harmed by sexual images.... No credible sociological or psychological study of this question has discerned any harmful effects whatever of a teenage male's viewing photos of nude women or of adult copulation" (p. 197). Mills further proposed that senseless religious moralizing is to blame for the fact that pornography has ever been stigmatized as immoral. He brazenly asserted: "When all the religious and moralistic blathering is dismissed, opponents of internet porn have failed utterly to document any empirical 'harm' to teenage males..." (p. 198).

Mills is demonstrably wrong in his assertion that no documented empirical evidence verifies that teenage males are harmed by pornography. Numerous studies document that, among other deleterious effects, viewing pornography "can lead to anti-social behavior," "desensitizes people to rape as a criminal offence," and "leads men and women to experience conflict, suffering, and sexual dissatisfaction" (Rogers, 1990). According to one study of rapists, half of those surveyed "used pornography to arouse themselves immediately prior to seeking out a victim" (1990). In addition, heavy exposure to pornography "encourages a desire for increasingly deviant materials which involve violence, like sadomasochism and rape" (1990).

Mills, Hitchens, Harris, and many of their fellow atheists are attempting to strip away all moral "regulations" from human sexuality. Make no mistake: **atheism justifies sexual conduct of any kind,** and those atheists who understand this point are demanding that all societal regulations on sex be abolished. As Joann Rodgers aptly summarized:

> Animals, insects, and bacteria, with their multiple desires, mutinous genders, alternative sex lives, and sometimes violent mating habits, behave in ways that we humans, **in our arrogance,** consider graceless if not immoral. And yet what we may consider **profane in nature is indeed profound.... With evolutionary biology as our guide,** however, we are better able to see what has long been concealed in our nature and nurture, and that the profound is **not at all profane** (2001, pp. 40-41, emp. added).

THE ATHEISTIC OBJECTION

Of course, atheists do not sit idly by while their philosophy is accused of grotesquely immoral implications. They fire back with the idea that millions have been abused, tortured, and murdered at the hands of "Christians." Atheistic apologists then proceed to detail horrible crimes that took place during the Salem Witch Trials, the Crusades, and the Spanish Inquisition. David Mills wrote: "The Crusades, the Inquisition, the witch burnings, the torture of 'infidels' were all carried out in the name of the Christian God. While it is unfair to hold Christianity responsible for perversions of its teachings, it is nonetheless indisputable that, historically more people have been slaughtered in the name of the Christian religion than for any reason connected to atheism" (2006, p. 48). Hitchens' book *god is not Great: How Religion Poisons Everything* contains copious examples of crimes against humanity perpetrated in the name of religion. The second chapter of his book is titled "Religion Kills." In it, he discussed several countries he visited. He stated: "Here then, is a very brief summary of the religiously inspired cruelty I witnessed in these six places" (2007, p. 18). The paragraphs that follow that statement document multiple tortures and murders done in the name of specific religions.

Hitchens and others can easily document atrocities performed in the name of religion. But does this prove that all religion is false, and that if a person can spot a flaw or comprehend a fallacy in one religion, then he has effectively disproved the validity of all religions? Absolutely not. Can you imagine what would happen if this type of argument were used in other areas of life? Apply such thinking to food: since many foods are poisonous and have killed people, all foods should be avoided. Apply the thinking to electricity: since many people have died while using electricity, all electrical use is detrimental to society. Or apply it to activities like swimming: many have drowned while swimming, thus all swimming leads to drowning and should be avoided. What if the logic were applied to surgery? Since it is true that thousands of people have died during or as a result of surgery, then all surgery should be avoided, because it leads to death or is in some way physically detrimental to society. Obviously, the ridiculous idea that **all** religion is detrimental to society, simply because it can be proven that **some** religions are, should be quickly discarded by any honest, thoughtful observer.

New Testament Christianity does not stand or fall based on the validity of competing religions. In fact, Hitchens and others are right in asserting that many religions are detrimental to society. But they are wrong to lump true Christianity in with the rest of the useless lot. New Testament Christianity is unique, logically valid, historically documented, and philosophically flawless. It does not crumble with those religions that are filled with "vain babblings and contradictions of what is falsely called knowledge" (1 Timothy 6:20). Instead, New Testament Christianity, as personified in the life of Jesus Christ, shines forth as **the truth** that makes men free (John 8:32).

Furthermore, it should be noted that atheism is not **discredited based on the behavior of its adherents**. Some atheists are kind to others, hard-working, and considerate. Does this prove that atheism is true? No. On the other hand, some atheists shoot their classmates because they consider them less fit. Does the brutal, immoral behavior of these individuals discredit atheism as a philosophy? Not necessarily. **No philosophy can be correctly assessed based solely on the behavior of those who claim to follow it.** Hitchens correctly stated: "The first thing to be said is that virtuous behavior by a believer is no proof at all of—indeed is not even an argument for—the truth of his belief" (2007, pp. 184-185).

Having said that, we must hasten to state that a philosophy can be correctly assessed by considering only the behaviors **which are based on the correctly derived, logical implications of the philosophy.** In regard to the crimes done in "the name of Christianity," even atheists admit that such crimes were justified by twisting the teachings of the New Testament. Notice that Mills conceded: "While it is unfair to hold Christianity responsible **for**

perversions of its teachings, it is nonetheless indisputable that, historically more people have been slaughtered in the name of the Christian religion than for any reason connected to atheism" (2006, p. 48, emp. added). Harris made a similar statement: "You probably think the Inquisition **was a perversion of the 'true' spirit of Christianity. Perhaps it was**" (2006, p. 11, emp. added). An honest reading of the New Testament lays bare the lucid fact that activities such as the witch hunts and inquisitions were not behaviors based on the logical implications of the teachings of Christ in the New Testament. Jesus taught people to treat others with love, kindness, and respect—the way they, themselves, wish to be treated (Matthew 7:12).

Notice, however, that the behaviors and views decried in this material about the fruits of atheism are directly derived from a proper understanding of atheism, and are propounded by the atheists themselves. Who said that atheistic evolution destroys all moral absolutes? Who stated that parents should have the option to kill a child a month after it is born? Who proposed that humans are no better than bacteria, and that 90% of the human population needs to be eliminated? Who suggested that sexual promiscuity, teen pregnancy, rape, and homosexuality are natural products of the evolutionary process? **Evolutionary atheists are the ones promoting these ideas**. Radical Christian fundamentalists are not building rhetorical straw men by concocting outlandish, grotesquely immoral behaviors out of thin air. On the contrary, the immoral actions and attitudes arising from atheistic evolution are clearly spelled out and advocated by the atheists themselves. If a person who claims to be a Christian kills a one-month-old child because the child is a hemophiliac, that person violates every principle derived from an accurate understanding of New Testament teaching. If an atheist does the same, he does so with the full force of a proper understanding of atheistic evolution justifying his behavior.

CONCLUSION

The concept of God is the only rational basis for an ultimate moral standard. When the concept of God is eradicated from a philosophy or society, that philosophy or society cuts off its ability to make moral decisions. In turn, it forfeits the ability to "eradicate" such actions as rape, theft, murder, or any other immoral vice. As John Paul Sartre appropriately commented, "Everything is indeed permitted if God does not exist, and man is in consequence forlorn, for he cannot find anything to depend upon either within or outside himself" (1961, p. 485). When the Bible succinctly stated, "The fool has said in his heart, 'There is no God,' they are corrupt, they have done abominable works, there is none who does good" (Psalm 14:1), it offered accurate, divine commentary on every person, society, or philosophy that would abandon the notion that God exists—"They are corrupt."

In truth, the false philosophy of naturalistic evolution fails on many accounts, not the least of which is its inability to provide a foundation for ethics. The denial of a divine, ultimate standard of morality throws one into hopeless confusion about how actions such as rape should be viewed. Naturalistic evolutionists who are honest with their theory's implications can say they do not "like" things like rape, or they think it is best that rape be stopped, or that they think it might be more beneficial to the majority for the action to be limited or eradicated, but they **have no grounds on which to say it is absolutely, morally wrong.**

In stark contrast to the foundationless ethics of naturalistic philosophy, the concept of God provides the perfect rationale on which to base moral determinations. There is a God who sees both "the evil and the good" (Proverbs 15:3). He will call every person into account for his or her actions (Revelation 20:12-15). Therefore each individual is responsible to that God for any actions he or she commits in violation of His moral standard found in the

Bible (Ephesians 3:3-4). Rape, murderous abortion, school slayings, genocide, and other such heinous crimes against humanity are not biological, evolutionary by-products passed down to humans from some mammalian precursor, nor are such crimes biological "malfunctions" caused by mutations. Such actions are sinful, morally reprehensible crimes against humanity and God by individuals who have **chosen** to ignore the ultimate moral standard God manifested in His Son Jesus Christ and recorded in His Word, the Bible.

THE IMMUTABILITY OF GOD

[NOTE: During his opening speech, Dan Barker listed 14 alleged Bible discrepancies as evidence against God's existence. His first claim (Part 1, p. 8) was that the Bible gives contradictory descriptions of God because it says that God changes and does not change. His allegation is refuted in the following article written by Caleb Colley in 2004.]

THE IMMUTABILITY OF GOD

by Caleb Colley, M.L.A.

The Bible plainly asserts that the qualities of God have never changed, and will never change. Consider a sampling of what the inspired writers penned concerning God's immutability:

- Psalm 90:2: "Before the mountains were brought forth, or ever You had formed the Earth and the world, even from everlasting to everlasting, You are God."

- Psalm 102:25-27: "Of old You laid the foundation of the Earth, and the heavens are the work of Your hands. They will perish, but You will endure; yes, they will all grow old like a garment; like a cloak You will change them, and they will be changed. But You are the same, and Your years will have no end."

- Malachi 3:6: "For I am the Lord, I do not change."

- Hebrews 13:8: "Jesus Christ is the same yesterday, today, and forever."

- James 1:17: "Every good gift and every perfect gift is from above, and comes down from the Father of lights, with whom there is no variation or shadow of turning."

Some assert that the concept of an unchanging God is ridiculous. As one critic put it,

> Christians believe that [a] their God is "unchanging." They also believe that [b] their God is jealous, as mentioned explicitly in Exodus 20:5, and that [c] their God is also full of wrath and anger (numerous citations can be found in the Bible which support this). If the Christian believes [a], [b], and [c] above, then according to them their God must always be jealous, angry and wrathful (i.e., God must be pretty miserable) [Thorn, 2000, parenthetical item in orig.].

Of course, the fact that our unchanging God has emotions such as anger and wrath (and emotions that are antithetical to anger and wrath, such as happiness and gladness, which Thorn ignored completely), based on His perfectly righteous nature, does not detract from His deity. After all, if God's nature did not cause sin to anger Him, and righteousness did not please Him, His nature, as revealed in the Bible, would be both false and irrelevant. God would be incapable of making decisions based on His objective standards, and would be unqualified to be our God.

God, in His relations with humans, is unchanging in that He opposes all sin and unrighteousness, while approving and appreciating righteous living, and giving all men the opportunity to be saved. God certainly is capable of changing His mind without changing His nature. For example, God tested Moses by telling him to get out of the way, so that God could destroy the "stiff-necked" nation of Israel, and make of Moses a great nation (Exodus 32:9-10). Moses, however, pleaded with God, and He "relented from the harm which He said He would do to His people" (verse 14). God knew ahead of time what Moses' answer would be, just as He knew that Abraham would do His will when He tested Abraham by commanding him to sacrifice his special son, Isaac (see Genesis 22; 1 Chronicles 28:9; Psalm 94:9-10; John 2:25). In this instance, God simply presented Moses (later labeled the meekest man in the entire world—Numbers 12:3) with the opportunity to become the ancestor of the divinely chosen people, but Moses refused, choosing to appeal to God's mercy. God considered Moses' humble appeal when He decided to preserve Israel; it was the unchanging nature of God that caused Him, in this particular instance, to act as He did (cf. Genesis 6:6; Jonah 3:10).

God had not promised a particular punishment to the people of Israel for their disobedience—God did not break a promise to Israel. God cannot lie, and He certainly did not do so in this case (see Colley, 2004a). God had merely told Moses what He intended to do, and reciprocated Moses' "repentance," on the behalf of the entire nation, with His own.

Inherent in the fact that God cannot lie (see Numbers 23:19; 1 Samuel 15:29; Romans 3:4; Hebrews 6:18) is the fact that His characteristics do not change. If they did, the righteous attributes of humans that please Him one day might not please Him on the next day, and humans would never know what to do in order to satisfy Him. Worse still, we might approach the judgment seat of Christ in the Day of Judgment (2 Corinthians 5:10), only to discover that God had created different rules, of which we were unaware.

To twist Exodus 32:9-14 into an attack on God's reliability, then, is blasphemous. Instead, we should understand the clear implications of the passage: (1) the fervent prayers of righteous people really do "avail much" (James 5:16); (2) it is unpleasant for God to destroy His creatures (2 Peter 3:9; see Keil, 1996, 1:468); and (3) God allows Himself to change His purpose when the actions of humans justify it (Jonah 3:10; see Coffman, 1985, p. 444).

Some assert that the Bible is not reliable because it makes evident that God changed the requirements for serving Him when He nailed the Old Law to the cross of Christ (Colossians 2:16). They assert that when God put away the Old Law and brought the New Law into effect, God evinced that He can change, so, even if He does exist, He cannot be trusted. Indeed, if it were true that God's changing of some requirements rendered His divine nature altered, then the biblical concept of God would be shattered, because, in that case, God frequently would have stood in complete contradiction of Himself. And so would Jesus when He spoke certain teachings while in human form. As one skeptic, writing for *Agnostic Review of Christianity*, commented: "If Jesus has always existed, has always been the same, and is also God, then this deity is psychotic. He issues laws that he ignores, commands people to obey these laws, rebukes them for trying to follow the laws, and practices situational ethics" ("Sticks and Stones…," n.d., emp. added). First-century gnostic Christians, in attempting to reconcile perceived differences between the character of the God of the Old Testament and the God of the New Testament, asserted that two distinct gods were responsible for the two testaments. They believed that the Old Testament god, Jehovah, was bumbling and inept, while the god revealed in the New Testament was the true god (see Layton, 1987, p. 134).

However, God did not change His nature in order to bring the New Testament into effect. The New Testament church, in which men can be saved from damnation, was in the mind of God from before the Earth was established; it was His eternal purpose (Ephesians 3:10-11). In fact, the Old Testament contains many prophecies concerning the church (e.g., Genesis 3:15; Isaiah 2:2-3; Daniel 2:44; see Silcox, n.d.), helping us to see that one purpose of the Old Law was to prepare humanity (in several different aspects, not the least of which was the establishment of Christ's lineage) for the coming of Christ and His Law (Luke 24:44; Galatians 3:24). When the Old Law was nailed to Christ's cross, the rules for obedience were changed in order to allow men to appropriate the blood of Christ to their souls (to wash away sin; see Acts 22:16). The blood of bulls and goats no longer was necessary in order to appease God's anger, because the perfect Lamb had been sacrificed once and for all (Hebrews 9:12; 1 Peter 3:18).

Finally, observe that the fact that God is not opposed to all change does not impose upon His immutability. He instituted the changing seasons (Genesis 1:14), and Psalm 102:25-26 illustrates that the Earth can be changed by an unchanging God, a fact that also was illustrated quite graphically by the Noahic Flood (Genesis 6-8). And, when we leave this life to slip into the timeless side of eternity, we will be changed (1 Corinthians 15:51-52).

God is not going to budge in His firm stand against sin. Ultimately, unforgiven sin will be punished (Romans 6:23; see Colley, 2004b). However, just as sin always has demanded strict punishment in every dispensation, God always has freely offered salvation to those willing to obey His message. God will pardon, through Christ's sacrifice, those who repent and obey Him.

DO CHILDREN INHERIT THE SIN OF THEIR PARENTS?

[NOTE: During his opening speech, Dan Barker insisted that the Bible gives contradictory descriptions of God's dealings with children and their parents' sins (Part 1, p. 8). His allegation is refuted in the following article I wrote in 2004.]

DO CHILDREN INHERIT THE SIN OF THEIR PARENTS?

Understanding the nature of God's interaction with man is no small task. The sincere Bible student often comes across things in the biblical text that are puzzling. Others, who are perhaps somewhat less sincere, twist these initially puzzling passages "to their own destruction" (as described in 2 Peter 3:16). One such idea that has been abused is the alleged contradiction between how Jehovah dealt (and still deals) with the children of sinful people. Steve Wells, author of the *Skeptic's Annotated Bible*, insists that there is a discrepancy in the Bible regarding this subject. He lists Exodus 20:5, which states: "For I, the Lord your God, am a jealous God, visiting the iniquity of the fathers on the children to the third and fourth generations of those who hate Me." Wells then presents Ezekiel 18:20 as a contradictory verse: "The soul who sins shall die. The son shall not bear the guilt of the father, nor the father bear the guilt of the son. The righteousness of the righteous shall be upon himself, and the wickedness of the wicked shall be upon himself" (Wells, 2003). [Barker used the very same argument (Part 1, p. 8).]

Is there a legitimate contradiction between these verses? Or, to pose the question differently, "Is there any possible way that both these statements can be true?" The fact of the matter is that both statements can be true, without a contradiction occurring. What Mr. Wells and others who twist these verses into an alleged contradiction do not recognize is that there is a difference between bearing the guilt of a parent, and suffering negative physical and emotional consequences due to that parent's bad decisions.

It often is the case that the children of wicked people suffer terribly. Sometimes these children suffer because the parent physically or emotionally abuses them (in direct violation of Scripture; cf. Matthew 7:12; Colossians 3:21). At other times, the child suffers as a result of the parent's irresponsible behavior. For instance, suppose a man addicted to gambling wastes his salary on gambling, instead of using it to feed his family. As a result, his children suffer hunger, shame, and poverty.

Yet, even though the children of sinful people often suffer physical consequences, they do not inherit the **sin** of those parents. The book of Jeremiah provides an interesting commentary on this subject. In Jeremiah 16:1-6, God told Jeremiah that the prophet should not take a wife and/or have children in the land of Israel. God explained His reasoning to Jeremiah as follows: "For thus says the Lord concerning the sons and daughters who are born in this place.... 'They shall die gruesome deaths; they shall not be lamented, nor shall they be buried, but they shall be as refuse on the face of the earth'" (16:3-4). Why was this going to happen? Wells is quick to refer to this chapter, especially verses 10 and 11 where the children of Israel pose the question, "Why has the Lord pronounced all this great disaster against us?" (vs. 10). Wells then records Jeremiah's answer: "'Because your fathers have forsaken Me,' says the Lord" (vs. 11). Wells, however, does not cite the very next verse (12), which states: "And you have done worse than your fathers...."

These Israelites were suffering due to the sins of their fathers—
and due to their own sins. Their children were going to die gruesome deaths. The skeptic is quick to seize upon this fact, and demand
that any time innocent children die, it is a travesty against justice
that a loving God never would permit (see Part 2, pp. 203-219).

Do children sometimes die horrible deaths due to their parents'
wrong decisions? Absolutely. The Israelites had adopted the practice of sacrificing their own children to a false god named Baal
(Jeremiah 19:5). The iniquity of the parents, then, can be visited
upon the children in the form of physical suffering. But do those
children bear the guilt of that sin? Absolutely not! Ezekiel wrote by
inspiration of the Holy Spirit: "The **soul** who sins shall die. The son
shall not bear the **guilt** of the father, nor the father bear the **guilt** of
the son" (Ezekiel 18:20, emp. added).

Notice the words "soul" and "guilt." Does the Bible ever insinuate, for example, that a child is guilty of idolatry because his parents
were idolatrous? No (read Matthew 18:3-5; Luke 18:16-17). Bearing the **guilt** of sin is altogether different than bearing the **physical
consequences** of the actions of others. As is often the case, the
skeptic has confused the two, and has alleged a biblical contradiction where, in fact, none exists. This is yet another example in which
the allegation against the Bible fails, but "the Word of the Lord
endures forever" (1 Peter 1:25).

DOES GOD "CREATE" EVIL?

[NOTE: To press his point that the Bible contains contradictions, Barker asserted that the Bible gives contradictory descriptions of God's being good, yet creating evil (Part 1, p. 9). His allegation is refuted in the following article written by Wayne Jackson in 1982.]

DOES GOD "CREATE" EVIL?

By Wayne Jackson, M.A.

Q. The text of Isaiah 45:7 seems to indicate that God "creates evil." Is this correct?

A. In Isaiah 45:7, the prophet wrote of God: "I form the light, and create darkness; I make peace, and create evil; I am Jehovah, that doeth all these things." On occasion, unbelievers appeal to this verse in an attempt to involve the Bible in a moral difficulty, since the text seems to suggest that God "created" evil. How should a Christian respond to such a charge?

First of all, the verse can have no reference to moral evil (wickedness) for such is opposed to the infinitely holy nature of God (Isaiah 6:3). Jehovah is a "God of faithfulness and without iniquity" (Deuteronomy 32:4). He is "not a God that hath pleasure in wickedness" (Psalm 5:4). Nor can it be supposed that this verse has to do with Jehovah's original creation, for at the termination of the creation week, the Lord saw "everything that he had made, and, behold, it was very good" (Genesis 1:31).

The context of Isaiah 45:7, along with several passages of similar import, reveals the truth of the matter. Jehovah—through the prophet Isaiah—prophetically announced to King Cyrus of Persia (a century-and-a-half before the monarch's birth!) His intention of using this pagan king as an instrument of His holy will. Within Isaiah 45:1-7 is a majestic affirmation of the universal sovereignty of the Almighty God; indeed, there is none like Him (vs. 5). He thus affirms: "I form light, and create darkness [i.e., control nature]; I make peace, and create evil [i.e., exercise control over the nations]; I am Jehovah that doeth all these things."

Notice how the word "evil" is used in obvious contrast to "peace." Isaiah simply was stating that Jehovah has the power to cause peaceful conditions to exist, or to bring about evil (i.e., destruction). Consider another verse. God warned the Israelites that if they made an alliance with Egypt, He would bring evil upon them [i.e., punishment (cf. Isaiah 31:1-2)]. Again, in describing the coming judgment upon ancient Babylon, the prophet declared: "Therefore shall evil come upon thee; thou shall not know the dawning thereof and mischief shall fall upon thee; thou shalt not be able to put it away; and desolation shall come upon thee suddenly, which thou knoweth not" (Isaiah 47:11). Thus, the **evil** that God sent was a desolation—a **desolation** due on account of their wickedness!

Scholars have observed that "evil" can be used with a purely secular meaning to denote physical injury (Jeremiah 39:12), or times of distress (Amos 6:3)—which is its significance in Isaiah 45:7 (see Harris, et al., 1980, 2:855).

DOES GOD TEMPT PEOPLE?

by Eric Lyons, M.Min.

During this debate, Dan Barker alleged that he "knows" the God of the Bible cannot exist because "there are mutually incompatible properties/characteristics of the God that's in this book [the Bible—EL] that rule out the possibility of His existence." Barker cited James 1:13 and Genesis 22:1 as proof that the God of the Bible cannot exist (Part 1, p. 9). Since James 1:13 says: "Let no man say when he is tempted, I am tempted of God: for God cannot be tempted with evil, neither tempteth he any man" (KJV), and Genesis 22:1 affirms that "God did tempt Abraham" (KJV) to sacrifice his son, Barker asserted that God is like a married bachelor or a square circle—He cannot logically exist.

If Genesis 22:1 actually taught that God really tempted Abraham to commit evil and sin, then the God of the Bible might be a "square circle," i.e., a logical contradiction. But, the fact of the matter is, God did not tempt Abraham to commit evil. Barker formulated his argument based upon the King James Version and only one meaning of the Hebrew word (*nissâ*) found in Genesis 22:1. Although the word can mean "to tempt," the first two meanings that Brown, Driver, and Briggs give for *nissâ* in their *Hebrew and English Lexicon of the Old Testament* is "to test, to try" (1993). Likewise, the *Theological Lexicon of the Old Testament* (1997) defines the word simply "to test" (Jenni and Westermann, 1997, 2:741-742). The *Theological Dictionary of the Old Testament* agrees that *nissâ* is best translated, whether in secular or theological contexts, as "test-ing" (Botterweck, et al., 1998, 9:443-455). For this reason, virtually all major translations in recent times, including the NKJV, NASB, ESV, NIV, and RSV, translate Genesis 22:1 using the term "tested," not tempted.

When David put on the armor of King Saul prior to battling Goliath, the shepherd realized: "I cannot walk with these, for I have not tested (*nissâ*) them" (1 Samuel 17:39, emp. added). Obviously, this testing had nothing to do with David "tempting" his armor; he simply had not tested or tried on Saul's armor previously. God led Israel during 40 years of desert wanderings "to humble...and test" them (Deuteronomy 8:2, emp. added), not to tempt them to sin. Notice also the contrast in Exodus 20:20 between (1) God test-ing man and (2) trying to cause man to sin. After giving Israel the Ten Commandments, Moses said: "Do not fear; for God has come to test (*nissâ*) you, and that His fear may be before you, so that you may not sin" (Exodus 20:20, emp. added). If one were to use Barker's reasoning that *nissâ* must mean "to tempt," regardless of the context, then he would have to interpret Exodus 20:20 to mean that God tempted Israel to sin, so that they would not sin.

When a person interprets the Bible, or any other book, with-out recognizing that words have a variety of meanings and can be used in various senses, a rational interpretation is impossible. Many alleged Bible contradictions, including several of those that Dan Barker mentioned in the debate, are easily explained simply by ac-knowledging that words are used in a variety of ways. Is a word to be taken literally or figuratively? Must the term in one place mean the exact same thing when in another context, or may it have dif-ferent meanings? If English-speaking Americans can intelligibly converse about running to the store in the 21st century by driving a car, or if we can easily communicate about parking on driveways, and driving on parkways, why do some people have such a difficult time understanding the various ways in which words were used in

Bible times? Could it be that some Bible critics like Barker are simply predisposed to interpret Scripture unfairly? The evidence reveals that is exactly what is happening.

Rather then contradicting James 1:13, Genesis 22:1 actually corresponds perfectly with what James wrote near the beginning of his epistle: "My brethren, count it all joy when you fall into various trials, knowing that the testing of your faith produces patience. But let patience have its perfect work, that you may be perfect and complete, lacking nothing" (1:2-4, emp. added). By instructing Abraham to sacrifice his promised son (cf. Hebrews 11:17), God gave Abraham another opportunity to prove his loyalty to Him, while Abraham simultaneously used this trial to continue developing a more complete, mature faith.

BIBLICAL IDEAS CONCERNING KILLING AND MURDER ARE NOT CONTRADICTORY

Dan Barker claimed that the God of the Bible cannot exist because biblical teachings regarding killing are contradictory. He stated:

> In Exodus 20:13, in the Ten Commandments: "Thou shalt not kill." In Leviticus 24:17 a different phrasing of it with a different Hebrew word: "He that killeth any man shall surely be put to death." However, we find in Exodus 32: "Thus says the Lord God, 'Put every man his sword by his side, slay every man his brother, his companion and neighbor." First Samuel 6: "The people lamented because the Lord had smitten many of the people with a great slaughter." The Bible is filled with examples of the biblical God committing, commanding, and condoning killing. The God of the Bible says, "Don't kill." The God of the Bible says, "Kill." He does not exist (Part 1, p. 9).

Is it true that the biblical position on killing is hopelessly contradictory and can be used as evidence that the God of the Bible cannot exist? Certainly not. The biblical injunctions about killing and murder are in perfect harmony with themselves, and with the principles of justice, and cannot be used as evidence against the God of the Bible.

First, according to Dan, the command to avoid killing in the Ten Commandments is a blanket statement that includes avoiding every type of killing. Yet, we must consider that just one chapter later, in Exodus 21:12-17, we read several injunctions pertaining to capital punishment in which the death sentence is prescribed for those who premeditatively murder another person due to malice, who kidnap a person to sell him, or who curse their father or mother. The original readers understood that the commandment in Exodus 20:13 did not mean that all killing was wrong, including capital punishment. They understood that certain qualifications, as are detailed in the rest of the Law, put limits, restrictions, and allowances on the term "kill." Barker would have us to believe that whoever wrote the book of Exodus was so ignorant that he did not catch contradictory statements that are separated by less than one chapter. Yet, such an idea is ridiculous in light of the remarkable accuracy and acumen of the Old Testament instructions (see Butt, 2007) that were used by the Jewish community for almost 1,500 years, many of which were the basis for the legal codes of modern nations. The arrogance of the current atheistic community to assume that the original readers of the Old Testament were so dim-witted as to accept contradictory statements less than a chapter apart is astounding. If a statement about killing is made, and then within a few verses, the statement is qualified and expounded upon, the allegation that all killing is being included in the original instruction cannot be maintained.

Second, Barker frequently uses this alleged contradiction in his writings as well as his debates. In his book, *godless*, he claimed that the commandment in Exodus 20:13 cannot be translated "Thou shalt not murder," because the Hebrew word *ratsach* sometimes means something other than murder. To prove his point, he listed the following five Hebrew words most commonly translated as "kill" or "murder":

> *muth*: (825) die, slay, put to death, kill
>
> *nakah*: (502) smite, kill, slay, beat, wound, murder
>
> *harag*: (172) slay, kill, murder, destroy
>
> *zabach* (140) sacrifice, kill
>
> *ratsach* (47) slay [23], murder [17], kill [6], be put to death [1] (Barker, 2008, p. 204).

To further "prove" his point, he listed several places in the Old Testament in which the term *ratsach* means something other than murder. He cited Deuteronomy 4:42, a verse that uses the term to refer to involuntary manslaughter. He also noted Numbers 35:30-31, in which the term is used for the justifiable capital punishment inflicted on a murderer. Barker's contention, then, is that if the term can ever be used to mean something besides murder, then it must be used that way in Exodus 20:13.

The fatal flaw in Barker's assertion is that of equivocation. "Equivocation is classified as both a formal and informal fallacy. It is the misleading use of a term with more than one meaning or sense **(by glossing over which meaning is intended at a particular time)**" ("Equivocation," 2009, emp. added). [NOTE: Although Wikipedia is not usually considered a scholarly source, equivocation is a commonly used concept and Wikipedia's wording was the most concise and clear of the various sources consulted.] Notice how Barker is equivocating in this instance. He is rightly saying that the term *ratsach* **might** be used for justified killing like capital punishment, but he is insisting that this definition **must** be used in Exodus 20:13. Yet, when we see the other definitions, such as murder, for the word *ratsach* that are available, we realize that the definition of murder fits the context of Exodus 20:13, not the concept of justifiable killing such as capital punishment. By forcing the word *ratsach* to have the same definition in all places, Dan alleges to have found a contradiction. Dan stated: "Modern preachers must be smarter than Hebrew translators if they claim that *ratsach* means 'murder' exclusively" (1992a, pp. 207-208). But the claim is not that the word means murder exclusively, but that in Exodus 20:13 the context shows that the word means murder. In truth, Barker must be smarter than the entire Hebrew nation and all linguists since the time of the Bible's writing to be able to prove that *ratsach* cannot mean murder in Exodus 20:13, when both the context and standard meanings of the word allow for such to be the case. His logical fallacy of equivocation, however, is plain to see and is inexcusable for a man who has been studying his Bible and debating for as many years as Dan has.

The only proper way to determine the meaning of a word with multiple meanings is to look at the context. In the context of Exodus 20:13 and other injunctions to avoid "killing," the clear meaning is that some types of killing, such as premeditated murder out of malice, are forbidden, while other types of killing, such as that done by the government as punishment for certain wrong doings, are permissible.

The use of our English word "kill" provides a good example of how words can be used. Suppose we say: "It is wrong to kill your neighbor," but then we say, "It is not always wrong for a policeman to kill his neighbor." Are these two statements contradictory? No. Not if in the first instance we use "kill" to mean intentionally, premeditatively killing out of malice, etc., but in the second we mean the policeman may shoot his neighbor if the neighbor was shooting at him, was holding hostages at gunpoint, etc. Biblical statements about killing, murder, and capital punishment are not contradictory.

Besides this alleged contradiction, Dan and his fellow atheists also contend that it is unfair for God to be in the position to decide when killing is justifiable or not. They contend that humans should have the same prerogative about deciding who lives and dies as God should have. Thus, they say, God cannot be in a position to determine when killing is justified if humans are not in this same position—the same rules must apply to God as to all humans. Barker opined: "Why is God special?" (2008, p. 204). Atheists continually overlook, however, the concept of authorization. Not everyone has the same authority to administer punishment. While it is true that a thief might deserve 10 years in prison, an **individual** cannot capture the thief, lock him in his basement for ten years and be considered moral. Only the government has the right to try the thief, find him guilty, and sentence him to prison. A **vigilante** cannot break into a federal penitentiary and kill all the inmates on death row, even though they are sentenced to death. Why? Because that individual does not have the **authorization** to kill those people. God has authority over life and death because He gives it, and He knows all the thoughts of those committing crimes and all the consequences of the punishment He administers (see Part 2, pp. 215-219). The atheists' contention that God and humans have the same prerogative over matters of life and death is logically flawed.

In conclusion, the biblical instructions regarding killing, when viewed in context and not equivocated, are clearly harmonious and without contradiction. Certain types of killing, such as premeditated murder done out of malice, are easily identified from the context as forbidden killing. While capital punishment administered by the proper authority is clearly not under discussion in the biblical statements against "killing." Alleged Bible contradictions that exhibit such poor scholarship and dishonesty should be viewed by the reasonable observer as evidence against atheism and for the Bible's accuracy and unity.

DEFENDING THE BIBLE'S POSITION ON SLAVERY

[NOTE: In his opening speech, Barker demanded that the Bible gives contradictory descriptions of God's attitude toward slavery (Part 1, pp. 9-10). His allegation is refuted in the following article I wrote in 2005.]

DEFENDING THE BIBLE'S POSITION ON SLAVERY

Through the millennia, some of the worst atrocities perpetrated on humans have been linked to the institution of slavery. Historically, slavery has not designated one particular ethnic group as its singular victim. The Hebrews were slaves to the Egyptians during the days of Moses. During the reign of King David, the Moabites were subjected to slavery (2 Samuel 8:2). Alexander the Great forced almost the entire inhabited world to cower and serve him. Truth be told, practically every nationality of people that exists today could point to a time in its past history when it fell victim to slavery. Hitting closer to home, the pages of history dealing with the formative years of the United States are despoiled with gruesome stories of ships carrying slaves sold to the Americas by their fellow Africans (and others, e.g., Arabians). These slaves frequently were packed so densely in lower ship decks that many of them died of disease or malnutrition. Those who lived to see the States soon learned that their fate hinged upon those who purchased them. Some slaves were ushered into homes with kind masters, decent living facilities, good food, and freedom to worship. Other slaves were purchased by cruel, greedy people who overworked them, abused them, underfed them, and allowed them no freedom.

Friction soon arose between those who wanted to maintain slavery, and those who wanted to outlaw the practice as inhumane and unjust. It can be argued convincingly that the American Civil War was fought primarily over this very issue. Politicians raged on both sides of the matter. Interestingly, so did religious people. Abolitionists, as well as pro-slavery advocates, went to the Bible to marshal arguments for their particular view. Abolitionists armed themselves with verses such as: "Therefore whatever you want men to do to you, do also to them: for this is the Law and the Prophets" (Matthew 7:12); or "There is neither Jew nor Greek, there is neither slave nor free, there is neither male nor female; for you all are one man in Christ Jesus" (Galatians 3:28). Religious pro-slavery activists fired impressive scriptural guns by quoting passages such as: "Servants, be submissive to your masters with all fear; not only to the good and gentle, but also to the harsh" (1 Peter 2:18); and "Servants, be obedient to those who are your masters according to the flesh, with fear and trembling, in sincerity of your heart, as to Christ" (Ephesians 6:5). Can we determine with accuracy what the Bible really says on the topic of slavery? Does the Bible condemn it as a social injustice? Does the Bible condone the practice? And how does the Bible's position on slavery mesh with the idea of a loving God?

For years, skeptics have railed against the written Word, insisting that its pro-slavery tendencies should alert any reader who has a scrap of common sense to the idea that an all-loving God could not have inspired such atrocious material. Morton Smith and R. Joseph Hoffman, in a book titled *What the Bible Really Says*, commented:

> [T]here is no reasonable doubt that the New Testament, like the Old, not only tolerated chattel slavery (the form prevalent in the Greco-Roman world of Paul's time) but helped to perpetuate it by making the slaves' obedience to their masters a religious duty. This biblical morality was one of the great handicaps that the emanci-

pation movement in the United States had to overcome. The opponents of abolition had clear biblical evidence on their side when they argued (1989, pp. 145-146, parenthetical item in orig.).

Following a similar line of thinking, Ruth Green wrote that "it was the Old and New Testaments of the Bible that were the authority for keeping humanity in serfdom for centuries and for legitimizing slavery in America, making a bloody civil war necessary to give slaves human rights under our Constitution" (1979, p. 351). Has the Bible been responsible for the oppression of slaves in the past? No, it has not. In fact, an in-depth look into the biblical account that reveals God's attitude toward slavery shows just the opposite.

SLAVERY IN THE OLD TESTAMENT

In Matthew 19:3-10, the Pharisees came to Jesus, attempting to trap Him with questions about the Old Law. They asked: "Is it lawful for a man to divorce his wife for just any reason?" Jesus informed them that divorce was not in God's plan from the beginning. Thinking they had trapped Him, they inquired: "Why, then, did Moses command to give a certificate of divorce and to put her away?" If it was in the Old Law, they suggested, then it must be God's ideal will. But Jesus' answer quickly stopped that line of thinking. He responded:

Moses, because of the hardness of your hearts, permitted you to divorce your wives, but from the beginning it was not so. And I say to you, whoever divorces his wife, except for sexual immorality, and marries another, commits adultery; and whoever marries her who is divorced commits adultery.

Jesus' point was crystal clear—some things permitted in the Old Testament did not necessarily represent the ideal. Due to the hardness of ancient Israel's heart, God tolerated (and regulated) some things under the Old Law that He did not endorse. As He did so, however, He progressively revealed His divine will to mankind, clarifying that will more fully through Christ.

Many of the injunctions found in the Old Testament pertaining to slavery fall into the category of regulating something that was "less than ideal." Even in the Old Testament, God desired that all people love their neighbors as themselves (Leviticus 19:18). Yet, in a time when God used the children of Israel as His arm of justice to punish evildoers, certain questions arose. What was to be done, for example, with the survivors of those wicked nations? What was to be done with a man who was so far in debt that he could not repay his lender? These issues, and others like them, necessitated that God institute some form of humane regulations for "slavery."

Often, those who attack the Bible skirt the real crux of the slavery issue. They point to verses in the Old Testament that offer a particular regulation for slavery. From there, they proceed to argue that the Bible is a vile book that does not condemn, but actually condones slavery. And, they argue, since all slavery is morally wrong, the Bible must not be the product of a loving God.

However, those who take such a position fail to consider that certain types of slavery are not morally wrong. For instance, when a man is convicted of murder, he often is sentenced to life in prison. During his life sentence, he is forced by the State to do (or not do) certain things. He is justly confined to a small living space, and his freedoms are revoked. Sometimes, he is compelled by the State to work long hours, for which he does not receive even minimum wage. Would it be justifiable to label such a loss of freedom as a type of slavery? Yes, it would. However, is his loss of freedom a morally justifiable situation? Certainly. He has become a slave of the State because he violated certain laws that were designed to ensure the liberty of his fellow citizen, whom he murdered. Therefore, one fact that must be conceded by anyone dealing with the Bible and its position on slavery is the fact that, under some conditions, slavery is not necessarily a morally deplorable institution.

Taking that into account, we also must ask: Who has the right to determine when slavery can be imposed on a certain person or group of people? The answer, of course, is God. In the Old Testament, immoral nations who practiced unspeakable evils surrounded the Hebrews. In order to rid the world of their destructive influence, the children of Israel dealt with them in several ways. One of those ways included forcing the wicked nations into slavery. Many of the slave regulations in the Old Testament deal with the treatment of individuals and nations who had committed crimes against humanity that were worthy of death. The wicked people were graciously allowed to live, but they were subjected to slavery, much like a lifetime prison sentence in modern criminal cases. Let us look more closely at this situation. In Leviticus 18:21,24 we read that the Lord told Moses to instruct the Israelites as follows: "And you shall not let any of your descendants pass through the fire to Molech.... Do not defile yourselves with any of these things; for by all these the nations are defiled, which I am casting out before you."

In order to understand this scenario, it is important that we understand what the phrase, "pass through the fire to Molech," means in verse 21. In brief, it means that the nations around the Israelites were burning their own children as human sacrifices to a pagan god named Molech (for further information on Molech and this practice, see Harrison, 1988, 3:401). Fitting this into our discussion, would it be morally permissible for God to allow a government (e.g., the Israelites) to punish those people who were viciously murdering their own children? We must answer in the affirmative. What punishment would be appropriate for a person who had committed such heinous crimes as to murder his or her own innocent children? The answer to that question rages even in our own society today when instances of child homicide arrive before the courts of our land. Legitimate answers often include the death penalty, or a life in prison in which many freedoms are revoked.

As additional evidence along these lines, in Exodus 22:1-3, the Bible discusses a situation in which a man was caught in the act of thievery. The thief was instructed to restore what he stole, returning four sheep, and five oxen, for every one stolen. The text further states: "He should make full restitution; if he has nothing, then he shall be sold for his theft" (vs. 3). Being sold into slavery was often a government-regulated punishment based on a criminal action. One can see, then, that it is morally permissible to revoke the freedoms of certain people or groups of people based on their inappropriate conduct.

Accordingly, many of the slavery regulations in the Old Testament pertained to people who deserved far worse. Dan Vander Lugt commented:

> Old Testament laws regulating slavery are troublesome by modern standards, but in their historical context they provided a degree of social recognition and legal protection to slaves that was advanced for its time (Exodus 21:20-27; Leviticus 25:44-46). We must keep in mind that on occasion it was an alternative to the massacre of enemy populations in wartime and the starvation of the poor during famine (2001, p. 1).

A MUTUALLY BENEFICIAL RELATIONSHIP

Frequently, "slavery" in Bible times was much more of an employer/employee relationship than an owner/slave situation. Even the words used to delineate between a hired servant and a slave are difficult to separate. As Herbert Lockyer noted:

> In the ancient world, service and slavery were closely related, so much so that one can scarcely distinguish the one from the other. The original words used for "servants" and "service" carry a variety of meanings between which it is not always easy to determine what is meant (1969, p. 197).

Arndt and Gingrich documented that the Greek word *doulos* meant "slave," but that it also was used "in a wider sense" to denote "any kind of dependence." In 2 Corinthians 4:5, the apostles are called the *douloi* (plural of *doulos*) of the Christians. Christ took on the form of a *doulos*, as stated in Philippians 2:7. Paul designates himself as a *doulos* of Christ in Romans 1:1, Philippians 1:1, Galatians 1:10, and numerous other passages (1967, pp. 205-206). The term can describe a person who is obligated in some way, whether voluntarily or involuntarily, to another person. Due to this broad use, various translations have employed a wide range of words to render the meaning of *doulos* in English. Using Romans 1:1 as a case in point, the NKJV has "bondservant," the New Living Translation has "slave," the KJV and ASV have "servant," and the Darby Bible has "bondman."

The Hebrew word *ebed* is similar to the Greek *doulos*, in that it can be translated as "slave" or "servant." In Exodus 4:10, Moses referred to himself as the "servant" (*ebed*) of God. Abraham called himself the *ebed* of the angels who came to visit him in Genesis 18:3. In Genesis 39:17-19, Potiphar's wife described Joseph as the Hebrew *ebed*, and Genesis 24:2 talks about the eldest *ebed* in Abraham's house, who "ruled over all he had."

The purpose of including this brief description of the two most common terms for a slave is to show that our modern use of the word "slave" generally evokes mental images of cruelty, injustice, and bondage against a person's will. While such ideas could be included in the biblical usage, they do not necessarily fit every time the words are used. Instead, the picture that we often see when the biblical words for "slave" are employed is a mutually beneficial arrangement similar to an employer/employee relationship. Job describes this relationship quite well:

> If I have despised the cause of my male or female servant (*ebed*) when they complained against me, what then shall I do when God rises up? When He punishes, how shall I answer Him? Did not

He who made me in the womb make them? Did not the same One fashion us in the womb? (Job 31:13-15).

Obviously, Job's dealings with his slaves provided a mutually acceptable situation for master as well as slave.

To illustrate further the true nature of much Old Testament slavery, Abraham's relationship with his slave Eliezer should be examined. In Genesis 15:2-3, Abraham lamented the fact that he was childless. In his dialogue with God, he stated that the heir of his wealth was Eliezer of Damascus. In verse three of chapter 15, Abraham described Eliezer as "one born in my house." Later, in Genesis 24:2, Abraham's oldest servant (probably Eliezer) "ruled over all that he had." Add to this the fact that Abraham armed 318 trained servants (Hebrew *ebed*) to bring back Lot after he had been captured (Genesis 14:14-15). If the slave/owner relationship was anything less than mutually trusting, Abraham most likely would not have intentionally armed his slaves.

Due to the mutually beneficial nature of much Old Testament slavery, some slaves did not even want to leave their masters. Deuteronomy 15:16-17 deals with that very situation:

And if it happens that he [a slave—KB] says to you, "I will not go away from you," because he loves you and your house, since he prospers with you, then you shall take an awl and thrust it through his ear to the door, and he shall be your servant forever. Also to your maidservant you shall do likewise.

Do the actions and words of Abraham's slaves, or those found in Deuteronomy 15, seem like the actions and words of tyrannized, oppressed people? Hardly. Rather, they seem more like the words and actions of people enjoying a mutually beneficial and consensual relationship.

Even during New Testament times, slavery often provided a mutually beneficial relationship to both owner and slave. As Paul Copan remarked:

> During Paul's time, the master-slave relationship provided sufficient benefits and opportunities, such that it dampened any thoughts of revolutionary behavior. One freed slave had inscribed on his tombstone: "Slavery was never unkind to me...." More often than not, it was the free workers rather than slaves who were abused by foremen and bosses. (After all, an owner stood to have an ongoing loss if he abused his slave.) [2001, p. 172, parenthetical item and emp. in orig.].

But suppose a master did abuse his slaves in Old Testament times, and those slaves decided to run away. In Deuteronomy 23:15-16, God made it unlawful for runaway slaves to be returned to their masters. The text states:

> You shall not give back to his master the slave who has escaped from his master to you. He may dwell with you in your midst, in the place **which he chooses** within one of your gates, **where it seems best to him**; you shall not oppress him (emp. added).

This passage is particularly revealing because it shows how costly cruelty to slaves was. It also shows that slaves had the freedom to choose where, and with whom, they wanted to live. Wright noted that this passage proves that

> [s]lavery as such is not protected or rendered sacrosanct under Israelite law. At the very least it can be said that such a law probably presumes that runaway slaves will be the exception, not the rule. This lends further weight to the view that normally slavery in Israel was not oppressively harsh. It would certainly not have been, if the spirit of the slavery laws of Exodus and Deuteronomy were put into practice (1983, pp. 181-182).

Add to this the fact that kidnapping a man and selling him as a slave was a crime punishable by death, as noted in Exodus 21:16: "He who kidnaps a man and sells him, or if he is found in his hand, shall surely be put to death." Certainly, any parallel to slavery in early America can be easily refuted.

Also note that the slavery regulated in the Bible had absolutely nothing to do with race, color, or ethnic background. While it is true that certain nations, as a whole, were captured and enslaved because of their wicked, idolatrous practices, it is not true that they were enslaved due to their allegedly inferior nationality. Leviticus 19:34 states: "But the stranger who dwells among you shall be to you as one born among you, and you shall love him as yourself; for you were strangers in the land of Egypt: I am the Lord your God." Deuteronomy 24:14 reads: "You shall not oppress a hired servant who is poor and needy, whether one of your brethren, or one of the aliens who is in your land within thy gates." And, although certain regulations applied only to Hebrews who found themselves enslaved (Deuteronomy 15:12-14; Exodus 21:2), it was not because they were a "superior" race or nationality, but simply because they were citizens of the nation of Israel (a similar concept would be the fact that a person who is born in the USA is not inherently any less or any more valuable than any other person, but, under the law system of the United States, that person would possess certain rights and privileges that a non-citizen would not enjoy). Deuteronomy 10:17-19 illustrates God's impartiality well:

> For the Lord your God is God of gods and Lord of lords, the great God, mighty and awesome, who shows no partiality nor takes a bribe. He administers justice for the fatherless and widow, and loves the stranger, giving him food and clothing. Therefore, love the stranger; for you were strangers in the land of Egypt.

The New Testament further underscores the idea of human equality in passages such as Galatians 3:28: "There is neither Jew nor Greek, there is neither slave nor free, there is neither male nor female; for you are all one man in Christ Jesus." Job's statement regarding his slave's equality—due to the fact that God formed him in the same way that God formed Job (31:15)—provides a perfect example of the biblical idea that all men possess the same inherent value. The idea that one nation or race is superior to another does not come from the Bible. Racism like that displayed by many during the slavery years of the United States has always been a sin (Acts 17:26-31).

A valid question naturally arises from the comment above, that, on occasion, nations as a whole were enslaved because of their wickedness. What about the children of those wicked men and women? Must they become slaves as well, suffering for their parents' evil actions? First, let us acknowledge that, even today, children often suffer because of their parents' poor decisions. Consider the sad and pitiful plight of a child whose father is an alcoholic or child abuser. That child will suffer physically, emotionally, and financially. Even in modern times, the children who are born in poverty or cruelty often remain slaves of those elements their entire lives. Second, let us ask a more pertinent question: Would it be better for that child to grow up in a country where the slave laws protected him or her, or would it be better for the child to have to "pass through the fire to Molech"? To ask is to answer, is it not? When nations were conquered by the Israelites, what was to happen to the nations' children who remained alive? They could be left to die on their own, or they could be given homes, food, and jobs. Which of the two options is more humane? Again, to ask is to answer. Furthermore, if the child grew up and did not like his master, he or she could simply run away and live wherever he or she wanted (Deuteronomy 23:15-16).

As we consider further the situation of slaves in ancient Israel, it is interesting to note that every slave was entitled (by God) to have a part in the Sabbath rest once every week. Exodus 20:10 states:

> [B]ut the seventh day is the Sabbath of the Lord your God. In it you shall do no work: you, nor your son, nor your daughter, nor your **manservant**, nor your **maidservant**, nor your cattle, nor your stranger who is within your gates (emp. added).

Along these same lines, every slave also was entitled to partake in the eight-day festivities surrounding the Feast of Weeks and the Feast of Tabernacles (Deuteronomy 16:9-17). The welcome rest provided on these occasions shows that God's regulations for slavery in Israel were humane and fair. Furthermore, the year of Jubilee provided freedom to "all the inhabitants" in the land of the children of Israel. [This provision included the bulk of the slaves, with possible exceptions such as those slaves who had chosen to stay with their masters and have their ears pierced as a sign of their situation.]

> And you shall consecrate the fiftieth year, and proclaim liberty throughout all the land to all its inhabitants. It shall be a Jubilee for you; and each of you shall return to his possession, and each of you shall return to his family (Leviticus 25:10).

Certainly, God kindly provided rest and freedom for slaves under the Old Testament in order to quell abuses that might arise.

SLAVES OF DEBT

Another aspect of Old Testament slavery had to do with severe debt accumulation. In Old Testament times, no bankruptcy legislation held sway over the Israelites. What was to be done for the person who was drowning in a sea of debt? Was his lender simply to wave his hand and forgive the debt? Would that be a fair situation for the lender? Hardly. Therefore, many of the slave situations arose because of such debt. Herb Vander Lugt commented:

> Remember too, at that time no nation had the ability to deal with people who had gotten themselves hopelessly in debt. So they were allowed to sell themselves into slavery (often temporarily) in exchange for release from their financial obligations (Ex. 21:2-4; Lev. 25:39-43; Dt.15:12) [1999, p. 11, parenthetical item in orig.].

Leviticus 25:47-49 provides an example of slavery caused by debt:

> Now if a sojourner or stranger close to you becomes rich, and one of your brethren who dwells by him becomes poor, and sells him-

self to the stranger or sojourner close to you, or to a member of the stranger's family, after he is sold he may be redeemed again. One of his brothers may redeem him; or his uncle or his uncle's son may redeem him; or anyone who is near of kin to him in his family may redeem him; or if he is able he may redeem himself.

Would it be fair for a society to allow a person who had accumulated a huge amount of debt to sell his labor to another person to pay that debt? Yes, it would. However, God—aware that abuse might arise in any situation—even regulated debt slavery, and provided for the rights and privileges of the slave to be guarded.

DIFFICULT LAWS TO UNDERSTAND

Admittedly, even with all the humane slave laws contained in the Old Testament, there are certain laws that we, in modern times, have a difficult time understanding. For instance, Exodus 21:20 reads:

And if a man beats his male or female servant with a rod, so that he dies under his hand, he shall surely be punished. Notwithstanding, if he remains alive a day or two, he shall not be punished; for he is his property.

In the first place, how could God allow a slave owner to beat his slave at all? To answer this question, we must remember who many of the Old Testament slaves were. They were members of the wicked, sinful nations who had been delivered into the hands of the Israelites because of their immorality. Suppose that a slave from one of those nations had made up his mind to do as much damage to his owner as possible. The slave had the option of running away to a gentler owner whenever he wished (Deuteronomy 23:15-16). However, suppose that he chose to stay and steal from the owner, or break the owner's equipment intentionally, or destroy the owner's crops. What could the owner do to stop such sabotage? Herb Vander Lugt put it like this:

Then, too, no matter how well the slaves were treated, some might have been rebellious and defiant. Forgetting that they were alive because they were taken as war captives instead of being executed, they might have blamed their master for their slave status. They might have shown their resentment by destroying property, abusing fellow slaves, or refusing to work. The master may have had no other way to bring his slave in line than to use physical punishment (1999, p. 17).

As appalling as it is to the sensitivities of most United States citizens, many countries still employ some type of beating or bodily harm to deter crime (some readers may recall the controversy over "caning" in Singapore in the early 1990s). When a modern-day prisoner violates rules while incarcerated, more stringent punishment (such as solitary confinement) often is required. If a slave deserved the death sentence, yet was allowed to live under certain conditions—and then did not comply with those conditions—would it be feasible to suggest that his death sentence could be reinstated? Even though it seems harsh to us, Exodus 21:20 does not militate against the justice of God.

In fact, the more closely the passage is scrutinized, the more it manifests the idea that God was protecting the slave. Concerning the punishment that a master would receive if he did beat his slave to death, Christopher Wright noted that the word "punished" as used here actually means "avenged." And,

in any other context [it] would mean that the guilty party would be liable to death himself at the hands of his victim's family.... This law's natural sense is that the murderous master was to be executed by the legal community on behalf of the slave, who had no family to avenge him (1983, p. 180).

While not all commentators are as confident as Wright is (that in this passage the death penalty is involved), there is no concrete case which argues that the death penalty is not at least a possibility in this situation. The authors of the *Pulpit Commentary* observed how this fear of punishment would protect the slave.

> Involving, as the death of the slave did, criminal proceedings, and, on conviction, severe punishment, the mere danger of a fatal result ensuing would be a powerful deterrent from exceptional violence.... The mere risk of incurring such a penalty would inspire salutary caution (Spence and Exell, n.d., p. 179).

Adding additional weight to the argument that the restriction in Exodus 21:20 was for the benefit of the slave, Burton Coffman wrote:

> This was a protective right granted to slaves that they should not be beaten to death! If that seems like a small blessing to us, let it be remembered that under the system in vogue all over the pagan world of that era, and extending down even till apostolical times, the Roman Law, in force all over the world, provided as a penalty against slaves, even for trivial and unintentional violations, that shame of the whole pagan world "flagellis ad mortem" (beaten to death), a penalty usually inflicted in the presence of all the other slaves of a master. God here provided that punishment should be meted out to a slave-owner for following that pagan custom (1985, pp. 309-310).

By way of summary, then, Exodus 21:20 documents that under certain circumstances, beating could be morally acceptable as punishment. This passage, however, provided rights that did not exist in other pagan cultures for the protection of the slave.

Exodus 21:26-27 provides another example of a law that seems difficult for us, in the present day, to understand as coming from a righteous God.

> If a man strikes the eye of his male or female servant, and destroys it, he shall let him go free for the sake of his eye. And if he knocks out the tooth of his male or female servant, he shall let him go free for the sake of his tooth (KJV).

Again, let it be noted that physical punishment might be the only solution to an unruly, rebellious slave who should have received the death penalty. However, something else of interest emerges from this verse that, rather than expressing the cruelty of Old Testament laws regulating slavery, shows instead God's care for those enslaved. The text states that the eyes and teeth of slaves should not be knocked out or destroyed. However, the nations around the Israelites did not adhere to any such standards. When the Philistines captured Samson, they "took him and put out his eyes; and brought him down to Gaza. They bound him with bronze fetters; and he became a grinder in the prison" (Judges 16:21). Also, when the Babylonian soldiers raided Israel, capturing King Zedekiah, "they killed the sons of Zedekiah before his eyes, put out the eyes of Zedekiah, bound him with bronze fetters, and took him to Babylon" (2 Kings 25:7). God's regulations for the treatment of slaves provided the slaves with many more rights than they had in the nations surrounding Israel.

Another of the most startling regulations concerning slavery is found in Leviticus 19:20-22:

> And whosoever lieth carnally with a woman, that is a bondmaid, betrothed to an husband, and not at all redeemed, nor freedom given her; she shall be scourged; they shall not be put to death, because she was not free. And he shall bring his trespass offering unto the Lord, unto the door of the tabernacle of the congregation, even a ram for a trespass offering (KJV).

Of course, skeptics have a heyday with this reading from the King James Version, which seems to indicate that if a free man has sexual intercourse with a slave woman who is betrothed, then the slave woman is to be scourged and the man simply supplies a ram as a trespass offering. However, upon further investigation, it can be seen that this passage says something far different.

In the first place, the translators of the KJV most likely mistranslated the part of the text "she shall be scourged." The ASV translators rendered the passage as follows:

And whosoever lieth carnally with a woman that is a bondmaid, betrothed to a husband, and not at all redeemed, nor freedom given her; they shall be punished; they shall not be put to death, because she was not free. And he shall bring his trespass-offering unto Jehovah, unto the door of the tent of meeting, even a ram for a trespass-offering.

The NKJV translators offered this reading:

Whoever lies carnally with a woman who is betrothed to a man as a concubine, and who has not at all been redeemed nor given her freedom, for this there shall be scourging; but they shall not be put to death, because she was not free. And he shall bring his trespass offering to the Lord, to the door of the tabernacle of meeting, a ram as a trespass offering.

A brief look at these three translations shows that the recipient(s) of the punishment is not as clearly delineated as the KJV indicates. Keil and Delitzsch, in their commentary on the Pentateuch, noted that the scourging "referred to both parties, as is evident from the expression, 'they shall not be put to death'" (1981, p. 422). G.J. Wenham has introduced another interesting solution regarding this passage by translating the disputed passage about scourging as "damages must be paid" (1979, p. 270). Concerning this translation he wrote:

This is the most problematic phrase in this law: literally, "there will be a *biqqôret*." The word *biqqôret* occurs only here in the OT, and its meaning is therefore quite uncertain.... Other renderings of *biqqôret* have less to commend them. "An inquiry shall be held" (RSV; cf. NEB) is vacuous: every legal dispute would have involved inquiry. "She shall be scourged" (AV) goes back to an old Jewish interpretation, probably based on the dubious derivation of *biqqôret* from *bâqâr*, "ox, i.e., an oxhide scourge" (pp. 270-271, emp. added).

Taking these things into account, it appears that the passage does not indicate that the female should be scourged apart from the guilty male. Rather, whatever punishment was inflicted should be applied equally, except for the fact that the guilty male alone shoulders the responsibility of supplying the ram for the trespass offering.

According to God, the Israelites did not have absolute control over their slaves, as is evinced by the instructions in Exodus 21:20,26-27 and Leviticus 19:20. This idea was a departure from the generally accepted notions of slavery in the Near East during the Israelites' day. "Any demeaning or oppressive treatment of slaves was condemned as wrong by biblical writers" (Copan, 2001, pp. 173-174). God's laws in the Old Testament not only regulated slavery (so that those enslaved would be given many rights that they otherwise would not have had), but they also supplied the means whereby fairness could be meted out with regard to criminal activity and debt. Every regulation of slavery in the Old Testament can be shown to be in harmony with the principles of justice and fairness.

SLAVERY IN THE NEW TESTAMENT

As we look into the New Testament, we see a strikingly different picture with regard to the biblical injunctions pertaining to slavery. The New Testament does not contain the specific regulations dealing with slavery that can be found in the Old Testament. In fact, for the most part, the New Testament says very little in its regulation of slavery. And herein lies one of the skeptic's primary challenges to the New Testament's stance on slavery. If the New Testament is supposedly a book inspired by an all-loving God, why does it remain virtually silent on slavery? Smith and Hoffman, in their attack on the Bible, stated:

> Slave-owning was the order of the day and, so far as we are told, Jesus never attacked the practice. He took the state of affairs for granted and shaped his parables accordingly.... If Jesus had denounced slavery, we should almost certainly have heard of his doing so (Smith and Hoffman, 1989, p. 143).

The other challenge to the New Testament's stance on slavery centers on the passages that teach slaves to be humble and obedient servants to their masters. In Colossians 3:22, Paul commanded: "Slaves, obey your earthly masters in everything, not only while being watched and in order to please them, but wholeheartedly, fearing the Lord" (NRSV). Although several modern translations insert the word "servants" at the first of this verse, "slaves" is probably a better translation of the Greek word *douloi* in this passage (Arndt and Gingrich, 1967, p. 205). Other similar passages include 1 Peter 2:18-20, 1 Corinthians 7:21-24, and Ephesians 6:5-9. Ruth Green, after presenting her case to suggest that the Bible condones slavery, wrote:

> Those who deny my contentions about the Bible should turn to the Epistles to see what Paul and Peter have to say about "servants" and masters. Here are only two examples: "Servants, be subject to your masters in all fear" (1 Peter 2:18). "Servants, be obedient to them that are your masters...with fear and trembling" (Ephesians 6:5). There are many more instructions about slavery in the Christian Holy Book (1979, p. 352).

Does the New Testament remain silent in its condemnation of all slavery? And why does it specifically instruct slaves to be obedient to their masters?

First, it must be acknowledged that many of the types of servanthood or slavery in the New Testament are identical to the morally permissible types discussed earlier in this article. For instance, much first-century slavery discussed in the Bible centered on the fact that a person had accrued massive debt, and thus had become a slave or servant due to this debt. As an example, in the Sermon on the Mount, Jesus said: "Agree with your adversary quickly, while you are on the way with him, lest your adversary deliver you to the judge, the judge hand you over to the officer, and you be thrown into prison. Assuredly, I say to you, you will by no means get out of there till you have paid the last penny" (Matthew 5:25-26). From Christ's comments, it can be ascertained that the person in this text who does not make the effort to agree with his adversary could risk being thrown into prison until that person "paid the last penny." This situation involved a revoking of individual freedoms due to the fact that the individual owed an unpaid debt—a debt that originally was owed to the adversary, or one that resulted from a fine imposed by a judge.

In Matthew 18:21-35, Jesus told a story about a servant who owed his master ten thousand talents. A talent was a huge sum of money that would be the modern equivalent of many thousands of dollars. It could easily have been the case that this servant had become a servant due to this enormous debt, or was being kept a servant because of the debt. Debt slavery was still a very real form of restitution in New Testament times. Such a condition absolutely cannot be used to argue that God is an unjust God for letting such take place.

Furthermore, it is a false notion that God condones something just because He mentions it without an immediate condemnation of it in the surrounding verses. Skeptics point to verses like 1 Peter 2:8 and Ephesians 6:5, and then insist that God condones abusive slavery because He instructs servants to be obedient to their masters. But, let us analyze that line of thinking. In Matthew 5:39, Christ instructed His listeners: "Do not resist an evil person. But whoever slaps you on your right cheek, turn the other to him also." Because Jesus told His listeners to be kind and turn the other cheek, does that mean that He condones the actions of the one who did the slapping? Absolutely not! Or what about the fact that Paul, through divine inspiration, instructed his readers to be subject to civil governments and to pay taxes to those governments. Was Paul condoning all practices of all governments to whom his readers would be subject and pay taxes? Certainly not. God never has condoned such unjustified behavior on the part of any individual or group.

BIBLICAL PRINCIPLES AND ABOLITION

As a concluding argument, let it be clearly stated that the principles set forth by Jesus and His apostles, if followed, would result in the abolition of all types of abusive relationships. Slavery would have been nonexistent if everyone from the first century forward had adhered to Jesus' admonition in Matthew 7:12: "Therefore, whatever you want men to do to you, do also to them." Any discussion of slavery would be moot if the world had heeded the words of Peter: "Finally, all of you be of one mind, having compassion for one another, love as brothers, be tenderhearted, be courteous" (1 Peter 3:8).

Truly, the teachings of the Lord and the apostles would have abolished slavery like no other social reform system ever known. As Herb Vander Lugt accurately observed:

> Jesus and the apostles didn't go on an anti-slavery crusade, because doing so would have been futile and a hindrance to their primary mission. The priority of Jesus was the provision of salvation. For the apostles it was the proclamation of the gospel. But both Jesus and the apostles undermined the basis for slavery by making it clear that God equally loves rich and poor, free and slave, male and female. The apostles also welcomed into the church and gave equal status to all who believed, regardless of race, gender, nationality, or social position (1999, p. 26).

Furthermore, an outright condemnation of kidnapping, or slave trading, is found in the New Testament. In 1 Timothy 1:9-10, Paul wrote:

> We also know that law is made not for the righteous but for lawbreakers and rebels, the ungodly and sinful, the unholy and irreligious; for those who kill their fathers or mothers, for murderers, for adulterers and perverts, for slave traders and liars and perjurers—and for whatever else is contrary to the sound doctrine... (NIV, emp. added).

Other versions render the Greek word *andrapodistais* as "kidnappers," or "menstealers," but it also is translated slave dealers or slave traders (Arndt and Gingrich, 1967, p. 63). Therefore, in keeping with the Old Testament injunction that anyone kidnapping and selling a person involves himself in immoral conduct, Paul certainly distinguished between certain types of slavery practices that were inherently wrong, and others that were not intrinsically sinful.

CONCLUSION

The fact is, certain types of "slavery" not only are permissible, but sometimes necessary to the well-being of a society at large. For the biblical stance on slavery to be condemned as unjust, it must be established that the specific regulations of slavery described in the text are immoral and unfair. However, when closely scrutinized, the biblical stance on slavery aligns itself with true justice. All regulations found therein were established for the just treatment of all parties involved. Many times, slavery as regulated in the Old Testament was a mutually beneficial relationship between servant and master, similar to an employee/employer relationship. Furthermore, slavery often was a substitute for the death penalty—which certain nations deserved. Debt accumulation caused many free persons to sell their labor and become slaves.

The skeptic's criticism that the New Testament does not speak against the abolition of slavery is misguided for any number of reasons. First, an attempt to generalize and condemn all types of slavery fails to take into account prison, personal debt, indentured servanthood, and a host of other morally permissible situations. Bankruptcy laws, prison terms, community service hours, and garnished wages are morally acceptable modern equivalents to certain types of slavery that were prevalent during the time of the biblical writers. Second, Jesus and the New Testament writers always condemned the mistreatment of any human being, instructing their followers to be kind, loving, and compassionate, whether they were slaves or masters of slaves.

In *The Social Record of Christianity*, atheist Joseph McCabe wrote: "Slavery is the last word that any Christian apologist ought to mention" (1935, p. 27). But he missed one of the main points in the Bible—that point being that everyone is a slave to something. As the apostle Paul wrote through inspiration:

> Do you not know that to whom you present yourselves slaves to obey, you are that one's slaves whom you obey, whether of sin leading to death, or of obedience leading to righteousness? But God be thanked that though you were slaves of sin, yet you obeyed from the heart that form of doctrine to which you were delivered. And having been set free from sin, you became slaves of righteousness (Romans 6:16-18).

Some people are slaves to drug addiction, sexual promiscuity, attitudes of pessimism and complaint, or any number of other vices. Others, however, are slaves to righteousness, teaching the Gospel, helping the sick, and taking care of the poor. We each must decide which master we will allow to control our lives. As the psalmist so beautifully stated it many years ago, "I had rather be a doorkeeper in the house of my God, than to dwell in the tents of wickedness" (Psalm 84:10).

God's injunctions and instructions pertaining to slavery have a clear ring of justice, compassion, mercy, and kindness to them. When analyzed fairly and fully, the idea of slavery gives the honest person one more piece of evidence that points to the perfection of the God of the Bible. The atheist's allegation that the biblical view of slavery is immoral cannot be sustained. Neither can it be shown that the Bible maintains contradictory positions regarding slavery.

DID JESUS COME TO BRING PEACE–OR TURMOIL?

[NOTE: In his list of alleged contradictions, Barker stated that the Bible gives contradictory descriptions of God and Christ being peaceful, while at the same time bringing about turmoil and war (Part 1, p. 10). His allegation is refuted in the following article written by Caleb Colley in 2004.]

DID JESUS COME TO BRING PEACE—OR TURMOIL?

by Caleb Colley, M.L.A.

Militant, violent, religious extremists have caused legitimate concern for America's security. In Palestine, on the very soil Jesus walked, people kill each other in warfare motivated by religion. Do the teachings of Christ authorize or encourage such behavior? In John 14:27, Jesus said: "Peace I leave with you, My peace I give to you; not as the world gives do I give to you. Let not your heart be troubled, neither let it be afraid." Some have charged that Jesus' promise of peace in that verse contradicts His message in Matthew 10:34: "Do not think that I came to bring peace on earth. I did not come to bring peace but a sword." Did Jesus come to Earth to bring peace—or turmoil?

Based on scriptural evidence, it is indisputable that Jesus wants His followers to have peace. The words "Christ" and "peace" are found together in the same verse no less than 24 times in the New King James Version. Consider Philippians 1:2: "Grace to you and **peace** from God our Father and Lord Jesus Christ." 2 Corinthians 1:2 reads: "Grace to you and **peace** from God our Father and the Lord Jesus Christ." Paul urged the Thessalonians, "Be at **peace** among yourselves" (1 Thessalonians 5:13). The message of Christ is called "the gospel of **peace**" (Ephesians 6:15), and Philippians 4:7 says that the peace of God "surpasses all understanding" and that peace will guard the hearts and minds of Christians. Jesus, Who is called the Prince of Peace in Isaiah 9:6, most definitely came to bring peace.

Could it also be that Jesus came to bring turmoil? Certainly. In the context of Matthew 10:34, Jesus was explaining to His disciples that the Gospel, in some cases, would cause division. A son would believe in Jesus, but his father might not. A mother would believe, but her daughter might refuse even to hear the Gospel. In Matthew 10:37-38, Jesus presented a hard truth: "He who loves father or mother more than Me is not worthy of Me. And he who loves son or daughter more than Me is not worthy of Me. And he who does not take his cross and follow after Me is not worthy of Me." Richard Lenski offered insight into the implications of the "turmoil" brought by Christ:

> The idea is this: if Christ had not come, the earth would have gone on undisturbed in its sin and its guilt until the day of its doom. Now Christ came to take away that sin and that guilt. At once war resulted, for in their perversion men clung to their sin, fought Christ and the gospel, and thus produced two hostile camps. Christ foresaw this effect and willed it. Emphatically He declared that He came to throw a sword on the earth. Better the war and the division, saving as many as possible, than to let all perish in their sin (1943, p. 415).

Many react with hostility to the Gospel. This is **not** because Christ's teaching promotes hostility (see Matthew 5:44; 7:12; John 13:14; 13:35), but because Jesus' teachings are highly controversial. In Matthew 10:34, Jesus did not mean to suggest that His purpose was to bring hostility or turmoil, but that hostility would, in some cases, be an **effect** of His teaching (Barnes, 1949, p. 115). It always will be the case that some people will respond negatively to Christ's teachings, for some always will prefer spiritual darkness to the light of Jesus (John 3:19). Christ, Who came to Earth to bring both peace and turmoil, never contradicted Himself.

SEEING GOD "FACE TO FACE"

by Eric Lyons, M.Min.

In his opening speech, Dan Barker alleged that He "knows" the God of the Bible cannot exist because "there are mutually incompatible properties/characteristics of the God that's in this book [the Bible—EL] that rule out the possibility of His existence" (2009). One of the supposed contradictions that Barker mentioned was that God claims invisibility, yet has been seen (Part 1, p. 10). Since biblical passages such as Exodus 33:20-23, John 1:18, and 1 John 4:12 teach that God cannot be seen, while other scriptures indicate that man has seen God and spoken to him "face to face" (Exodus 33:11; Genesis 32:30), allegedly "the God of the Bible does not exist."

Although in modern times words are regularly used in many different senses (e.g., hot and cold, good and bad), Barker, like so many Bible critics, has dismissed the possibility that the terms in the aforementioned passages were used in different senses. Throughout Scripture, however, words are often used in various ways. In James 2:5, the term "poor" refers to material wealth, whereas the term "rich" has to do with a person's spiritual well-being. In Philippians 3:12,15, Paul used the term "perfect" (NASB) in different senses. Although Paul had attained spiritual maturity ("perfection") in Christ (vs. 15), he had not yet attained the perfect "final thing, the victor's prize of the heavenly calling in Christ Jesus" (Schippers,

1971, 2:62; cf. Philippians 3:9-11). Similarly, in one sense man has seen God, but in another sense he has not.

Consider the first chapter of John where we learn that in the beginning Jesus was with God and "was God" (1:1; cf. 14,17). Though John wrote that Jesus "became flesh and dwelt among us" (1:14), he indicated only four sentences later that "no one has seen God at any time" (1:18; 1 John 4:12). Was Jesus God? Yes. Did man see Jesus? Yes. So in what sense has man not seen God? No human has ever seen Jesus in His true image (i.e., as a spirit Being—John 4:24—in all of His fullness, glory, and splendor). When God, the Word, appeared on Earth 2,000 years ago, He came in a veiled form. In his letter to the church at Philippi, the apostle Paul mentioned that Christ—Who had existed in heaven "in the form of God"—"made Himself of no reputation," and took on the "likeness of men" (Philippians 2:6-7). Mankind saw an embodiment of deity as Jesus dwelt on Earth in the form of a man. Men saw "the Word" that "became flesh." Likewise, when Jacob "struggled with God" (Genesis 32:28), He saw only a form of God, not the spiritual, invisible, omnipresent God Who fills heaven and Earth (Jeremiah 23:23-24).

But what about those statements which indicate that man saw or spoke to God "face to face"? Jacob said, "I have seen God face to face" (Genesis 32:30). Gideon proclaimed: "I have seen the Angel of the Lord face to face" (Judges 6:22). Exodus 33:11 affirms that "the Lord spoke to Moses face to face, as a man speaks to his friend." First, although these men witnessed great and awesome things, they still only saw manifestations of God and a part of His glory (cf. Exodus 33:18-23). Second, the words "face" and "face to face" are used in different senses in Scripture. Though Exodus 33:11 reveals that God spoke to Moses "face to face," only nine verses later God told Moses, "You cannot see My face; for no man shall see Me, and live" (33:20). Are we to believe (as Barker and other critics assert) that the author of Exodus was so misguided that he wrote contradictory statements within only nine verses of each other? Certainly not! What then does the Bible mean when it says that God "knew" (Deuteronomy 34:10) or "spoke to Moses face to face" (Exodus 33:11)? The answer is found in Numbers 12. Aaron and Miriam had spoken against Moses and arrogantly asked: "Has the Lord indeed spoken only through Moses? Has He not spoken through us also?" (Numbers 12:2). God then appeared to Aaron and Miriam, saying: "If there is a prophet among you, I, the Lord, make Myself known to him in a vision; I speak to him in a dream. Not so with My servant Moses; He is faithful in all My house. I speak with him face to face, even plainly, and not in dark sayings; and he sees the form of the Lord" (Numbers 12:6-8, emp. added). Notice the contrast: God spoke to the prophets of Israel through visions and dreams, but to Moses He spoke, "not in dark sayings," but "plainly." In other words, God, Who never showed His face to Moses (Deuteronomy 33:20), nevertheless allowed Moses to see "some unmistakable evidence of His glorious presence" (Jamieson, et al., 1997), and spoke to him "face to face, as a man speaks to his friend" (33:11), i.e., He spoke to Moses plainly, directly, etc.

The Bible does not reveal "mutually incompatible characteristics of God" as Barker has alleged. His assertions in no way prove that the God of the Bible does not exist or that the Bible is unreliable. In truth, Barker's comments merely reveal that he is a dishonest interpreter of Scripture. If Barker can work "side by side" with a colleague without literally working inches from him (Barker, 2008, p. 335), or if he can see "eye to eye" with a fellow atheist without ever literally looking into the atheist's eyes, then Barker can understand that God could speak "face to face" with Moses without literally revealing to him His full, glorious "face."

WERE THE IRON CHARIOTS TOO POWERFUL?

[NOTE: Barker's list of alleged Bible discrepancies consumed almost two-thirds of his opening speech. At one point, he claimed that the Bible gives contradictory descriptions of God's power, because of a statement about the Israelite's failure to conquer their neighbors who possessed iron chariots (Part 1, p. 11). I refuted his allegation in the following article written in 2004.]

WERE THE IRON CHARIOTS TOO POWERFUL?

It has been suggested that the Bible is filled with contradictions. One of the supposed contradictions is between Joshua 17:18 and Judges 1:19. Let us look closely at these verses and their contexts to see if any real contradiction exists.

> Joshua 17:18: "But the mountain country shall be yours. Although it is wooded, you shall cut it down, and its farthest extent shall be yours; for you shall drive out the Canaanites, though they have iron chariots and are strong."

> Judges 1:19: "So the Lord was with Judah. And they drove out the mountaineers, but they could not drive out the inhabitants of the lowland, because they had chariots of iron."

After reading the two verses, it may look like they contradict one another. Did the children of Israel defeat the Canaanites with their chariots of iron as Joshua apparently had said they would, or were the chariots just too powerful for the people of Judah to overcome?

These two passages have several plausible ways of reconciliation. And, please remember that the **exact way** to reconcile any contradiction need not be pinpointed, as long as a **possible way** can be provided. The rest of this brief answer will deal with only two of the many possible ways to reconcile the passages.

The first way to reconcile the passages is to show that Joshua was informing his listeners that they had the power to drive out the Canaanites **only if** they would follow God faithfully and be confident in His promises. Judges chapter 2:1-3 says:

> Then the Angel of the Lord came up from Gilgal to Bochim, and said: "I led you up from Egypt and brought you to the land of which I swore to your fathers; and I said, 'I will never break My covenant with you. And you shall make no covenant with the inhabitants of this land; you shall tear down their altars.' But you have not obeyed My voice. Why have you done this? Therefore I also said, 'I will not drive them out before you; but they shall be thorns in your side, and their gods shall be a snare to you.' "

God's promise through Joshua was not an unconditional guarantee that the children of Israel would possess all of the land they had been promised. It was conditional, based upon the faithfulness of the Israelites and their obedience to God's commandments. After all, God never would force the Israelites to clear the wooded areas against their will. Neither would He force them to conquer the iron chariots. The two verses under discussion easily could be dealing with land that God chose not to clear of its previous inhabitants because of the disobedience of the people of Judah.

A second possible solution could be that the children of Israel did conquer the mountain country and succeeded in driving out its inhabitants for a brief time, but they were unable to maintain control of the cities. Thus, by the time referred to in Judges 1, the cities already could have been retaken by the chariots of iron.

As a final word, notice that Joshua said that "the mountain country" and "its farthest extents" were the promised possession of the Israelites. In Judges 1:19, the children of Israel did, indeed, drive out "the inhabitants of the mountains." Unless we force the phrase "its farthest extents" in Joshua 17:18 to read "lowland" as in Judges 1:19, then there is absolutely no hint of a contradiction, and this entire explanation is unnecessary.

[NOTE: The way Dan quoted Judges 1:19, he implies that the text reads that "he" means God could not drive out the chariots. The actual text makes clear that it was Judah that failed to remove the Canaanites, not God.]

DOES GOD DWELL IN LIGHT OR DARKNESS?

by Eric Lyons, M.Min.

In the debate, Dan Barker spent nearly two-thirds of his opening 15-minute speech alleging that the Bible's portrayal of God is contradictory. Barker alleged several discrepancies, including that God cannot logically dwell in light and darkness. Twelve minutes and five seconds into his first speech, Dan Barker asserted:

> Does God live in light or does God live in darkness? First Timothy 6: "The King of kings, Lord of Lords dwelling in the light which no man can approach." James 1:17: He's "the Father of lights" and on and on we see God is light. There's no darkness in him at all. However, in 1 Kings 8: "Then spake Solomon: "The Lord said that he would dwell in the thick darkness." First Samuel 22: "He made darkness pavilions round about Him, dark waters and thick clouds of the sky." Psalm 18:11: "He made darkness his secret place." So, God lives in light. God lives in darkness (Part 1, p. 11).

Do these verses paint a contradictory picture of God? Not at all.

First, the Bible uses the terms "light" and "darkness" in several ways and in a variety of contexts. God's dwelling place in the spiritual realm of the heaven of heavens is filled with "unapproachable light" (1 Timothy 6:16), because His unrestrained glory illuminates it (Revelation 21:23). God made light in the physical Universe during the six-day Creation and "called the light Day, and the darkness He called Night" (Genesis 1:5). He made the Sun, Moon, and stars on day four of Creation, thus making Him the "Father of lights" (James 1:17). Jesus was miraculously transfigured before three of His apostles and "His face shone like the sun, and His clothes became as white as the light" (Matthew 17:2). The psalmist referred to light in the sense of divine instruction: "The entrance of Your words gives light; it gives understanding to the simple" (119:130). Conversely, the psalmist referred to those who "do not know, nor... understand," as those who "walk about in darkness" (82:5). While addressing the subjects of sin and righteousness, the apostle John used the terms light and darkness symbolically: "God is light (i.e., holy) and in Him is no darkness (i.e., sin)" (1 John 1:5). This same apostle referred to Jesus as "the Light" throughout his gospel account (1:4-9; 8:12; 9:5; 12:34-36,46), and Matthew recorded that Jesus spoke of His disciples as "the light of the world" (5:14-16), reflectors of His righteousness.

Notice that Barker never hinted at the different ways in which the word "light" and "darkness" are used in Scripture. He simply positioned a phrase like that found in James 1:17 regarding God being the Creator ("Father") of lights against the poetic statement found in Psalm 18:11 ("He made darkness his secret place") and expected his listeners to believe they are contradictory. But the fact is, God being the Father of the Sun, Moon, and stars made on day four, has no bearing whatsoever on the question of whether God dwells in darkness or light. What God has created and where God dwells are two different things. One cannot fault Scripture when a critic compares apples and oranges. For there to be a legitimate contradiction, the same thing must be under consideration.

Second, the passage in 1 Kings 8:12 that Barker noted ("The Lord said that he would dwell in thick darkness"—KJV) is not discussing God's dwelling place in the heaven of heavens. First Kings 8:12-13, along with 2 Chronicles 5:13-14, discuss God's presence in the physical temple of God in Jerusalem. Just as "the cloud covered the tabernacle of meeting, and the glory of the Lord filled the tabernacle" in the days of Moses (Exodus 40:34), so "the house of the Lord [the temple], was filled with a cloud" (2 Chronicles 5:13). Similarly, the highly poetic wording in Psalm 18 and 1 Samuel 22 (a quotation of Psalm 18) pictures God, not on His majestic, glorious throne in heaven, but as One Who "came down" from heaven (Psalm 18:9), "flew upon the wings of the wind" (18:10), and delivered his servant David from his enemies while making "darkness His secret place" and "His canopy...dark waters" (18:11). As H.C. Leupold commented:

> The picture is that of a violent storm—a figure so frequently used in the Scriptures to furnish the accompaniment of God's approach, He Himself being as it were housed in the storm. From the time of Sinai onward these figures become standard (cf. Exod. 19:16-18; Judg. 5:4,5; Ps. 68:7;77:16-18; Is. 29:6; 30:27ff.; etc.). As the storm sweeps near, He is in it. The thick storm clouds are the material upon which He rides (1959, pp. 166-167).

Once again, when a person takes the time to carefully inspect Dan Barker's allegation that the Bible paints a contradictory picture of God, the sincere truth seeker will discover that his charges are vacuous. Time and again, both in this debate and in his writings, Barker has disregarded the fact that for a legitimate contradiction to exist, one must be referring to the same person, place, or thing, at the same time, in the same sense (for more information, see Lyons, 2003 and 2005).

DOES GOD ACCEPT HUMAN SACRIFICE?

Dan further claimed that the God of the Bible cannot exist because the Bible presents contradictory information about God's acceptance of human sacrifice. Barker said: "Does He [God—KB] accept human sacrifice? In some verses, 'Yes,' in some verses, 'No.' Remember the thing about when [sic] Abraham; He asked Abraham to sacrifice his son Isaac" (Part 1, p. 11).

This brief statement is the only one that he gave as "evidence" of this alleged Bible contradiction. In our debate he did not cite any verses that he believes show this contradiction. But in chapter 13 of his book *godless*, he made the same claim and listed several verses. On page 240, he quoted Deuteronomy 12:31: "Thou shalt not do so unto the Lord thy God: for every abomination to the Lord, which he hateth, have they done unto their gods; for even their sons and their daughters they have burnt in the fire to their gods." Barker then quoted Genesis 22:2: "And he [God—KB] said, Take now thy son, thine only son Isaac, whom thou lovest, and get thee into the land of Moriah; and offer him there for a burnt offering upon one of the mountains which I will tell thee of" (KJV). Dan does not offer any comments on these two verses, other than to list them as contradictory.

On close inspection, however, it becomes evident that these two verses cannot be contradictory. From the biblical narrative in Genesis 22, it is clear that God never intended to allow Abraham to kill his son. When Abraham got to the top of the appointed mountain, before he killed his son, God stopped him and showed him a ram caught in a thicket that was provided as a sacrifice instead of Isaac. God knew that He would stop Abraham before the sacrifice (see Part 2, pp. 191-194), and thus never planned to accept a human sacrifice in this instance. If Isaac was never sacrificed, due to God's intervention, then it cannot be claimed that God accepted human sacrifice on this occasion. In fact, since God stepped in and commanded Abraham not to sacrifice his son (Genesis 22:12), Abraham would have been sinning if he had continued with the sacrifice. It is impossible to claim that God accepted the human sacrifice of Isaac when the Bible specifically states that He prevented it. [NOTE: At this point in the discussion, Barker generally changes the argument, as he did in this debate, and demands that it was immoral for Abraham to follow God's commands. That allegation is dealt with in Part 2, pp. 203-216. It is important to stay focused on Barker's original allegation of contradiction before moving on to refute his allegation that God is immoral.]

EXODUS 22:29

In addition to the incident with Isaac, Barker cited Exodus 22:29 as an example of God accepting human sacrifice. In *godless*, he quoted this verse on page 240: "For thou shalt not delay to offer the first of thy ripe fruits, and of thy liquors; the firstborn of thy sons shalt thou give unto me." With all due respect to Barker, either he has intentionally misled the reader by citing this verse, or he is unaware of its true meaning. Based on his background of Bible study and his claims of biblical knowledge, the former, unfortunately, seems to be the case.

Exodus 22:29 was never intended to mean that the Israelites were supposed to sacrifice their firstborn sons to God. In fact, Exodus 13:13 says, "And all the firstborn of man among your sons you shall redeem." What did it mean to redeem the firstborn son? It meant that the Israelites were to give to the Lord five skekels of silver when the firstborn son was one month old (see Numbers

18:16). What was the purpose of redeeming the firstborn son? Moses explained that it was a memorial of the process by which God delivered the Israelites from Egyptian bondage (Exodus 13:14-15). It is inexcusably poor scholarship for any person who has read the book of Exodus to make such an uninformed statement as to demand that Exodus 22:29 speaks of human sacrifice. We should remember, however, that Barker has admitted his belief that honesty is not always the best tactic for dealing with Christianity or the Bible (Part 2, pp. 63-64).

JEPHTHAH'S VOW

As further "evidence" of a Bible contradiction in regard to human sacrifice, Barker cited the story of Jephthah that is found in Judges 11:30-39. In that biblical narrative, Jephthah made a vow to God that, if God would give him victory against his enemies, then Jephthah would sacrifice the first thing that came out of his house upon his return. Jephthah defeated his enemies and his only daughter was the first thing that greeted him. Jephthah was very sorry for his vow, but the text says that he "carried out his vow with her which he had vowed" (Judges 11:39).

In regard to Jephthah's vow, there are at least two insurmountable problems with presenting this as an example of God accepting human sacrifice. First, there is considerable evidence that the girl was not killed, she simply was dedicated to the Lord, remained unmarried, and had no children (for a more thorough discussion of Jephthah's vow, see Miller, 2003). Second, there is no indication that God approved of Jephthah's vow. If Jephthah offered his daughter as a literal burnt offering, he disobeyed God's instructions in the Law of Moses (Leviticus 18:21; 20:2-5; Deuteronomy 12:31; 18:10). The Jephthah incident cannot be used to show that God either asked for human sacrifice, or approved of it.

SAUL'S DESCENDANTS

Furthermore, Barker cited 2 Samuel 21:8-14 as an example of God accepting human sacrifice. Barker quoted those verses as follows: "But the king [David] took the two sons of Rizpah…and the five sons of Michal…and he delivered them into the hands of the Gibeonites, and they hanged them in the hill before the Lord: and they fell all seven together, and were put to death in the days of harvest… And after that God was intreated for the land" (2008, pp. 240-241). Again, this narrative offers no proof that God ever accepted human sacrifice. Was it the case that God sometimes demanded that sinful people who deserved capital punishment be put to death for their sins? Yes, it was (see Miller, 2002). Could it be, then, that the descendants of Saul were guilty of offenses that deserved the death penalty? Yes.

Notice that the text indicates that the ones who were hanged were "men" (2 Samuel 21:6), who would have been old enough to be responsible for their moral decisions. Furthermore, notice that the text indicates that Saul's "house" or "household" was a bloodthirsty house (2 Samuel 21:1), apparently implying that many of his relatives were involved in his murderous plots. In 2 Samuel 16:5-14, the Bible introduces a wicked man named Shimei who was "from the family of the house of Saul" (2 Samuel 16:5). And Saul's wickedness is documented throughout the book of 1 Samuel. Could it be that Saul's descendants who were hanged had followed in the wicked paths of many from the "house of Saul" and deserved the death penalty? Yes. Thus, it is once again impossible to use this passage to "prove" that God accepted human sacrifice.

THE DEATH OF CHRIST

Finally, Barker alleges that the sacrifice of Christ provides an example of God accepting human sacrifice. He cited Hebrews 10:10-12 and 1 Corinthians 5:7 as evidence. Once more, Barker is guilty of egregious textual manipulation and dishonesty. Did God approve of the sinful actions of those who killed Jesus? Absolutely not. In fact, Peter explained that those who killed Jesus had done so with "lawless hands" (Acts 2:23). He further explained that they had to repent of their sins or they would be lost forever (Acts 2:38). While God used the sinful actions of Jesus' murderers to bring about His purposes (Acts 3:17-19), He never condoned those actions. Those who murdered Jesus violated God's law; they did not accomplish their dastardly deeds at God's request, nor with His approval.

Barker is well aware of this truth. In fact, he has spoken in other places about Christ's atoning sacrifice. In his book *Losing Faith in Faith*, Barker stated:

> Christians do know how to think; but they don't start deep enough. A thoughtful conclusion is the synthesis of antecedent presuppositions or conclusions. The propitiatory nature of Christ's sacrificial atonement, for example, is very logical. Logical, that is, if you first accept the existence of sin, the fall of humankind, the wrath of God and divine judgment. If you don't buy the premises, then, of course, the conclusion cannot be logical (1992a, p. 60).

Barker, of course, does not "buy the premises," but his denial of them does not make them any less logical or true. And if they are true, then he acknowledges that the sacrifice of Christ, although perpetrated by sinful men acting against God's will, fits logically into the scheme of redemption.

CONCLUSION

God has never accepted human sacrifice. The examples that Barker listed fail completely to manifest a contradiction in the Bible concerning God's policy toward the practice. Barker's lack of knowledge, or his intentional dishonesty, is evident throughout his discussion of the biblical view of human sacrifice. Since no contradiction exists, the accusation of a Bible contradiction is unfounded, and cannot be used against the Bible or the existence of God. Let us all be gravely reminded that those who twist the Scriptures, and force them to seemingly say what they do not say, do so at their own eternal peril (2 Peter 3:16).

DOES GOD REALLY KNOW EVERYTHING?

by Eric Lyons, M.Min.

Numerous passages of Scripture clearly teach that God is omniscient. The psalmist declared that God "knows the secrets of the heart" (44:21), that His eyes "are in every place" (15:3), and that "His understanding is infinite" (147:5). Of Jehovah, the psalmist also wrote:

> O Lord, You have searched me and known me. You know my sitting down and my rising up; You understand my thought afar off. You comprehend my path and my lying down, and are acquainted with all my ways. For there is not a word on my tongue, but behold, O Lord, You know it altogether.... Such knowledge is too wonderful for me; it is high, I cannot attain it. Where can I go from Your Spirit? Or where can I flee from Your presence? If I ascend into heaven, You are there; if I make my bed in Sheol, behold, You are there (139:1-4,6-8).

The New Testament reemphasizes this truth: "God is greater than our heart, and knows all things" (1 John 3:20). Not only does He know the past and the present, but the future as well (Acts 15:18; cf. Isaiah 46:10). According to the Bible, there is nothing outside of the awareness of God.

Dan Barker, however, alleged in this debate that the Bible paints a contradictory picture of God and His knowledge (Part 1, p. 11). Whereas some scriptures indicate that God knows the future, supposedly, the God of the Bible cannot exist because other passages reportedly teach that God does not know the future. Twelve minutes and 54 seconds into his first speech, Barker exclaimed:

> Look what God said after he stopped it [Abraham's sacrifice of Isaac—EL]. He said: "Lay not thine hand upon the lad, neither do thou any thing unto him: for I know now, I now know, that you fear God, seeing that you have not withheld thy son." I know now? I thought God knew everything. The Bible says God knows the future but here He is saying, "I didn't even know." The Bible even says that God searches and understands all the imaginations of the heart. The God of the Bible knows the future. The God of the Bible does not know the future (Part 1, p. 11).

Is Barker correct? Does the Bible paint a contradictory picture of God's knowledge? Do some passages testify to the omniscience of God, while others indicate that He is finite in His understanding?

The kind of language found in Genesis 22:12 actually is present throughout Scripture. As early as Genesis chapter three, God asked Adam, "Where are you?" (3:9). In Genesis four, He asked Cain, "Where is Abel your brother?" (4:9). The book of Job reveals that at the beginning of God's first speech to Job, God asked the patriarch, "Where were you when I laid the foundations of the earth?" (38:4, emp. added). Are we to assume questions like these or statements like those found in Genesis 22:12 and 18:21 ("I will know") imply a lack of knowledge on God's part?

First, one must acknowledge that questions often are asked and statements frequently are made for a variety of reasons. Are we really to assume that the Creator of heaven and Earth was ignorant of Adam's whereabouts when He asked him, "Where are you?" (Genesis 3:9)? Are we to believe that God did not know where Job was when He made the world (Job 38:4)? Certainly not! What father, having seen his son dent a car door, would imply ignorance by asking, "Who did that?" Obviously, the father did not ask the question to obtain information, but to see if the son would admit to something the father knew all along. On occasion, Jesus used questions or made statements for the same purpose. When He questioned the Pharisees' disciples and the Herodians regarding whose inscription was on a particular coin, it clearly was not because He did not know (Matthew 22:15-22). Likewise, when Jesus asked the multitude that thronged Him, "Who touched Me?" (Luke 8:45), it was not because the woman who touched Him was hidden from Him (Luke 8:47). Jesus knew the woman who was made well by touching His garment before she confessed to touching Him (Mark 5:32). His question was intended to bring attention to her great faith and His great power (Mark 5:34). In no way are the questions God asks or the statements He makes an indication of Him being less than omniscient.

Second, the term "know" (Hebrew *yada*, Greek *ginosko*) or one of its derivatives (i.e., knew, known, etc.) is used in Scripture in a variety of ways. Several times it is used in reference to a man and woman having sexual intercourse (Genesis 4:1,17,25; Judges 11:39; 19:25). Jesus used the term to refer to His regard for His sheep (i.e., people—John 10:27). In contrast to the way of the wicked that will perish, the psalmist wrote that God "knows" (i.e., approves, takes delight in, etc.) the way of the righteous (Psalm 1:6). Paul used the term "know" in Ephesians 3:19 in the sense of knowing "experimentally what intellectually is beyond our powers of knowing"—the love of Christ (Jamieson, et al., 1997). The fact is, like so many words in Scripture (and in modern times) the word "know" has a variety of meanings. What's more, neither Dan Barker nor any Bible critic can prove that the term "know" in Genesis 22:12 directly contradicts God's omniscience.

Third, the Bible's usage of phrases such as "now I know" (Genesis 22:12) or "I will know" (Genesis 18:21) in reference to God actually are for the benefit of man. Throughout the Bible, human actions (such as "learning") frequently are attributed to God for the purpose of helping us better understand His infinity. When Jehovah "came down to see the city and the tower" built at Babel

(Genesis 11:5), it was not for the purpose of gaining knowledge. Anthropomorphic expressions such as these are not meant to suggest that God is not always fully aware of everything. Rather, as in the case of Babel, such wording was used to show that He was "officially and judicially taking the situation under direct observation and consideration" (Morris, 1976, p. 272). Almighty God visited Sodom and Gomorrah likely "for appearance' sake, that men might know directly that God had actually seen the full situation before He acted in judgment" (p. 342). "These cities were to be made ensamples to all future ages of God's severity, and therefore ample proof given that the judgment was neither rash nor excessive (Ezek 18:23; Jer 18:7)" (Jamieson, et al., 1997). Similarly, in the case of God testing Abraham regarding Isaac, although God already knew what Abraham would choose to do, there still was a reason to allow Abraham the opportunity to actually show his great faith and know that God indeed had witnessed (in real time and not just in His foreknowledge), Abraham's actions. God came "to know" of Abraham's faith by actual experiment. The meaning of the phrase, "now I know" (Genesis 22:12), therefore, "is not that God had, by the events of this probation, obtained information regarding Abraham's character that He did not previously possess; but that these qualities had been made apparent, had been developed by outward acts" (Jamieson, et al.).

Similar to how God instructs man to pray and make "known" to Him our petitions for our benefit (Philippians 4:6), even though He actually already knows of our prayers and needs before they are voiced (Matthew 6:8), for our profit the all-knowing God sometimes is spoken of in accommodative language as acquiring knowledge.

THE FANG ARGUMENT: A REFUTATION

Dan frequently uses an argument that he calls FANG. The letters in FANG stand for the Freewill Argument for the Non-existence of God. To summarize this argument, Barker claims that a being can only be defined as personal if it has free will (Part 1, pp. 11-12). He then claims that God cannot have free will because, he asserts, "Free will, if it exists, requires that you not know the future" (2008, p. 127). He further states:

> However, if you are omniscient, you already know all your future choices and you are not free to change what you know in advance. You cannot make decisions. You do not have a period of uncertainty and flexibility before selecting. You do not have free will. If you do change what you thought you knew in advance, exercising the prerogative of omnipotence, then you were not omniscient in the first place. You can't have both free will and omniscience. If God is defined as having free will and knowing the future, then God does not exist (2008, pp. 127-128).

Barker's FANG argument has several problems. First, he has extreme difficulty maintaining that a personal being must have free will, because he does not believe humans have free will. Barker's atheistic evolutionary assumptions force him to believe that humans are products of nature that do not possess an independent mind capable of truly making any choice that is not directed by genes and nature. In his debate with Peter Payne, Barker stated: "I happen to think that we have the illusion of freewill.... I'm a strict determinist. We are natural creatures. The material world is all there is. We actually don't have what we would call libertarian freewill" (Barker and Payne, 2005). If humans do not have free will, then they cannot be personal beings. Knowing the absurdity of this conclusion, Barker must somehow change the definition of free will to allow humans to be personal beings and still be completely controlled by their alleged naturalistic origins.

How does Barker accomplish this? He simply changes the definition of free will. He states: "I am a determinist, which means that I don't think complete libertarian free will exists. Since we don't know the future...we have the *illusion* of free will, which to me is what 'free will' actually means" (2008, p. 128, italics in orig.). Notice the extremely devious switch in which having the illusion of something now means that a person actually has it. Suppose that we used this type of thinking in the real world. Suppose a man is in the desert dying of thirst and suddenly he sees a mirage in which he has the illusion that he is drinking a tall glass of water. Does he actually have the water because he has the illusion of it? Certainly not. Will the illusion of the water save him from dying of thirst? No. Having a thing, and having the illusion of that thing, are very different situations, indeed. In essence, then, Dan's FANG argument falls apart because of his incoherent assertion that a personal being must have free will, but humans are personal beings, yet they do not have free will.

There are other reasons why FANG is false. Remember that, according to Barker, "Free will, if it exists, requires that you not know the future." This statement, however, is simply an assertion, with no factual or logical backing. Who says that free will requires that you not know the future? Is there a logical syllogism that Barker has produced that proves the statement to be true? No, there is not. Dan merely tosses the statement out there, sounding very confident in his assertion, expecting the listener or reader to accept what he says, but he does not prove the validity of his major premise. A mere assertion, however, proves nothing.

In fact, free will does not require that a person be ignorant of the future. Could a person know what would happen in the future, have the ability and power to change it, but still choose what he knew would happen? Yes. The life of Jesus Christ gives a perfect case in point. In Isaiah 53:9, the Bible says that the Messiah would not lie. This prophecy was written about 700 years before Jesus walked the Earth. According to Dan, that must mean that since God knew Jesus (God in the flesh) would not lie, then Jesus did not have the ability or choice to lie. Yet, when we look to the New Testament, we see that Jesus was tempted in all ways like other humans (Hebrews 4:15), but He did not sin. Did Jesus have the ability to lie? Yes. Did He have the opportunity to lie every day of His life on Earth? Yes. But did Jesus know that He would not lie? Yes. We see, then, that foreknowledge of an event does not rob a person of the ability to change the event. It is not that God, by knowing His future actions, cannot change them. It is simply that He does not choose to change them.

At this point in the discussion, the atheist might raise an objection. He might say that using the biblical example of Jesus to reinforce the fact that free will does not require ignorance of the future is unacceptable, since the atheist does not acknowledge that the Bible is God's Word. This objection is plagued by a serious problem. Where did the idea originate that God is omnipotent and omniscient? The atheist has used the Bible's description of God to construct the FANG argument. If the Bible was used to construct the "problem," how could a person object to using the Bible to solve the problem? In reality, the skeptic often wants to use the Bible when it is convenient, but reject the Bible when the text clears up an alleged contradiction. One of the primary purposes of the Bible is to show the consistency of God's characteristics. To say that God has qualities (derived from the Bible) that are inconsistent, and then to completely ignore the explanation given that reconciles them, is dishonest.

Furthermore, even if a person were to reject the factual validity of the prophecies and the life of Jesus, the example of Jesus would still provide a valid hypothetical situation that would disprove Barker's statement: "free will requires that you not know the future." Even if we were to say that, hypothetically, there was a person named Jesus who knew he would never lie, but had the opportunity and ability to lie every day of His life, that would be sufficient to prove Barker's assertion false [NOTE: Just for the record, the historicity and deity of Christ has been established as fact, see Butt & Lyons, 2006.]

Additionally, the FANG argument fails because it equates the **knowledge** of the future with the **cause** of the future events. Suppose a person knows that at 12:00 p.m. tomorrow he will choose to drink coffee instead of tea. At 12:00 p.m. the next day, he chooses coffee. What caused him to choose coffee? According to FANG, the cause of his choice must be his knowledge of the future. But, if you ask him what caused him to choose coffee, he might say that he hates tea, is allergic to tea, likes coffee better, etc. His knowledge of the fact that he would choose coffee did not force him to choose coffee, nor did it take from him the ability to change his mind. To further illustrate this fact, consider the idea of God's omnipresence in relation to the actions of humans. According to the biblical definition, used by Barker to form FANG, does God know all future actions of every human? Yes. So, God knew that you would be reading this information at this moment. Does the fact that God knows in advance what a person will do **cause** that person's actions? No, because foreknowledge does not equal causality.

The FANG argument in no way accomplishes its stated purpose of disproving God's existence. It is incoherent based on Dan Barker's own concept of human free will. It is invalid based on the fact that its basic foundational assumption is false: free will does not demand that a person must be ignorant of the future. The FANG argument turns out to be nothing more than the False Assertion for the Nonexistence of God.

NAZIS WERE NOT COMMUNISTS OR ALL ATHEISTS, WHICH IS BESIDE THE POINT

During my opening speech, I focused the audience's attention on the reality that atheism is powerless to account for the fact that objective morals exist. I quoted William Provine and Charles Darwin, both of whom are on record as saying that atheistic evolution cannot provide a foundation for ethics. To illustrate that point, I stated: "So that means that if the atheistic communists of the Nazi Germans—if they killed six million Jews—what Darwin said was, you just do what feels the best to you" (Part 1, p. 17). In his 10-minute rebuttal, Dan stated that I had said that Hitler was an atheistic communist. [Actually, I did not say Hitler, but the Nazi Germans.] He correctly noted that the Nazis were not all atheists nor were they communists. Barker then stated that Hitler "was a really lousy Christian" (Part 1, p. 22), but none-the-less implied that Hitler was a Christian. At the time I made the statement, I was fully aware that the Nazis were not communists, and I also understood that many of them were not atheists. This simply was a misstatement, which I admitted immediately when he pointed this out.

There are three important points to make about this particular exchange. First, and most importantly, whether or not the Nazi Germans were atheists or communists had nothing to do with the point that was being made about objective moral values. The point was simply that atheism cannot maintain that the Nazis were morally wrong for killing six million Jews. Knowing atheism's weakness in this area, Dan diverted attention from the real issue, using a red-herring argument, and failed to satisfactorily deal with the point that without a divine Lawgiver, the Nazis' actions are as morally right as any other actions. Second, I could have (and should have) simply used the name of Stalin and communistic Russia under his regime to make the point. Barker admits that Stalin was an atheist (2008, p. 113). In reality, the point never rested on the Nazis' atheism or communism.

Third, for Barker to insinuate that Hitler was a Christian, even a lousy one, shows that he has missed one of the major teachings of Christianity. A person is not a Christian based on a self-applied label, or one that society may apply. A person is a Christian who follows the example and teachings of Jesus Christ. Jesus made this clear when he stated: "You are my friends **if** you do what ever I command you" (John 15:14, emp. added). Jesus again made the point: "Not everyone who says to Me, 'Lord, Lord,' shall enter the kingdom of heaven, but **he who does the will of My Father** in heaven" (Matthew 7:21, emp. added). In discussing His relationship with His true followers, Jesus declared: "A disciple is not above his teacher, nor a servant above his master. It is enough for a disciple **that he be like his teacher**" (Matthew 10:24-25, emp. added). A disciple of Christ, also called a Christian, is one who not only wears the name of Christ, but also follows His teachings. Even a cursory comparison of the actions of Adolf Hitler and the teachings and example of Jesus Christ shows that Hitler was no Christian.

GEOGRAPHY AS THE MOST IMPORTANT PREDICTOR OF RELIGION?

Dan noted that "there are other reasons besides reason and truth that people come to their faith." He continued:

> The most obvious one is geography. Geography is the greatest single predictor of what religion a person will have. If you were born in Baghdad, you can pretty much predict what religion that person will have. If you were born in Tennessee, you can pretty much predict what kind of person you are going to be with your religion, generally. It's the highest predictor (Part 1, p. 23).

While it may be true that geography is the highest predictor of a person's religion, it is important to understand what Barker is trying to say and why it has no bearing on the truth of the proposition that God exists. The implication is that if most people in an area hold a certain religious belief, then the mere fact that it is the "traditional" belief of that area should cast disparaging light on the belief or at least should call into question the honesty and intellectual rigor of those who hold the belief.

When Barker's statement is studied critically, however, it becomes apparent that he is making a moot point. So what if the biggest predictor of a person's religion is geography? Does that mean that when geography is the biggest predictor of those who will hold a certain belief, then that belief is false? If that were the case, we could simply lump atheism in with all other "religions" and say that geography is the single biggest predictor of whether a person will claim atheism. Polls indicate that those born in China or the former Soviet Union, and certain other areas of Europe, are much more likely to be atheists than other areas of the globe ("Major Religions of the World…," 2007). So what does that mean about atheism? We are forced by rationality to agree that it means nothing other than the fact that most people, including atheists, adopt the beliefs of the people nearest to them. It says nothing whatever about the truth of the beliefs.

Suppose we were to suggest that geography is the single biggest predictor of whether a person will know his or her multiplication tables by age 12? Would that mean that all those who learned their "times tables" hold an incorrect view of the world? Of course not. Would it mean that the local knowledge of multiplication casts suspicion on the truth of the math being done? No. It has absolutely no bearing on the accuracy of the multiplication tables. Again, suppose that we said that geography is the single most important indicator of whether a person understands how germs are passed. Does that mean that all those people who wash their hands because that is "what their mothers taught them about germs" have been taught wrong? Certainly not.

In truth, everyone knows that geography has nothing to do with truth claims. Is it the case that truth seekers often break away from their culturally held beliefs, forsake false ideas, and embrace the truth that God exists, the Bible is His Word, and Jesus is His Son? Yes. Is it also true that many forsake the cultural truths that they were taught as children, reject the reality of God's existence, and exchange that belief for false worldviews like atheism and agnosticism? Yes, that happens as well.

In logic, there is a common fallacy known as a "red herring." The term comes from the idea of dragging a fish across an animal's scent trail in an attempt to throw the hounds off the scent. In logic, a "red herring" is a device used to divert the attention of the audience from the real point that is being addressed. When we look at Barker's use of the "geography" idea, something smells very fishy.

IS GOD IMMORAL FOR KILLING INNOCENT CHILDREN?

Dan Barker and many of his atheistic colleagues claim that atheism offers the world a superior system of morality when compared to the moral system presented in the Bible. In fact, near the end of Dan's ten-minute rebuttal speech, he stated: "We can know that the atheistic way is actually a superior intellectual and moral way of thinking" (Part 1, p. 24). One primary reason Dan gave for his belief that the Bible's morality is flawed is that the Bible states that God has directly killed people, and that God has authorized others to kill as well. In Dan's discussion about Abraham's sacrifice of Isaac, Dan said that Abraham should not have been willing to obey God's command. Dan stated: "By the way, Abraham should have said, 'No, way. I'm better than you [God—KB], I'm not going to kill my son'" (Part 1, p. 11).

In his book *godless*, Barker said: "There is not enough space to mention all of the places in the bible where God committed, commanded or condoned murder" (2008, p. 177). The idea that God is immoral because He has killed humans is standard atheistic fare. In his *Letter to a Christian Nation*, Sam Harris cited several Bible verses in which God directly or indirectly caused people to die. He then stated: "Anyone who believes that the Bible offers the best guidance we have on questions of morality has some very strange ideas about either guidance or morality" (2006, p. 14). In his landmark atheistic bestseller, *The God Delusion*, Richard Dawkins wrote the following as the opening paragraph of chapter two:

The God of the Old Testament is arguably the most unpleasant character in all fiction: jealous and proud of it; a petty, unjust, un-forgiving control-freak; a vindictive, **bloodthirsty ethnic cleanser**; a misogynistic, homophobic, racist, **infanticidal, genocidal, fili-cidal**, pestilential, megalomaniacal, sadomasochistic, capriciously malevolent bully (2006a, p. 31, emp. added).

After listing several Old Testament verses pertaining to the conquest of Canaan, Dawkins referred to God as an "evil monster" (p. 248). Christopher Hitchens wrote that God's actions and instructions in the Old Testament had caused "the ground" to be "forever soaked with the blood of the innocent" (2007, p. 107).

Is it true that atheism offers a superior morality to that found in the Bible? And is the God of the Bible immoral for advocating or directly causing the deaths of millions of people? The answer to both questions is an emphatic "No." A close look at the atheistic claims and accusations will manifest the truth of this answer.

ATHEISM CANNOT MAKE "MORAL" JUDGMENTS

The extreme irony of the atheistic argument against God's morality is that atheism is completely impotent to define the term "moral," much less use the concept against any other system. As I have documented copiously (pp. 72-74; 87-88), atheism cannot offer a foundation for ethical thinking. And as C.S. Lewis pointed out (see p. 73), if there truly are cases of justice and injustice, then God must exist. Furthermore, we will show that the God of the Bible never is unjust in His dealings with humanity. On the contrary, the atheistic position finds itself mired in injustice at every turn.

STRESS "INNOCENT"

Generally, the atheistic argument against God's morality begins with blanket statements about all of God's actions or commands that caused anyone to die. When the case is pressed, however, the atheistic argument must be immediately qualified by the concepts of justice and deserved punishment. Could it be that some of God's actions were against people who had committed crimes worthy of death? Atheist Sam Harris believes that the mere adherence to certain beliefs could be a legitimate cause for putting some people to death (2004, pp. 52-53). Almost the entirety of the atheistic community admits that certain actions, such as serial killing, theft, or child abuse, deserve to be punished in **some** way. They do not all agree with Harris that the death penalty may be appropriate, but they would argue that some type of punishment or preventive incarceration should be applied to the offender.

Once the atheistic community admits that people who break certain laws should be punished, then the only questions left to decide are **how** they should be punished and **to what extent**. The atheists may quibble with God's idea of divine punishment, but it has been sufficiently demonstrated that their arguments cannot be reasonably defended (see Lyons and Butt, 2005, 25[2]:9-15; see also Miller, 2002). Knowing that the idea of justice and the concept of legitimate punishment can effectively be used to show that their blanket accusations against God are ill founded, the atheists must include an additional concept: innocence.

The argument is thus transformed from, "God is immoral because He has killed people," to "God is immoral because He has killed **innocent** people." Since human infants are rightly viewed by atheists as the epitome of sinless innocence, the argument is then restated as "God is immoral because He has killed innocent human infants." Dan Barker summarized this argument well in his debate with Peter Payne. In his remarks concerning God's commandment in Numbers 31 for Moses to destroy the Midianites, he stated: "Maybe some of those men were guilty of committing war crimes. And maybe some of them were justifiably guilty, Peter, of committing some kind of crimes. **But the children? The fetuses?**" (2005, emp. added).

It is important to note, then, that a large number of the instances in which God caused or ordered someone's death in the Bible were examples of divine punishment of adults who were "justifiably guilty" of punishable crimes. For instance, after Moses listed a host of perverse practices that the Israelites were told to avoid, he stated: "Do not defile yourselves with any of these things; for by all these the nations are defiled, which I am casting out before you. For the land is defiled; therefore I visit the **punishment of its iniquity** upon it, and the land vomits out its inhabitants" (Leviticus 18:24-25, emp. added).

Having said that, it must also be recognized that not all the people God has been responsible for killing have been guilty of such crimes. It is true that the Bible documents several instances in which God caused or personally ordered the death of innocent children: the Flood (Genesis 7), death of the first born in Egypt (Exodus 12:29-30), annihilation of the Midianites (Numbers 31), death of the Amalekites (1 Samuel 15), etc. Using these instances, atheists claim that God cannot be moral because He kills **innocent** children. The atheists then insist that modern-day atheism would never approve of such, and thus atheism is morally superior to the morality of the biblical God.

ATHEISM HAS NO MORAL QUALMS ABOUT KILLING INNOCENT CHILDREN

A closer look at atheistic morality, however, quickly reveals that atheists do not believe that it is morally wrong to kill **all** innocent children. According to the atheistic community, abortion is viewed as moral. Dan Barker, in his debate with John Rankin, said that abortion is a "blessing" (Barker and Rankin, 2006; see also Barker, 1992a, pp. 135, 213). One line of reasoning used by atheists to justify the practice is the idea that humans should not be treated differently than animals, since humans are nothing more than animals themselves. The fact that an embryo is "human" is no reason to give it special status. Dawkins wrote: "An early embryo has the sentience, as well as the semblance, of a tadpole" (Dawkins, 2006a, p. 297).

Atheistic writer Sam Harris wrote: "Many of us consider human fetuses in the first trimester to be **more or less like rabbits**; having imputed to them a range of happiness and suffering that does not grant them full status in our moral community" (2004, p. 177, emp. added). Isn't it ironic that Dan Barker protested to Peter Payne that God could not cause the death of an unborn human "fetus" and still be considered moral, and yet the bulk of the atheistic community adamantly maintains that those fetuses are the moral equivalent of rabbits (see pp. 88-99)?

It is clear, then, that atheism does not have moral constraints against killing all innocent babies, but rather only those innocent babies that the atheistic community considers "worthy" to live. How in the world would a person make a moral judgment about which children were "worthy to live?" Singer, Harris, and others contest that a child's age in utero, mental capability, physical disability, or other criteria should be used to formulate the answer. Dan Barker has given his assessment about how to make such moral decisions. He claimed that "morality is simply acting with the intention to minimize harm." He further insisted that the way to avoid making mistakes in ethical judgments is to "be as informed as possible about the likely consequences of the actions being considered" (2008, p. 214).

Using Barker's line of reasoning, if God knows everything, then only He would be in the best possible situation to know all the consequences of killing infants. Could it be that all the infants born to the Amalekites had degenerative genetic diseases, or were infected with an STD that was passed to them from their sexually promiscuous mothers? Could it be that the firstborn children in Egypt had some type of brain damage, terminal cancer, hemophilia, etc.? The atheistic community cannot accuse God of immorally killing infants and children, when the atheistic position itself offers criteria upon which it purports to morally justify such killing. Once again, the atheistic argument must be further qualified. The argument has moved from: "God is immoral because He killed people," to "God is immoral because He killed innocent babies," to "God is immoral because He killed innocent babies that we feel would not have met our atheistically based criteria for death." Ultimately, then, the atheistic position is arguing that atheists, not God, should be the ones who decide when the death of an innocent child is acceptable.

ATHEISM TAKES "ALL THAT THERE IS" FROM INNOCENT CHILDREN

As with most logically flawed belief systems, atheism's arguments often double back on themselves and discredit the position. So it is with atheism's attack on God's morality. Supposedly, God is immoral for killing innocent children. Yet atheists believe the death of certain innocent children is permissible. Have we then simply arrived at the point where both atheistic and theistic morality are equally moral or immoral? Certainly not.

One primary difference between the atheistic position and the biblical position is what is at stake with the loss of physical life. According to atheism, this physical life is all that any living organism has. Dan Barker stated: "Since **this is the only life we atheists have**, each decision is crucial and we are accountable for our actions right now" (2008, p. 215, emp. added). He further commented that life "is dear. It is fleeting. It is vibrant and vulnerable. It is heart breaking. It can be lost. It will be lost. But we exist now. We are caring, intelligent animals and can treasure our brief lives." Since Dan and his fellow atheists do not believe in the soul or any type of afterlife, then this brief, physical existence is the sum total of an organism's existence. If that is the case, when Barker, Harris, Singer, and company advocate killing innocent babies, in their minds, they are taking from those babies all that they have—the entirety of their existence. They have set themselves up as the sovereign tribunal that has the right to take life from their fellow humans, which they believe to be **everything** a human has. If any position is immoral, the atheistic position is. The biblical view, however, can be shown to possess no such immorality.

PHYSICAL LIFE IS NOT "ALL THERE IS"

Atheism has trapped itself in the position of stating that the death of innocent children is morally permissible, even if that death results in the loss of everything that child has. Yet the biblical position does not fall into the same moral trap as atheism, because it recognizes the truth that physical life is not the sum total of human existence. Although the Bible repeatedly recognizes life as a privilege that can be revoked by God, the Giver of life, it also manifests the fact that death is not complete loss, and can actually be beneficial to the one who dies. The Bible explains that every person has a soul that will live forever—long after physical life on this Earth is over (Matthew 25:46). The Bible consistently stresses the fact that the immortal soul of each individual is of much more value than that individual's physical life on this Earth. Jesus Christ said: "For what profit is it to a man if he gains the whole world, and loses his own soul? Or what will a man give in exchange for his soul?" (Matthew 16:26).

Although the skeptic might object, and claim that an answer from the Bible is not acceptable, such an objection falls flat for one primary reason: the skeptic used the Bible to formulate his own argument. Where is it written that God is love? In the Bible, in such passages as 1 John 4:8. Where do we learn that the Lord did, indeed, kill or order the death of babies? Once again, that information comes directly from the Bible. Where, then, should we look for an answer to this alleged moral dilemma? The answer should be: the Bible. If the alleged problem is formulated from biblical testimony, then the Bible should be given the opportunity to explain itself. As long as the skeptic uses the Bible to formulate the problem, we certainly can use the Bible to solve the problem. One primary facet of the biblical solution is that every human has an immortal soul that is of inestimable value.

With the value of the soul in mind, let us examine several verses that prove that physical death is not necessarily evil. In a letter to the Philippians, the apostle Paul wrote from prison to encourage the Christians in the city of Philippi. His letter was filled with hope and encouragement, but it was also tinted with some very pertinent comments about the way Paul and God view death. In Philippians 1:21-23, Paul wrote: "For to me, to live is Christ, and to **die is gain**. But if I live on in the flesh, this will mean fruit from my labor; yet what I shall choose I cannot tell. For I am hard pressed between the two, having a desire **to depart** and be with Christ, **which is far better**" (emp. added).

Paul, a faithful Christian, said that death was a welcome visitor. In fact, Paul said that the end of his physical life on this Earth would be "far better" than its continuation. For Paul, as well as for any faithful Christian, the cessation of physical life is not loss, but gain. Such would apply to innocent children as well, since they are in a safe condition and go to paradise when they die (see Butt, 2003a).

Other verses in the Bible show that the loss of physical life is not inherently evil. The prophet Isaiah concisely summarized the situation when he was inspired to write: "The righteous perishes, and no man takes it to heart; merciful men are taken away, while no one considers that the righteous **is taken away from evil. He shall enter into peace**; they shall rest in their beds, each one walking in his uprightness" (57:1-2, emp. added). Isaiah recognized that people would view the death of the righteous incorrectly. He plainly stated that this incorrect view of death was due to the fact that most people do not think about the fact that when a righteous or innocent person dies, that person is "taken away from evil," and enters "into peace."

The psalmist wrote, "Precious in the sight of the Lord is the death of His saints" (Psalm 116:15). Death is not inherently evil. In fact, the Bible indicates that death can be great gain in which a righteous person is taken away from evil and allowed to enter peace and rest. God looks upon the death of His faithful followers as precious. Skeptics who charge God with wickedness because He has ended the physical lives of innocent babies are in error. They refuse to recognize the reality of the immortal soul. Instead of the death of innocent children being an evil thing, it is often a blessing for that child to be taken away from a life of hardship and evil influence at the hands of a sinful society, and ushered into a paradise of peace and rest. In order for a skeptic to legitimately charge God with cruelty, the skeptic must prove that there is no immortal soul, and that physical life is the only reality—neither of which the skeptic can do. Failure to acknowledge the reality of the soul and the spiritual realm will always result in a distorted view of the nature of God. "The righteous perishes...while no one considers that the righteous is taken away from evil."

We then could ask who is moral: the atheist who has no problem approving of the death of innocent children, while believing that he is taking from them the only life they have? Or an all-knowing God Who takes back the physical life He gave the child, exchanging it for an eternal life of happiness?

WHY NOT KILL ALL THE CHRISTIANS AND BABIES?

Once the atheistic position is forced to concede that it advocates the killing of babies, and that **if** there is an afterlife, then the biblical description of God's activities could be moral, then the atheist often shifts his argument in a last ditch effort to save face. If death can be, and sometimes is, better for the innocent child or for the

Christian, why not kill all children and execute all Christians as soon as they come up out of the waters of baptism (see Lyons and Butt, n.d.)? The atheist contends that if we say that death can be a better situation for some, then this position implies the morally absurd idea that we should kill every person that death would benefit.

Before dealing with this new argument, it should be noted that we have laid the other to rest. We have shown that it is impossible for atheism to accuse God of immorality in his dealings with innocent children. Since atheism's attack against God's character has failed on that front, the maneuver is changed to accuse the follower of God of not carrying his belief about death to its alleged logical conclusion by killing all those who would benefit. One reason that atheists argue thus is because many of them believe that humans have the right to kill those who they deem as "expendable." Of course, atheism does not base this judgment on the idea that certain **babies** or other **innocent people** would benefit, but that **society** at large would benefit at the **expense** of those who are killed. Here again, notice that God is allegedly immoral because He "sinned" against innocent children by taking their lives, yet atheism cares nothing for innocent children, but for the society of which they are a part. In truth, atheism implies that once a certain category of people, whether unborn babies, hemophiliacs, or brain-damaged adults, is honestly assessed to be "expendable," then humans have the moral right, and sometimes obligation, to exterminate them. The atheist berates the Christian for not taking his beliefs far enough, in the atheist's opinion. If certain people would benefit from death, or in atheism's case, society would benefit from certain people's death, then the atheist contends we should be willing to kill everyone who would fall into that category. If we are not so willing, then the atheist demands that our belief involves a moral absurdity. Yet, the fact that death is beneficial to some cannot be used to say we have the **right** to kill all those that **we think** it would benefit.

What Humans Do Not Know

One extremely significant reason humans cannot kill all those people that we think might benefit from death is because we do not know all the consequences of such actions. Remember that Dan Barker stated that the way to make moral decisions was to "try to be as informed as possible about the likely consequences of the actions being considered" (2008, p. 214). Could it be that human judgments about who has the right to live or die would be flawed based on limited knowledge of the consequences? Certainly. Suppose the hemophiliac child that Singer said could be killed to make room for another more "fit" child possessed the mind that would have discovered the cure for cancer. Or what if the brain-damaged patient that the atheistic community determined could be terminated was going to make a remarkable recovery if he had been allowed to live? Once again, the biblical theist could simply argue that God is the only one in the position to authorize death solely based on the fact that only God knows all the consequences of such actions. The atheistic community might attempt to protest that God does not know everything. But atheism is completely helpless to argue against the idea that **if** God does know everything, then only He is in the position to make the truly moral decision. Using Barker's reasoning, when God's actions do not agree with those advocated by the atheistic community, God can simply answer them by saying, "What you don't know is...."

It is ironic that, in a discussion of morality, Barker offered several rhetorical questions about who is in the best position to make moral decisions. He stated: "Why should the mind of a deity—an outsider—be better able to judge human actions than the minds of humans themselves...? Which mind is in a better position to make judgments about human actions and feelings? Which mind has more credibility? Which has more experience in the real world? Which mind has more of a right?" (1992a, p. 211). Barker intended his rhetorical question to elicit the answer that humans are in a better position to make their own moral decisions, but his rhetoric failed completely. If God is all-knowing, and if God has been alive to see the entirety of human history play out, and if only God can know all of the future consequences of an action, then the obvious answer to all of Barker's questions is: God's mind.

Additionally, there is no possible way that humans can know all the good things that might be done by the Christians and children that live, even though death would be better for them personally. The apostle Paul alluded to this fact when he said that it was better for him to die and be with the Lord, but it was more needful to the other Christians for him to remain alive and help them (Philippians 1:22-25). Books could not contain the countless benevolent efforts, hospitals, orphanages, soup kitchens, humanitarian efforts, and educational ventures that have been undertaken by Christians. It is important to understand that a strong Christian example is one of the most valuable tools that God uses to bring others to Him. Jesus noted that when Christians are following His teachings, others see their good works and glorify God (Matthew 5:13-16). Furthermore, the lives of children offer the world examples of purity and innocence worthy of emulation (Matthew 18:1-5). While it is true that death can be an advantageous situation for Christians and children, it is also true that their lives provide a leavening effect on all human society.

Ownership and Authorization

The mere fact that only God knows all consequences is sufficient to establish that He is the sole authority in matters of human life and death. Yet, His omniscience is not the only attribute that puts Him in the final position of authority. The fact that all physical life originates with God gives Him the prerogative to decide when and how that physical life should be maintained. In speaking of human death, the writer of Ecclesiastes stated: "Then the dust will return to the earth as it was, and the spirit will return **to God who gave it**" (12:7, emp. added). The apostle Paul boldly declared to the pagan Athenians that in God "we live and move and have our being" (Acts 17:28). If God gives life to all humans, then only He has the right to say when that life has accomplished its purpose, or under what circumstances life may be legitimately terminated.

In addition to the fact that God gives life, and thus has the authority to take it, He also has the power to give it back if He chooses. Throughout the Bible we read of instances in which God chose to give life back to those who were dead, the most thoroughly documented example of that being the resurrection of Jesus Christ (Butt, 2002, 22[2]:9-15). In fact, Abraham alluded to this fact during his preparations to sacrifice Isaac. After traveling close to the place appointed for the sacrifice, Abraham left his servants some distance from the mountain, and said to them: "Stay here with the donkey; the lad and I will go yonder and worship, and **we** will come back to you" (Genesis 22:5). Notice that Abraham used the plural pronoun "we," indicating that both he and Isaac would return. The New Testament gives additional insight into Abraham's thinking. In Hebrews 11:17-19, the text states: "By faith Abraham, when he was tested, offered up Isaac, and he who had received the promises offered up his only begotten…accounting that **God was able to raise him up, even from the dead**…" (emp. added). Since God gives physical life to all, and since He can raise people from the dead, then any accusation of injustice that fails to take these facts into view cannot be legitimate.

CONCLUSION

It is evident that atheism has no grounds upon which to attack God's character. Atheists contend that a loving God should not kill innocent babies. But those same atheists say that killing innocent babies could be a blessing under "the right" circumstances. Atheists contend that God is immoral for taking the lives of innocent children. Yet the atheist believes that it is permissible to take the lives of innocent children, when doing so, according to their belief, means that those children are being robbed of the sum total of their existence. Yet, according to the biblical perspective, those children are being spared a life of pain and misery and ushered into a life of eternal happiness. Atheism contends that its adherents are in a position to determine which children should live and die, and yet the knowledge of the consequences of such decisions goes far beyond their human capability. Only an omniscient God could know all the consequences involved. The atheist contends that human life can be taken by other humans based solely on reasoning about benefits to society and other relativistic ideas. The biblical position shows that God is the Giver of life, and only He has the authority to decide when that life has accomplished its purpose. In reality, the atheistic view proves to be the truly immoral position.

THE GOODNESS OF GOD AND AN ETERNAL HELL

In his writings and debates, Dan contends that a loving God could not send people to hell forever. In fact, Dan often uses the idea of hell to argue that the God of the Bible is presented as an immoral dictator Who does not exist, but Who is simply the concoction of the men who wrote the Bible. During his ten-minute rebuttal in our debate, Dan stated:

> And if he [God] wants to prove what a big, macho man he is by sending someone like me to hell, then let him do it. Fine. I go to hell gladly, proudly, knowing that I have resisted somebody like—a dictator like that who would create a hell in the first place.

> Think about it. Any system of thought that's based to any extent upon a threat of violence—which is what hell is—it's a threat of eternal torture. Any system of thought that has that thought in it that scares the minds of children, who go to bed at night wondering if they're going to go to hell is a morally bankrupt system.

> You should not be proud to hold that Bible under your arm. It is morally bankrupt and you're better than that (Part 1, p. 24).

Renowned agnostic, Bertrand Russell, stated:

> There is one very serious defect to my mind in Christ's moral character, and that is that He believed in hell. I do not myself feel that any person who is really profoundly humane can believe in everlasting punishment (1957, p. 17).

Russell's self-defined sense of humanness balked at the idea of an everlasting punishment, which he offered as one of his primary reasons for rejecting Jesus (since Jesus taught about an everlasting hell). Russell further noted:

> Christ certainly as depicted in the Gospels did believe in everlasting punishment, and one does find repeatedly a vindictive fury against those people who would not listen to His preaching.... I really do not think that a person with a proper degree of kindliness in his nature would have put fears and terrors of that sort into the world.... I must say that I think all this doctrine, that hell-fire is a punishment for sin, is a doctrine of cruelty. It is a doctrine that put cruelty into the world and gave the world generations of cruel torture; and the Christ of the Gospels, if you could take Him as His chroniclers represent Him, would certainly have to be considered partly responsible for that (pp. 17-18).

Barker and Russell both "feel" that there exists an irreconcilable moral dilemma between a loving God and an eternal Hell. That dilemma, however, has been created more from a sense of emotional discomfort than from an honest study of morality and God's nature. As J.P. Moreland accurately stated when questioned about the eternality of conscious punishment, many people "tend to evaluate whether it's [eternal punishment—KB] appropriate based on their feelings or emotional offense to it" (as quoted in Strobel, 2000, p. 172, parenthetical comment added). He went on to state: "The basis for their evaluation should be whether hell is a morally just or morally right state of affairs, not whether they like or dislike the concept" (p. 172). The alleged moral dilemma presented by Barker and Russell is one that is based on emotions, not on accurate assessments of morality and justice. Upon further investigation, there proves to be no dilemma at all.

God is Love

It would be extremely difficult for a person to read the Bible and miss the fact that God is described as a loving and caring Creator. In 1 John 4:7-8, the writer declared that love issues directly from God and that, in fact, "God is love." First John 4:16 states: "And we have known and believed the love that God has for us. God is love, and he who abides in love abides in God, and God in him." Throughout the Scriptures, God's love for His creatures is repeated time and time again. One of the most familiar passages of Scripture, known even to the masses, is John 3:16, which declares: "For God so loved the world that He gave His only begotten Son, that whoever believes in Him should not perish but have everlasting life."

It is here, however, that a very important point must be made. Our "politically correct" society has influenced many people to believe that a loving person would never cause harm or discomfort to the object of his love. In an interview with Lee Strobel, J.P. Moreland addressed this issue when he observed: "

> Yes, God is a compassionate being, but he's also a just, moral, and pure being. So God's decisions are not based on modern American sentimentalism.... People today tend to care only for the softer virtues like love and tenderness, while they've forgotten the hard virtues of holiness, righteousness, and justice (as quoted in Strobel, p. 174).

What does the Bible mean when it says that God is love? In today's society, the concept of love often is misunderstood. Many people today think that a "loving person" is one who always tries to keep others out of **every** pain or discomfort. Punishment is often looked upon as an "unloving" thing to do. But that is not the case. In fact, a loving person often will **cause** pain to others in order to accomplish a greater good. For instance, suppose a mother tells her four-year-old son to stop trying to put the hairdryer into his little sister's bath water, but the child continues his mischievous and dangerous activity? That child most likely will be punished. Maybe he will get a swift swat on the leg, or have to sit in the corner of a room. The pain or discomfort inflicted on the child is for his own good and/or the good of his sister. This mother loves her children, but still punishes them. In fact, the Proverbs writer noted that a parent who **does not discipline** his/her child (which includes corporal punishment) simply **does not love** that child (Proverbs 13:24; cf. 22:15; 23:13-14; 29:15).

God is Just

God is not a one-sided Being. He has many different attributes that must be considered. One of those attributes is love. But another is His justice. Psalm 89:14 states that "righteousness and justice" are the foundation of God's throne. Deuteronomy 32:3-4 declares: "For I proclaim the name of the Lord: ascribe greatness to our God. He is the Rock, His work is perfect; for all His ways are justice, a God of truth and without injustice; righteous and upright is He."

What is justice? Justice is the principle that crime must be punished. It is not difficult to recognize justice. Suppose a certain judge in a large U.S. city let every murderer walk away from his courtroom without any punishment. Even though many of the murderers had killed several people in cold blood, the judge would just wave his hand, pat the murderer on the shoulder, and say something like, "I am feeling very generous and loving today, so you are free to go without any punishment." The judge obviously would not be administering justice, and he should promptly be relieved of his position. In the same way, if God did not provide punishment for the sinful actions that humans commit, then justice could not be the foundation of His throne.

It can be shown, then, that a loving person could punish those that he loves, and that justice demands that some type of punishment or penalty must be paid for actions that break the law. But the problem still remains that **eternal** punishment seems to some to be too harsh and permanent to come from a loving God.

There is one other principle of justice that needs attention at this juncture. Punishment almost always lasts longer than the actual crime. When a gunman walks into a bank, shoots two tellers, robs the bank, and is apprehended, tried, and found guilty, his punishment is of a much longer duration than his crime. The actual shooting and looting might have taken only three minutes to accomplish, but he most likely will pay for those three minutes with the remainder of his life in prison. Those who contend that hell will not be eternal say that forever is "too long." But once a person concedes that punishment can (and generally does) last longer than the crime, his argument against an eternal hell becomes self-defeating. Once a person admits that punishment can last longer than the crime, it is simply a matter of who gets to decide how long the punishment should be.

The skeptic and others admit that punishment can be longer than the crime, but then they contest that "forever" is too long. Who says forever is too long? Would a hundred years be too long to punish a child molester? What about two hundred? It soon becomes obvious that determinations of "too long" are arbitrarily made by those (like skeptics and infidels) who want to reject the God of the Bible or the hell of the Bible.

In his debate with renowned atheistic philosopher, Antony Flew, Thomas B. Warren pressed this point masterfully. Before one of the debating sessions, Warren gave Flew a list of questions to be answered (a facet of the debate that was agreed upon before the debate started). One of the questions was a "true or false" question that read as follows: "It is not possible that the justice of God would entail any punishment for sin." To this question Flew answered "false," indicating that it is possible that the justice of God would entail some punishment for sin. The next "true or false" question issued by Warren stated: "It is possible that this infinite justice of God might entail at least one minute of punishment when this life is over"—to which Flew answered "true." Warren then commented:

> He answered "true." Now note, it might entail at least one minute of punishment and not be out of harmony—the basic concept of God would not be self-contradictory. What about two minutes, Dr. Flew? What about three minutes, four minutes, an hour, a day,

a year, a month, a hundred years, a million years? Where do you stop? Would a billion years be long enough? Could God punish a man a billion years and still be just and loving? You can see that he has given up tonight…. He has shown his inability to answer these questions in harmony with the atheistic position and the implications which follow from it. He himself is on record as saying when a man cannot do that, then it is clear that he holds a false position (1977, p. 150).

Once the point is conceded that a loving God could punish sin with at least one minute of punishment after this life, then the only question left to answer is: Who is in the best position to determine how long punishment should be? Would it not be a righteous judge who knew every detail of the crime, including the thoughts and intents of the criminal? God is exactly that. He is not motivated by selfishness, greed, or other vice, but sits on a throne of righteousness (Psalm 89:14). Furthermore, He knows **all** the facts of the case (Proverbs 15:3) and the intents and thoughts of the lawbreakers (Psalm 44:21). Only God is in a position to determine how long sin should be punished.

Furthermore, it is ironic that those who are claiming that "forever" is "too long" to punish people for sins, have themselves sinned. Of course a person who is guilty of sin is going to want to lessen the punishment of that sin. Once again we must ask, would a person guilty of sin be in a better position to determine how long sin should be punished than a sinless, perfect God (1 John 1:5)? To ask is to answer.

Yet again, the idea that eternity is "too long" only tugs at human emotions when dealing with punishment, never with reward. Who would argue that heaven cannot be eternal because God would be unjust to reward us for "too long." On the contrary, the eternality of heaven and hell stand and fall together. And both are rooted in the justice and mercy of God. When Christ spoke to the people of His day about the ultimate fate of humanity in eternity, He stated that the wicked would "go away into everlasting (*aionios*) punishment, but the righteous into eternal (*aionios*) life" (Matthew 25:46). The Greek word *aionios*, rendered "eternal" in the English, is the same Greek word (*aionios*) rendered earlier as "everlasting." Observe that precisely the same word is applied to the **punishment** of the wicked as to the **reward** of the righteous. Those who are willing to accept Christ's teaching on heaven should have no trouble accepting His teaching on hell.

CONCLUSION

Those who argue that a loving God cannot punish impenitent sinners for eternity, simply have neglected to realize the heinousness of sin. What could possibly be so bad that it would deserve an eternity of punishment? God's answer to that is simple—unforgiven sin. Adam and Eve's sin brought into the world death, disease, war, pestilence, pain, and suffering. The cumulative weight of the sin of mankind from that day until the Day of Judgment was, and is, **so overwhelming** that it cost God the lifeblood of His only Son.

To see the atrociousness of sin, cast your eyes back 2,000 years to the excruciating violence, mockery, and torture perpetrated on the only human ever to live a perfect life without sin—Jesus Christ (Hebrews 4:15). Does God want the wicked to be punished for eternity in hell? Absolutely not! Scripture speaks expressly to that point. "The Lord is not slack concerning His promise, as some count slackness, but is longsuffering toward us, not willing that any should perish but that all should come to repentance" (2 Peter 3:9). Again, Paul wrote that God "desires all men to be saved and to come to the knowledge of the truth" (1 Timothy 2:4). The Old Testament prophet Ezekiel recorded the words of God concerning the wicked: "'Do I have any pleasure at all that the wicked should die?' says the Lord God, 'and not that he should turn from his ways and live?'" (Ezekiel 18:23). The answer to that rhetorical question is a resounding "No." God does not want the wicked to die in their sins and be lost forever in eternal punishment. God will not, however, override the freewill of humans, and **force** them to accept His free gift of salvation. Nor will He contradict His Word, and save those who have not "obeyed the gospel" (2 Thessalonians 1:7) by coming into contact with the blood of Christ (Ephesians 1:7).

WAS EVE CREATED PERFECT?

During the question and answer session, Dan Barker asked if God created Eve perfect. I answered that God created her sinless with the capacity to choose between right and wrong. I illustrated my answer by saying that a company could produce a car that worked perfectly, but that would not stop a person from driving the car off a cliff. Just because the car has the capacity to be driven off the cliff, does not mean that there is an imperfection in its construction. Dan countered by saying that my answer was insufficient: since Eve chose wrong, then God must be responsible for creating her with some type of flaw. Dan's argument is that if Eve did something wrong, or had an evil desire, then it must be due to her composition (Part 1, pp. 32-33).

Dan's conclusion, however, is unwarranted by the evidence. Is it possible for a supernatural Creator to create a being that has the capacity to originate something that was not a part of its initial make up? Certainly. The real question is simply: "Is God capable of creating a being with genuine freewill?" There is no valid reason to conclude that God cannot create a totally free moral agent who can originate his/her own desires that are not a part of his/her original composition.

Since Dan framed his question using the Bible, it is appropriate to use the Bible to answer the question. The Bible offers clear evidence to support the conclusion that evil desires and imperfection were concocted by humanity's free moral agency, and were not a part of the original creation. James 1:14 states: "But each one is tempted when he is drawn away by his own desires and enticed." The phrase "his own desires" indicates that each person originates such evil desires and they are not inherent in his make up or forced upon him by his Creator. Solomon once wrote: "Truly, this only I have found: that **God made man upright,** but they have sought out many schemes" (Ecclesiastes 7:29, emp. added). According to Jeremiah 7:31, the Israelites offered their children as burnt offerings to idols, something that God says did not "come into" His heart. In essence, God was telling the sinful Israelites that they originated the idea of burning their children in sacrifice to idols and such did not come from their Creator. The same sentiments are found in Jeremiah 19:5.

Can creative, human minds originate evil desires that were not a part of the original creation? Yes. There is nothing logically or rationally inconsistent with this answer. One reason that Dan Barker has a problem with the answer is that he believes that humans **cannot** have freewill. Barker's atheistic, evolutionary assumptions force him to believe that humans are products of nature and therefore do not possess independent minds capable of making any choice that is not directed by genes and environment. In his debate with Peter Payne, Barker stated: "I happen to think that we have the **illusion** of freewill.... I'm a **strict determinist.** We are natural creatures. The material world is all there is. We actually don't have what we would call libertarian freewill" (Barker and Payne, 2005, emp. added). In his book, *godless,* Barker stated: "I am a **determinist,** which means that I don't think complete libertarian free will exists (2008, p. 128, emp. added).

It is easy to see why Barker feels forced to conclude that Eve must have been created with some type of flaw. He believes that humans are merely products of their genes, and that all their actions are determined strictly by the natural processes at work in the body. If he admits that Eve could have been created perfectly, and yet her free, creative mind could have originated an evil desire, then his entire "strict deterministic" philosophy crumbles. Therefore, in order to maintain his determinism, he must deny that any person could truly originate anything. His concept of determinism, however, is false (see Butt, 2009), and his application of it to Eve is unfounded.

The irony of the situation is that the entire purpose of a debate like the one in which he and I participated, is for free moral agents to assess the arguments and arrive at logical conclusions. If people cannot really make their own decisions, why would Dan spend 25 years of his life trying to convince his fellow humans to agree with him? His actions admit that Eve could have originated her own evil desires, even though his false philosophical view will not allow it.

DEFENDING THE BIBLE'S POSITION ON PRAYER

In their efforts to discredit the Bible, skeptics often attack its teachings concerning prayer. They claim that certain statements made by Jesus regarding prayer can be proven to be inaccurate, and thus all rational people should reject both Jesus and the Bible. Skeptics routinely quote Jesus' words, "If you ask anything in My name, I will do it" (John 14:14). After quoting this verse, the skeptic usually mentions praying parents who asked God, in the name of Jesus, to save their sick children; but the children died in spite of the prayer. The skeptic then argues that the children's death is proof positive that Jesus was a liar and His statements about prayer cannot be true. In addition to John 14:14, skeptics often use Matthew 21:22 in a very similar way. In fact, Dan Barker, during the audience question and answer period in our debate, quoted this verse: "And all things, whatever you ask in prayer, believing, you will receive" (Part 1, p. 53). According to the skeptic, if a person asks for a million dollars every day, truly believes in his heart that he will get it, and tacks the name of Jesus on the end of the prayer, then if God does not answer that prayer, Jesus lied and the Bible is false.

Is it true that the Bible's teaching on prayer cannot be reconciled with what we see happening in daily life? Did Jesus make false statements to His disciples about the efficacy of prayer? Is the skeptics' interpretation of Jesus' statements accurate and justified? The answer to these questions is a resounding "No." An honest, critical look at the Bible's teachings regarding prayer reveals that its teachings are internally consistent and correspond perfectly with reality.

QUALIFYING A STATEMENT

Most of us understand the concept of attaching qualifying remarks to a statement. For instance, hypothetical syllogisms constructed with "if-then" clauses are good examples of qualification. Suppose a person named Bill makes the statement: "If John works for eight hours, then I will give John $50." If John demands payment from Bill without doing the work, he has misunderstood the qualifier. He could contend that Bill said: "I will give John $50." Even though, technically speaking, John's quotation is correct, his argument would fail because he disregarded the qualifying statement: "If John works for eight hours." Without the first condition being met, the person making the statement is not responsible for fulfilling the second condition.

The skeptic readily understands this concept, since it must be incorporated to understand the skeptics' own writings. For instance, Dan Barker, in *godless*, included a chapter titled "Dear Theologian." The chapter is a satirical letter supposedly from God to theologians. In that chapter, Dan has God saying: "I created the universe with all kinds of natural laws that govern everything from quarks to galactic clusters" (2008, p. 149). Are we to conclude that Dan really believes that God created the world and its natural laws? Of course not. We must qualify Dan's statement by saying that he does not really believe in God, and that his "letter" is satire. Again, in *godless*, Dan made the statement: "What has theology ever provided? Theology has given us hell" (p. 220). From Dan's statement, should we conclude that Dan really believes in hell and that he credits theology with originating it? Certainly not. Dan does not believe in heaven, hell, God, or Satan. Whatever statements a person chooses to pick out of Dan's book to "prove" he believes in God or hell must be qualified by other statements elsewhere in his books, other writings, or debates that show he certainly does not believe in the existence of God or hell. In a similar way, even a superficial reading of the

New Testament shows that many of Jesus' statements concerning prayer are qualified by certain criteria that must be met in order for that prayer to be effective.

IN THE NAME OF JESUS

A systematic study of everything the Bible says on prayer is beyond the scope of this article. A look at a few Bible verses on the topic, however, will show that the skeptics' attack on prayer is ill-founded and vacuous. In truth, John 14:14, one of the skeptics' favorite verses to quote along these lines, can be used to show one of the primary "qualifying" concepts concerning prayer. In that verse, Jesus told His disciples: "if you ask anything **in My name**, I will do it" (emp. added). It is extremely important that we understand how the Bible uses the phrase "in Jesus' name." The way the skeptic understands this verse, the phrase means that as long as a person puts the words "in Jesus' name" at the end of a prayer, then God is obligated to answer that prayer positively. Attaching Jesus' name on the end of a prayer, however, is not what the Bible means when it says that a prayer is to be offered "in Jesus' name." The phrase "in Jesus' name" means that whatever is being said or done must be done **by the authority** of Jesus. Earnest Bible students have long understood this to be the proper use of the phrase. In fact, Colossians 3:17 makes this clear: "And whatever you do in word or deed, do all in the name of the Lord Jesus, giving thanks to God the Father through Him." This verse does not mean that you should proclaim before every action or sentence that what follows is being done "in Jesus' name." It means that whatever actions are taken or words are spoken should be **in accord with Jesus' teachings and by His authority**.

To illustrate, suppose a man bangs on your door and yells: "Open this door in the name of the Law." Should you open the door for this man? That depends. If he truly is a policeman who has a warrant and has been authorized by the government to enter your house, then you should. However, if he is a civilian off the street who simply added the phrase "in the name of the Law" to his sentence to make it sound more forceful, then you should not open the door. The phrase "in the name of the Law" only has force if the person using it is actually authorized by the government to perform the action. In the same way, the phrase "in Jesus' name" (or "in the name of Jesus") only has power if what is being prayed for truly is authorized by Jesus. For instance, if a person prayed, "Lord, please forgive me of my sins even though I will not forgive others of their sins, in Jesus' name, Amen," would Jesus comply with such a request? No, because He explained that God will forgive only those people who are willing to forgive others (Matthew 6:14-15). Including the phrase "in Jesus' name" does not give a prayer some magical power that allows the request to bypass the authority and teachings of Christ.

In the book of Acts, we see an extremely effective illustration of this truth. Paul, Peter, and the other apostles were preaching and doing miracles "in the name of Jesus." Their healing activities were authorized by Christ, and their message was inspired by the Holy Spirit. Seeing how effectively Paul accomplished such miracles, "some of the itinerant Jewish exorcists took it upon themselves to call the name of the Lord Jesus over those who had evil spirits, saying 'We adjure you by the Jesus whom Paul preaches'" (Acts 19:13). The itinerant Jewish exorcists had fallen into the same misunderstanding as the modern skeptic. They thought that by simply tacking Jesus' name onto their activities, that would qualify as doing things "in Jesus' name." The result of their misuse of Jesus' name quickly became apparent. When seven sons of Sceva attempted to invoke Jesus' name, the evil spirit answered: "'Jesus I know, and Paul I know; but who are you?' Then the man in whom the evil spirit was leaped on them, overpowered them, and prevailed against them, so that they fled out of that house naked and wounded" (Acts 19:14-16). Simply adding Jesus' name to actions or requests that Jesus has not authorized does not qualify as doing something "in Jesus' name" as the Bible instructs. [NOTE: Even though the skeptic does not believe the story in Acts to be true, he cannot deny that the story provides a valid illustration and explanatory commentary on what the Bible means by saying or doing something "in Jesus' name." If the skeptic is going to attack the Bible's position on prayer, he or she must allow the Bible to explain itself.]

ACCORDING TO GOD'S WILL

It is inexcusable for a person to claim to attack the Bible's position on prayer, but then to avoid many of the paramount concepts associated with the Bible's teaching on the subject. You can know that any person who pulls verses out of context about prayer, and does not turn to primary passages, such as Matthew 6:9-15, is either unaware that such passages are in the Bible, or is intentionally being intellectually dishonest. If you really want to know what Jesus taught on prayer, you simply must consider **all** that He taught about prayer, not just the few scattered verses skeptics want to rip from their contexts.

In Jesus' instructions to His disciples regarding prayer, He explained that they should include in their prayers the idea that God's will should be done (Matthew 6:10). The apostle John, who would have been well-aware of Jesus' teaching on prayer, stated: "Now this is the confidence that we have in Him, that if we ask anything **according to His will**, He hears us. And if we know that He hears us, whatever we ask, we know that we have the petitions that we have asked of Him" (1 John 5:14-15, emp. added). Notice that if we do not include verse 14 of 1 John 5, we could make the passage say, "whatever we ask, we know that we have the petitions that we have asked of Him." Yet to do that would be to leave off the important qualifying statement that the request should be in accordance with God's will, and should be offered from a heart that is humble enough to accept God's will—even if that means that the request is denied. When the skeptic pulls snippets of verses from the gospel accounts concerning prayer, he or she is guilty of leaving off just such important qualifying information.

When we consider the idea of praying "according to God's will," we can see how important this qualifier is. No requests will be granted that attempt to violate or circumvent God's ultimate will. For instance, suppose a person were to pray: "God, please save my mother even though she does not believe in Jesus Christ and refuses to repent of her sins, please let her go to heaven anyway, in Jesus' name, Amen." Would God grant that petition? The Bible is clear that He certainly would not, because to do so would be to violate His ultimate will that salvation is through the name of Jesus (Acts 4:12).

Furthermore, certain events and actions in this physical world are required for God to accomplish His will on this Earth. For example, if one of Jesus' apostles had asked God to spare the life of Jesus and not let Him die on the cross, that request would not have been in accord with God's ultimate will and would not have been answered in the affirmative. Mark 8:33 provides an excellent example of this when Peter rebuked Jesus for predicting His own death. Jesus responded to Peter, saying: "Get behind Me, Satan! For you are not mindful of the things of God, but the things of men." Whereas Peter most likely thought his actions were in accord with God's will, they were not. To further illustrate, the many events in the life of the Old Testament character Joseph may have seemed unfair at the time. No doubt Joseph prayed to be freed from slavery or to be released from jail. But at the end of Joseph's life, we see that God's will was to make him a great leader in Egypt and to save the Jewish nation through him. Joseph recognized this, and said to his brothers who had sold him into Egypt: "Do not be afraid, for am I in the place of God? But as for you, you meant evil against me; but God meant if for good, in order to bring it about as it is this day, to save many people alive" (Genesis 50:20). Joseph's slavery and incarceration were the vehicles by which God brought Joseph to power, accomplishing His will.

The Skeptic's Response

Knowing that the Bible plainly teaches that prayer must be according to God's will, Dan Barker has attempted to respond. He stated: "It does no good to claim that many prayers are unanswered because they are not 'according to his will.' Even prayers that are clearly in line with the expressed 'will of God' are rarely successful. Even if this reasoning were valid, it makes prayer useless as a means of changing nature" (1992a, p. 108). First, it should be noted that Dan often **conveniently neglects** to inform his audiences that he knows the Bible includes statements that qualify Jesus' statements that Dan and his fellow skeptics take out of context. Second, notice that Dan made sure that he included the phrase "the **expressed** 'will of God.'" The question then arises, does God have certain plans that He has not expressed to humans, but that are part of His will on Earth? Absolutely. Moses wrote: "The secret things belong to the Lord our God, but those things which are revealed belong to us and to our children forever, that we may do all the words of this law" (Deuteronomy 29:29). Is there any indication that God revealed to any humans His plans for Joseph before they were carried out? No. Is there any indication that God told any humans about His conference with Satan and His plan for Job prior to the events? None. Is God obligated to express to humans all the various facets of His will? Certainly not. That is one of the points Jesus was attempting to make in His teachings on prayer. Even though we may not know the specific will of God for our lives, we must pray with a heart that is ready to accept the events God allows, understanding that God has a will to which we are not always privy.

Notice that Dan is forced to concede the point, but then attempted to attack prayer from a different angle when he stated: "Even if this reasoning were valid, it makes prayer useless as a means of changing nature" (1992a, p. 108; see also Templeton, 1996, p. 147). It is important to be clear that once the skeptic is honest enough to admit that certain qualifications do apply to prayer, he must alter the entire argument against it. Instead of the Bible's position being internally inconsistent or at odds with reality, the skeptic must drop back and demand that, even though it **cannot be proven to be such**, it is "useless."

Again, however, the skeptics' assertion that praying according to God's will renders the prayer useless to change nature is groundless. Could it be possible that multiple outcomes to certain events or situations fit into God's will? Surely. To illustrate, suppose that a father was getting a child a drink from the refrigerator. The father had various nutritious options from which to choose including juice, milk, or water. Could the child request water and that option be according to the father's will? Sure. If the child requested juice, could that option be equally as acceptable as water? Yes. But suppose the child requested something not in the refrigerator, or something harmful to drink. While those options would be outside the father's will, the other three choices of milk, water, or juice would all be possibilities. Thus, if the child wanted juice, and asked for it, then the child's request (prayer) would be effective. [NOTE: The skeptic may attempt to say that since God knows everything, He should know what His children want before they ask. But the Bible articulates this very point in Matthew 6:8. While it is true that God knows everything (Psalm 139:1-6), it is also true that God has instructed His children to ask for what they desire (Matthew 7:7). Numerous reasons could be given for why God wants His children to present their requests to Him. One is simply that God wants humans to understand their dependence on Him (Acts 17:28).]

To illustrate, there are several biblical examples in which God's will for people involved considerable latitude in what He could allow to happen. For instance, 2 Kings 20:1-11 gives us the story of Hezekiah's terminal sickness. The prophet Isaiah informed Hezekiah that he was going to die. Hezekiah then turned his face to the wall and prayed that the Lord would extend His life. The Lord listened to his prayer and extended Hezekiah's life for fifteen years. Here we have an example of two outcomes both of which were consistent with God's will on Earth: Hezekiah living and Hezekiah dying. Without Hezekiah's prayer, he would have died of his sickness. Because of his prayer, however, God intervened and allowed Hezekiah to live. Contrary to the skeptics' false assertion, Hezekiah's prayer certainly did have the power to "change nature." It is also interesting to note that Hezekiah's sickness was healed through **natural** means. Isaiah instructed the king's attendants to place a poultice of figs on Hezekiah's boil. When they did so, Hezekiah recovered. This story provides an excellent example of a person who prayed according to God's will. That prayer drastically altered nature, and God worked through natural means to accomplish His purpose. [NOTE: While the skeptic may refuse to accept the truthfulness of this Bible story, he cannot refute the fact that the story provides at least a theoretical explanation as to how a person could pray in accordance with God's will and alter the course of nature.]

BELIEVING YOU WILL RECEIVE

Another widely recognized qualification for effective prayer is that the one praying must honestly believe that God can and will grant the prayer, if it is according to His will. As Jesus stated in Matthew 21:22: "And all things, whatever you ask in prayer, **believing**, you will receive" (emp. added). Of course, this verse does not mean that believing is the only prerequisite for having a prayer answered. Factors that we have mentioned such as asking by the authority of Jesus and according to God's will are necessary as well. But this verse and others teach us that belief is a necessary component of effective prayer. According to James 1:5-8:

> If any of you lacks wisdom, let him ask of God, who gives to all liberally and without reproach, and it will be given to him. **But let him ask in faith, with no doubting**, for he who doubts is like a wave of the sea driven and tossed by the wind. For let not that

man suppose that he will receive anything from the Lord; he is a double-minded man, unstable in all his ways (emp. added).

It is often the case that the skeptic will contend that millions of good Christian people regularly pray for things they that do not receive. The skeptic usually stresses that the people truly believed that they would receive them, and yet their prayers were ineffective. The skeptic claims to know for a fact that the petitioners in question honestly believed their prayers would be answered positively. Yet it must be stressed that the skeptic has no possible way of knowing who, in their hearts, truly believe that God will answer their prayers. Even some who claim to believe in the outcome could be harboring doubts about God's power and promises in regard to prayer. In truth, a person would need to be able to search people's hearts and minds to be an accurate judge of belief. And since the Bible explains that only God is capable of knowing the secrets of the heart (Psalm 44:21), then only He would be in a position to gage a person's true belief. While it is true that other factors such as praying according to God's will and by the authority of Christ influence the effectiveness of prayer, it is also true that fervent belief in God's willingness and ability to answer a prayer are also necessary for the prayer to be successful.

THE PRAYER OF A RIGHTEOUS MAN OR WOMAN

The Bible writers stress throughout the text, from the Old Testament to the New, that sinful, rebellious people should not expect to have God answer their prayers in a positive way. Only penitent, obedient followers of Christ are promised God's listening ear and His active hand in their lives. As James 5:16 states: "The effective, fervent prayer of a **righteous** man avails much" (emp. added). Peter stated:

> He who would love life and see good days, let him refrain his tongue from evil, and his lips from speaking guile; let him turn away from evil and do good; let him seek peace and pursue it. For the eyes of the Lord are on the righteous, and his ears are open to

their prayers; but the face of the Lord is against those who do evil (1 Peter 3:10-12).

The unnamed blind man Jesus healed summarized this position well when he stated: "Now we know that God does not hear sinners, but if anyone is a worshiper of God and does His will, He hears him" (John 9:31). The writer of Proverbs noted: "The Lord is far from the wicked, but He hears the prayer of the righteous" (15:29).

The book of Ezekiel provides further evidence that humility before God is a required element of effective prayer. During Ezekiel's day, the elders and leaders of the Jewish nation had begun to worship idols. Yet, in their troubled times, they also attempted to seek the true God along with their idols. Ezekiel 14:1-4 states:

> Now some of the elders of Israel came to me and sat before me. And the word of the Lord came to me saying, "Son of man, these men have set up their idols in their hearts, and put before them that which causes them to stumble into iniquity. Should I let Myself be inquired of at all by them? Therefore speak to them, and say to them, 'Thus says the Lord God: "Everyone of the house of Israel who sets up his idols in his heart, and puts before him what causes him to stumble into iniquity, and then comes to the prophet, I the Lord will answer him who comes, according to the multitude of his idols, that I may seize the house of Israel by their heart, because they are estranged from Me by their idols.""

The Bible clearly and plainly teaches that those who are not faithfully following God are not promised an answer to their prayers. It should also be noted along these lines that, although many people feel that they are faithful followers of Christ, they have not obeyed God's will (see Lyons and Butt, n.d.). As Jesus stated:

> Not everyone who says to Me, "Lord, Lord," shall enter the kingdom of heaven, but he who does the will of My Father in heaven. Many will say to Me in that day, "Lord, Lord, have we not prophesied in Your name, cast out demons in Your name, and done many wonders in Your name?" And then I will declare to them, "I

never knew you; depart from Me, you who practice lawlessness!" (Matthew 7:21-23).

It is often the case that a bulk of the people who skeptics claim are faithful followers of Christ simply have not obeyed God and, according to the Bible's teachings, should not expect Him to answer their prayers because of their rebellious lives.

SELFISH MOTIVES AND DESIRES

Suppose that a person prays that God will give him ten thousand dollars every day for the rest of his life **so that he can spend that money only on himself to gratify his physical pleasures**. Even if he adds the phrase, "in Jesus' name" to the end of that prayer, and honestly believes that God will answer the prayer, is God obligated to comply with such a request? The way the skeptic has twisted the Scriptures, he or she must contend that God is bound to grant such an absurd appeal. Yet an elementary understanding of the biblical doctrine of prayer quickly sets such a conclusion on its head. One of the key concepts regarding prayer centers on the reason for which the petitioner is making the request. If the one making the request is driven by selfish, impure motives, then he or she cannot expect God to grant the plea. James made this point abundantly clear when he wrote: "You lust and do not have. You murder and covet and cannot obtain. You fight and war. Yet you do not have because you do not ask. You ask and do not receive, because you ask amiss, that you may **spend it on your pleasures**" (4:2-3, emp. added). Selfish ambitions unmotivated by a sense of spiritual concern nullifies the effectiveness of prayer.

Acts 8:9-25 provides an adequate illustration of this truth. In this passage, a man named Simon had been practicing sorcery in the city of Samaria. Many of the Samaritans had been convinced by his deceptive, "magic" tricks. When Philip visited the area, however, and preached the Gospel of Jesus Christ, a host of the Samaritans believed and obeyed the truth, including Simon the sorcerer. After a while, the apostles came to the area and laid their hands on some of the disciples for the purpose of imparting spiritual gifts to them. When Simon saw this power, he offered the apostles money, requesting to purchase the ability to give people spiritual gifts. Apparently, he had not purged himself of old habits of selfish ambition. Peter rebuked Simon and explained that he needed to repent and beg God to forgive him of the wicked thoughts and intents of his heart. Simon's request for the power to impart the gifts of the Holy Spirit was denied, not only because it violated the will of God, but also because it was issued out of purely selfish motives.

Jesus further documented the fact that prayers which issue from selfish motivations will not be effective. In the Sermon on the Mount, He stated: "And when you pray, you shall not be like the hypocrites. For they love to pray standing in the synagogues and on the corners of the streets, that they may be seen by men. Assuredly, I say to you, they have their reward" (Matthew 6:5). The hypocrites' showy prayers designed to garner public approval negated the effectiveness of their requests.

PERSISTENCE

The persistence of the petition is another factor that the Bible indicates has a bearing on the efficacy of prayer. In Luke 18:1, the gospel writer stated: "Then He [Jesus—KB] spoke a parable to them, that men **always ought** to pray and not lose heart" (emp. added). The parable Jesus told in this context was about a widow who made a request to an unjust judge. Her request was noble and right, but the unjust judge did not feel obligated to comply with her appeal. Due to her persistence, however, and her "continual coming" to the judge, he finally granted her petition. Jesus then commented that if an unjust judge can be swayed by persistence, how much more effective is the persistent prayer of a virtuous person when addressed to the righteous Judge of all the Earth.

Additionally, Jesus told of a man who visited his neighbor at midnight requesting bread to feed a guest. Initially, the neighbor refused the request, but eventually he complied. Jesus stated: "I say to you, though he will not rise and give to him because he is his friend, yet **because of his persistence** he will rise and give him as many as he needs" (emp. added). Jesus then coupled this parable with the instructions to be persistent in requests to God (vss. 9-13). In fact, throughout the Scriptures, persistence plays a prominent role in effective prayer (see Philippians 1:4; 1 Thessalonians 5:17; Ephesians 6:18; Luke 2:37).

THE PRAYER EXPERIMENT

In *The God Delusion*, Richard Dawkins caustically attacked the concept of the effectiveness of prayer to accomplish any real world results. He focused primarily on a "prayer experiment" in which approximately 1,800 heart patients were divided into three groups: "Group 1 received prayers and didn't know it. Group 2 (the control group) received no prayers and didn't know it. Group 3 received prayers and did know it" (2006a, p. 66). The results of the experiment suggested that the prayers that were offered for groups 1 and 3 did not favorably affect the successful results of their surgery or recovery. Dawkins focused on these negative results, insinuating that such an experiment proves that prayer is useless and the Bible's teaching on the topic is at odds with reality. Dawkins quoted one of the religious people who had offered some of the prayers, who stated that the results did not dissuade him from his belief in the efficacy of prayer. Dawkins then sarcastically retorted: "Yeah, right: we know from our faith that prayer works, so if evidence fails to show it we'll just soldier on until finally we get the result we want" (2006a, p. 66).

Dawkins' assessment of the experiment, however, shows a glaring ignorance of the Bible's true position concerning prayer, and a complete failure to approach the subject with any type of scholarly rigor.

Every critique of a scientific experiment must certainly include a knowledge and understanding of the factors that would "skew" the results of the study. For instance, if the Bible plainly says that the prayers of a righteous person and those of an unrighteous person differ in their efficacy, then such information must be considered in order for an accurate assessment of any prayer experiment to take place. Furthermore, if the Bible specifically details that the motives driving a particular request have a bearing on the answer, then the "experimental" format in which the prayers were offered would itself be called into question and would adversely affect the accuracy of the report. In addition, if the Bible clearly states that those who are praying must truly believe that God, according to His will, will comply with the request, then the level of belief held by each of the members in the "prayer groups" must be factored into the critique of the experiment.

Please do not misunderstand what I am saying. It is impossible to know or compare the faithfulness of a prayer group, much less each individual's level of belief. Nor would it be feasible to attempt to study the various lives of the ones who were being prayed for and try to systematically document how their health or sickness would factor into God's will on this Earth. I am not suggesting that the experiment could have been arranged better so that more accurate results could have been obtained. A negative result to prayer cannot prove that prayer is ineffective, but only that at least one of the biblical criteria was lacking. I am suggesting, however, that Dawkins' failure to comprehensively view the Bible's qualifications about prayer, and his dishonest (or ignorant) glossing over of the true facts concerning prayer, would not be tolerated in any critique of a scientific experiment, and should be shown to have absolutely no value in discrediting the Bible's position on prayer. [NOTE: It is unfortunate that even some religious people have so misunderstood the Bible's teachings about prayer that they would even attempt such an experiment. We would be wise to consider that many people who profess to be defending the Bible's position on subjects such as prayer are actually doing more harm than good by misrepresenting the truth.]

CONCLUSION

To document the millions of incidents in which people's prayers have been answered positively would be virtually impossible. The Bible offers a multitude of examples in which the prayers of God's faithful followers were answered, and modern Christians could detail countless examples of such in their personal lives. It is true, however, that God does not always respond positively to all those who petition him. The skeptic delights in pulling out scattered verses, misrepresenting the Scriptures' true position on prayer, and demanding that the Bible cannot be God's Word, since its teachings concerning prayer are "contradictory" and do not accurately represent what occurs in the real world. A critical look at the skeptics' claims, however, quickly and clearly reveals that much is amiss with their allegations. It is only the feeble straw man built by the skeptic's own imagination that can be effectively demolished. An accurate representation of the Bible's position concerning prayer reveals complete internal consistency and perfect correspondence to real world events. The Bible explains that prayer is not a magic incantation that can be spouted out to accomplish selfish ambitions. Instead, the effective prayer comes from a righteous person, who prays persistently, by the authority of Christ, according to God's will, out of unselfish motives, believing he or she will receive the petitions requested.

COMMENT ON THE LAST QUESTION

everal of the atheists in the audience disliked my answer to the last question so much that they booed rather loudly. I am not sure what they were reacting to so forcefully, but after asking some of my supporters who were there, I think I need to clarify the answer. Some of those who attended thought that I was equating abortion and birth control. That was never my intent, and I attempted, in my answer, to make sure I was not misunderstood. I was not saying that all birth control is the equivalent of an abortion. Nor was I saying that all forms of birth control are immoral and homicidal, like abortion is. I said "What is often **lumped in with** birth control? Abortion" (Part 1, p. 54).

Due to my familiarity with the way Dan Barker uses the two terms together, I did not feel the need to expound upon my connecting them. For instance, in *Losing Faith in Faith*, Dan stated: "Most religions have consistently resisted progress—including abolition of slavery; women's right to vote and to choose **contraception and abortion**; medical developments such as anesthesia…" (1992a, p. 135). Notice how Barker closely tied the two together, labeling them both as "progress," implying that abortion is not only morally acceptable, but morally superior to not having the option. In Barker's debate with John Rankin, Barker called abortion a "blessing."

In hindsight, it might have been more effective to have shown, using such quotes, that Dan is a proponent of abortion, and then to have explained that he and other atheists view abortion as a viable means to control the human population (see Part 2, pp. 94-99). It might also have been better received if I had stated more clearly that I was not equating all birth control to abortion. But if the atheists in the audience had a problem with the fact that atheism can have no moral objections to murdering children to reduce the population, then they need to revisit their philosophy and take that up with Dan Barker.

DARWIN, EVOLUTION, AND RACISM

Eric Lyons & Kyle Butt

During the debate, one minute and 30 seconds into Kyle's rebuttal speech, he pointed out to Dan that Adolf Hitler was attempting to breed a superior Arian **race** of humans (Part 1, p. 25). I suggested that this plan fit perfectly with Darwin's understanding of natural selection, especially in light of Darwin's subtitle to his major work *The Origin of Species by Means of Natural Selection **or the Preservation of Favored Races in the Struggle for Life**. In short, I suggested that Darwin thought some **races** of humans were evolutionarily superior to others, and this idea led Hitler to attempt to eliminate those he deemed to be inferior.

In Barker's five-minute closing arguments, he addressed this idea, and stated: "When Darwin talked about favored races, in those days the word 'race' did not mean human 'race,' like Hitler might have used it. In his day the word 'race' was just a synonym for animal species. He wasn't talking about favored 'races' like whites over blacks or something" (Part 1, p. 56). According to Barker, Darwin did not make a distinction between various human races, but simply between the human race and animal races. Barker's statement was not backed by any documented definition from Darwin or his contemporaries, and, in truth, is patently false.

Darwin **did** distinguish between various human races, or "species of men," and he believed that some were superior to others (1871, p. 395). Although he steered clear of these ideas in *The Ori-*

gin of Species, his second major work on evolutionary theory, *The Descent of Man and Selection in Relation to Sex*, published in 1871, did address the issue.

Darwin began the first chapter of *The Descent of Man* with these words: "He who wishes to decide whether man is the modified descendant of some pre-existing form, would probably first enquire whether man varies, however slightly, in bodily structure and in mental faculties; and if so, whether the variations are transmitted to his offspring in accordance with the laws which prevail with the lower animals" (1871, p. 395). Later, in his chapter titled "On the Affinities and Genealogy of Man," Darwin wrote:

> At some future period, not very distant as measured by centuries, the **civilised races** of man will almost certainly exterminate, and replace, the **savage races** throughout the world. At the same time the anthropomorphous apes, as Professor Schaaffhausen has remarked, will no doubt be exterminated. The break between man and his nearest allies will then be wider, for it will intervene between man in a more civilised state, as we may hope, even than the Caucasian, and some ape as low as a baboon, instead of as now between the **negro** or **Australian** and the gorilla (p. 521, emp. added).

Clearly, Darwin was convinced that the more "civilized races" (e.g., Caucasian) would one day exterminate the more "savage races," which he considered to be less evolved (and thus more ape-like) than Caucasians. Darwin believed that "the Negro" and "Australian" are more of a sub-species, somewhere between Caucasians and apes. [NOTE: In addition to Darwin's racist comments in *The Descent of Man*, he also included sexist statements. His evolutionary views led him to believe that "[t]he chief distinction in the intellectual powers of the two sexes is shown by man's attaining to a higher eminence, in whatever he takes up, than can woman—whether requiring deep thought, reason, or imagination, or merely the use of the senses and hands…. [T]he average of mental power in man must be above that of woman…. [M]an has ultimately become superior to woman" (pp. 873-874).]

One of Darwin's closest friends and defenders, the prominent, 19th-century English biologist Thomas Huxley, was even more direct in his evolutionary-based racist remarks. In his 1865 essay, "Emancipation—Black and White," Huxley remarked:

> It may be quite true that some negroes are better than some white men; but **no rational man, cognisant of the facts, believes that the average Negro is the equal, still less the superior, of the white man**. And, if this be true, it is simply incredible that, when all his disabilities are removed, and our prognathus relative has a fair field and no favour, as well as no oppressor, he will be able to compete successfully with his bigger-brained and smaller jawed rival, in a contest which is to be carried on by thoughts and not by bites. The highest places in the hierarchy of civilisation will assuredly not be within the reach of our dusky cousins, though it is by no means necessary that they should be restricted to the lowest (emp. added).

According to "Darwin's Bulldog," as Huxley was called, the "Negro" is not equal to "the white man." The alleged smaller-brained, big-jawed "Negro" supposedly cannot compete on the same playing field with the white man. Huxley espoused the false notion that "[t]he **highest places** in the hierarchy of civilisation will assuredly not be within the reach of our dusky cousins" (1865, emp. added). Little did Huxley know that less then 150 years later an African-American would sit in the **highest office** of the most wealthy and powerful nation on Earth.

The fact is, Darwinian evolution implies that some groups of humans are closer to our alleged ape-like ancestors in their mental faculties than others. Thus, some groups of humans supposedly are superior to others. The Bible teaches exactly the opposite. There are not different species or races of men; there is just one human race—an intelligent people (see Lyons, 2002)—that God created "in His image" in the beginning (Genesis 1-2; see Lyons and Thompson,

2002), both "male **and female**" (Genesis 1:27, emp. added). All of humanity descended from Adam and Eve, the first couple (1 Corinthians 15:45; Genesis 3:20), and later Noah, through whom the Earth was repopulated after the Flood (Genesis 6-10). Whether we are red, yellow, black, or white, we share equal value as human beings, God's image-bearers (Genesis 1:26-28; cf. Romans 10:12). What's more, all men stand on equal footing before God as sinners (Romans 3:10,23) in need of a Savior (John 8:24; Mark 16:15-16).

CONCLUSION

Barker's attempt to vindicate Darwin of racist ideas was founded on groundless assertions and is easily disproven. Darwin used the term "race" to distinguish between Caucasians, Negros, and Aborigines, exactly as was suggested in Kyle's statement concerning the implications of Darwin's evolution. As with many of Barker's assertions in the debate, we encourage the discerning listener/reader to ask a simple question: Does Barker provide a valid argument or supply documentation for the assertion he is making? The majority of the time, the answer is a resounding, "No."

CONNECTING THE DOTS

One of Dan's favorite accusations in his writings and debates is to insist that his opponent "didn't connect the dots." By this, Dan suggests that the arguments used by his opponents do not make an adequate case to draw the conclusion they are defending. In our debate, Dan stated: "What Kyle did tonight was he talked a lot, but he didn't connect any dots. Did you notice that? Our debate is, does the God of the Bible exist? He didn't give us any evidence for that God. You quoted a bunch of Bible verses. But the point of the Bible itself being reliable is a very important point" (Part 1, p. 57).

First, it should be noted that Dan consumed almost 10 minutes of his first 15-minute speech quoting Bible verses that he alleged to be contradictory. If anyone "quoted a bunch of Bible verses" it was Dan. I responded by answering his allegation that the Bible is contradictory by addressing one of those, and moving on to additional evidence. Due to the very limited time constraints, the refutation of the remaining alleged discrepancies has been included in this book. By showing that Dan's charge of biblical discrepancy is false, I effectively addressed two-thirds of his opening statements and showed that the Bible is reliable—the very thing he insisted must be done in order to prove the existence of the God of the Bible. [NOTE: It should also be mentioned that Dan is one of the world's leading atheistic debaters. If he filled almost two-thirds of his opening speech with 14 alleged discrepancies in the Bible, he must believe that this is some of the strongest evidence that is available against the God of the Bible. So, in dealing with alleged discrepancies, and showing that they have no merit, we have effectively demolished one of the lines of argument that the atheistic community perceives as its strongest.]

Second, I offered two lines of evidence in my opening speech—that design in the natural world demands an intelligent Designer and that objective morality demands a moral standard outside of humans. The design argument corresponds with the God of the Bible's attributes of intelligence and omniscience. And the morality argument verifies that the intelligent Creator must be a personal Being, just as the Bible portrays, Who can understand and demand conformity to a certain moral code.

To further connect the dots between the God Who I was defending and that God being the God of the Bible, I noted that in order to falsify belief in this God, one would have to prove that Jesus Christ did not come to Earth, did not die on the cross, and did not rise from the dead (Part 1, p. 31). Thus, I not only showed that the law of design and the reality of a moral code perfectly match the picture of the God of the Bible, but that God's existence can be falsified simply by disproving the existence of Jesus Christ and the events that happened to Him in first-century Palestine. Of course, Dan alleged that he can disprove Jesus' existence, but he certainly cannot (see Butt and Lyons, 2006).

Dan's contention that the dots were not connected was shown to be vacuous during the audience question period. One member of the audience asked me, "What makes your God of the Bible more legitimate than any other God in any other myth?" Included in my answer was the statement that "the God of the Bible has opened Himself up for falsifiability in the historicity of Jesus Christ."

Not only did I show that Dan's assertion that the Bible is unreliable is false, I further showed that the picture that the Bible paints of God perfectly corresponds to what we see in the natural world.

I then connected God with the person of Jesus Christ, and nailed down the fact that the two stand or fall together. Since it can be shown that atheism's attacks on both the Creator God and the person of Jesus Christ have failed miserably, then it can also be proven that God, the God of the Bible, exists.

DO ATHEISTS REALLY WANT PEOPLE TO THINK FOR THEMSELVES?

In Dan's closing remarks, he repeated a statement that he often makes in his debates and his writings. He said: "Most Christians are afraid that people will think for themselves. Most atheists are afraid that they won't" (Part 1, p. 59). According to Dan, atheism offers people freedom to think "outside the box" of religion. Supposedly, the atheistic philosophy is unimpaired by dogmatic teachings and is the only philosophy that allows people to let their minds follow the evidence wherever it may lead. Dan's proffer of freethought, however, is nothing more than an illusion that Dan, in his writings, has shown to be false.

In *Losing Faith in Faith*, Barker discussed a book that he wrote for children that contained these words: "No one can tell you what to think. Not your teachers. Not your parents. Not your minister, priest, or rabbi. Not your friends or relatives. Not this book. You are the boss of your own mind. If you have used your own mind to find out what is true, then you should be proud! Your thoughts are free!" (1992a, p. 47). Noble sentiments, indeed!

But, as one digs deeper into Barker's book, it quickly becomes clear that those sentiments do not find a willing practitioner in the person of Dan Barker or in the atheistic philosophy in general. In his chapter on prayer, Barker wrote:

> Don't ask Christians if they think prayer is effective. They will think up some kind of answer that makes sense to them only. Don't ask them, **tell** them: "You know that prayer doesn't work. You know you are fooling yourself with magical conceit." No matter how they

reply, they will know in their heart of hearts that you are right (1992a, p. 109, emp. in orig.).

From Barker's statement about what should be "told" to those who believe in prayer, it is easy to see that he does not necessarily believe his previous statement that "no one can tell you what to think," or that a person should use his own mind "to find out what is true." In fact, what Barker is really trying to say is that a person should only think for himself if such thinking will lead him to believe that there is no God, or that prayer does not work, or that all religion is nonsense. If thinking for himself leads a person to believe in the efficacy of prayer or the existence of God, then that person should be "told" what to believe.

Furthermore, Dan wrote an entire chapter titled, "What is a Freethinker?" At the end of this chapter, Barker said, "Freethought allows you to do your own thinking…. Freethought is truly free" (1992a, p. 136). Obviously, Mr. Barker wants everyone who comes in contact with freethought to believe that it is an avenue of thinking that allows each individual to go where his or her thoughts lead.

Upon further investigation, however, Barker's brand of freethought is not so free after all. On the very first page of his chapter on freethought, he contends, "No one can be a freethinker who demands conformity to a bible, creed, or messiah." So, according to Mr. Barker, since he and his group of freethinkers do not think they see enough evidence for the Bible's inspiration, then all "freethinkers" must reject conformity to the Bible. What happened to the idea that freethought allows you "to do your own thinking"? Again, on the same page he wrote, "Freethinkers are naturalistic" (p. 133), meaning that freethinkers cannot believe in anything outside the realm of what can be measured using the senses. What if certain evidences compel a person to believe in a supernatural deity? According to Barker's idea of freethought, a person is not free to follow that type of evidence. Once again, freethought proves to be much less "free" than we have been told.

Another telling statement from Barker's pen comes on page 134, where he says, "Individuals are free to choose, within the limits of humanistic morality." His "freethought," then, allows a person to choose freely any set of ethical and moral standards, **as long as those standards conform to the "humanistic morality"** adopted by Barker and his fellow "freethinkers." But what if those moral standards fall outside the realm of "humanistic morality?" Then a freethinker must choose some other standard—or cease to be a freethinker.

In one of his concluding paragraphs, Barker states: "A multiplicity of individuals thinking, free from the restraints of orthodoxy, allows ideas to be tested, discarded or adopted" (p. 135). Barker subtly omits the other restraints such as naturalism and humanism, from which freethinkers are not free. In essence, freethinkers, according to Dan Barker, are those people **who think like him** and his fellow freethinkers. If a person does not think like the humanistic, naturalistic Dan Barker, then that person must be an enslaved thinker, not a freethinker.

In reality, "freethought" is a misnomer and is not free after all. In fact, it is one of the "least free" ways to think that is available in the marketplace of ideas. In actuality, the only thing that can ever make a person free is the truth (John 8:32). The Bible insists that each person weigh the evidence for himself or herself. First Thessalonians 5:21 states: "Test all things; hold fast what is good." From the statements quoted above, it is evident that Dan Barker and his fellow freethinkers are not really interested in freedom but, rather, are interested in forming a group of "freethinkers" that toes the party line on such false concepts as naturalism and humanism.

APPENDIX

During the course of the debate, Dan Barker made several statements that require explanation and refutation. Due to the brief nature of these statements, and the lengthy amount of time that would be involved in responding to them, I have chosen to simply refer the reader to additional materials that adequately address the assertions he made. The references for this section are listed immediately following.

In Part 1, p. 5, Barker stated: "And I guess, thank you, Charles Darwin. None of us would be here, right, if it weren't for evolution, the fact of evolution." In reality, evolution is not a fact; it is a theory that has been shown to be false, (see: Thompson, 2001; Butt and Lyons, 2009; Sarfati, 1999 and 2002). Barker made similar statements in Part 1, p. 20, that are answered by the above listed resources as well.

In Part 1, p. 22, Barker commented: "If we want to go back to the tradition, women should not vote, women should stay home, women should not go to college, women don't even own their own property. This all comes out of the Bible, by the way." Again, Barker's assertion that his statements are backed by the Bible is false. Alvin Schmidt has some excellent material manifesting the truth that the Bible has helped exalt and dignify women in the cultures where Christianity has spread (2001).

Additionally, Barker claimed that the Messianic prophecies, especially in Matthew, were inaccurate (Part 1, pp. 42-43). That claim is refuted in the book *Behold! The Lamb of God* (Butt and Lyons, 2006), in Wayne Jackson's article "Did Isaiah Prophesy the Virgin Birth of Christ?" (n.d.), and in the book *Rays of Messiah's Glory*, by David Baron (2000).

REFERENCES

Baron, David (2000 reprint), *Rays of Messiah's Glory* (Jerusalem, Israel: Kern Ahvah Meshihit).

Butt, Kyle and Eric Lyons (2006), *Behold! The Lamb of God* (Montgomery, AL: Apologetics Press).

Butt, Kyle and Eric Lyons (2009), "Darwin in Light of 150 Years of Error," [On-line], URL: http://www.apologeticspress.org/articles/240057.

Jackson, Wayne (no date), "Did Isaiah Prophesy the Virgin Birth of Christ?", [On-line], URL: http://www.christiancourier.com/articles/461-did-isaiah-prophesy-the-virgin-birth-of-christ.

Sarfati, Jonathan (1999), *Refuting Evolution* (Green Forest, AR: Master Books).

Sarfati, Jonathan (2002), *Refuting Evolution 2* (Green Forest, AR: Master Books).

Schmidt, Alvin (2001), *Under the Influence: How Christianity Transformed Civilization* (Grand Rapids, MI: Zondervan).

Thompson, Bert (2001), "Is Evolution a 'Fact' of Science?," [On-line], URL: http://www.apologeticspress.org/articles/1985.

REFERENCES

"Abortion" (2008), *Merriam-Webster Dictionary,* [On-line], URL: http://www.merriam-webster.com/dictionary/abortion.

American Heritage Dictionary of the English Language (2000), (Boston, MA: Houghton Mifflin), fourth edition.

"Animal Sex: No Stinking Rules" (no date), *Live Science,* [On-line], URL: http://www.livescience.com/bestimg/index.php?URL=&cat=polygamous.

Arndt, William and F.W. Gingrich (1967), *A Greek-English Lexicon of the New Testament and Other Early Christian Literature* (Chicago, IL: University of Chicago Press).

Barker, Dan (1992a), *Losing Faith in Faith: From Preacher to Atheist* (Madison, WI: Freedom From Religion Foundation).

Barker, Dan (1992b), *Maybe Right, Maybe Wrong: A Guide for Young Thinkers* (Amherst, NY: Prometheus).

Barker, Dan (2006), "How to be Moral Without Religion," [On-line], URL: http://www.ffrf.org/about/bybarker/CASH1.mp3.

Barker, Dan (2008), *godless* (Berkeley, CA: Ulysses Press).

Barker, Dan and John Rankin (2006), "Evolution and Intelligent Design: What are the Issues?," [On-line], URL: http://www.ffrf.org/about/bybarker/ID_Debate.mp3.

Barker, Dan and Peter Payne (2005), *Does Ethics Require God?* [On-line], URL: http://www.ffrf.org/about/bybarker/ethics_debate.php.

Barker, Dan and Rubel Shelly (1999), *Barker/Shelly Debate: Does God Exist?* (Brentwood, TN: Faith Matters).

Barnes, Albert (1949), *Notes on the New Testament: Matthew and Mark* (Grand Rapids, MI: Baker).

Botterweck, G. Johannes, Helmer Ringgren, and Heinz-Josef Fabry (1998), *Theological Dictionary of the Old Testament* (Grand Rapids, MI: Eerdmans).

Bryner, Jeanna (no date), "Are Humans Meant to be Monogamous?" *Live Science*, [On-line], URL: http://www.livescience.com/mysteries/080319-llm-monogamy.html.

Brown, Francis, S.R. Driver, and Charles B. Briggs (1993), *A Hebrew and English Lexicon of the Old Testament* (Electronic Database: Biblesoft).

Burke, Barbara (1974), "Infanticide," *Science*, 185:653.

Butt, Kyle (2002), "Jesus Christ—Dead or Alive?," *Reason & Revelation*, [On-line], URL: http://www.apologeticspress.org/articles/121.

Butt, Kyle (2003a), "Do Babies Go to Hell When They Die?," [On-line], URL: http://www.apologeticspress.org/scrspeak/2003/ss-03-18.htm.

Butt, Kyle (2003b), "What 'We All Know' About a Lie," [On-line], URL: http://www.apologeticspress.org/articles/1839.

Butt, Kyle (2004), "The Skeptic's Faulty Assumption," [On-line], URL: http://www.apologeticspress.org/articles/2230.

Butt, Kyle (2007), *Behold! The Word of God* (Montgomery, AL: Apologetics Press).

Butt, Kyle (2009), "The FANG Argument: A Refutation," [On-line], URL: http://www.apologeticspress.org/articles/240121.

Butt, Kyle and Dan Barker (2009), *Does the God of the Bible Exist?* (Montgomery, AL: Apologetics Press).

Butt, Kyle and Eric Lyons (2006), *Behold! The Lamb of God* (Montgomery, AL: Apologetics Press).

Coffman, James Burton (1985), *Commentary on Exodus* (Abilene, TX: ACU Press).

Colley, Caleb (2004a), "God Cannot Lie," [On-line], URL: http://www.apologeticspress.org/articles/2561.

Colley, Caleb (2004b), "God's Mercy and Justice," [On-line], URL: http://www.apologeticspress.org/articles/1860.

"Columbine" (2008), [On-line], URL: http://home.arcor.de/hbredel/Buch/Columbine-English/ columbine-english.html.

Copan, Paul (2001), *That's Your Interpretation: Responding to Skeptics Who Challenge Your Faith* (Grand Rapids, MI: Baker).

Craig, William Lane (no date), *Pain and Suffering Debate*, Part 1, [On-line], URL: http://www.youtube.com/watch?v=8ZTG5xyefEo.

Cullen, Dave (1999), "Kill Mankind. No One Should Survive," *Salon.com*, [On-line], URL: http://www.salon.com/news/feature/1999/09/23/journal/print.html.

Dahmer, Lionel (1994), *A Father's Story* (New York: William Morrow).

Darwin, Charles (1859 reprint), *The Origin of Species by Means of Natural Selection or The Preservation of Favoured Races in the Struggle for Life* (New York: The Modern Library).

Darwin, Charles (1860), *On the Origin of Species By Natural Selection or the Preservation of Favored Races in the Struggle for Life* (New York: The Modern Library), second edition.

Darwin, Charles (1871), *The Descent of Man* (New York: Modern Library, reprint).

Darwin, Charles (1958), *The Autobiography of Charles Darwin*, ed. Nora Barlow (New York: W.W. Norton).

Dawkins, Richard (1996), *The Blind Watchmaker* (New York: W.W. Norton).

Dawkins, Richard (2006a), *The God Delusion* (New York: Houghton Mifflin).

Dawkins, Richard (2006b), *The Selfish Gene* (Oxford: Oxford University Press), 30th Anniversary Edition.

The Declaration of Independence (1776), National Archives, [On-line], URL: http://www.archives.gov/national_archives_experience/charters/declaration.html.

Doyle, Alister (2006), *"Birds and Bees May Be Gay: Museum Exhibition,"* [On-line], URL: http://news.yahoo.com/s/nm/20061012/sc_nm/environment_homosexuality_ dc;_ylt=AhEiR4DtDaCUi1h7KCssWv ms0NUE;_ylu=X3oDMTA3ODdxdHBhBHNlY wM5NjQ-.

"Dr. Eric R. Pianka: University of Texas at Austin" (2006), [On-line], URL: http://www.geocities.com/tetrahedronomega/brenmccnnll.blogspot. com-2006-03-dr.html.

"Equivocation" (2009), *Wikipedia*, [On-line], URL: http://en.wikipedia. org/wiki/Equivocation.

"Excerpts from Student Evaluations" (1999), [On-line], URL: http:// www.zo.utexas.edu/courses/bio357/357evaluations.html.

Fudge, Edward (1982), *The Fire That Consumes* (Houston, TX: Providential Press).

Green, Ruth H. (1979), *Born Again Skeptic's Guide to the Bible* (Madison, WI: Freedom from Religion Foundation).

Harris, R.L. G.L. Archer, and B.K. Waltke, (1980), *Theological Wordbook of the Old Testament* (Chicago, IL: Moody).

Harris, Sam (2004), *The End of Faith* (New York: W.W. Norton).

Harris, Sam (2006), *Letter to a Christian Nation* (New York: Alfred A. Knopf).

Harrison, R.K. (1988), "Molech," *International Bible Encyclopedia*, ed. Geoffrey W. Bromiley (Grand Rapids, MI: Eerdmans).

Harrub, Brad and Bert Thompson (2002), "Creationists Fight Back! A Review of *U.S. News and World Report*," *Reason & Revelation*, 22[9]:65-71, September, [On-line], URL: http://www.apologeticspress.org/articles/2094.

Harrub, Brad and Bert Thompson (2004), "The Origin of the Brain and Mind—Parts 1 & 2," [On-line], URL: http://www.apologeticspress. org/articles/1.

Harrub, Brad and Dave Miller (2004), "'This is the Way God Made Me': A Scientific Examination of Homosexuality and the 'Gay Gene,'" *Reason & Revelation*, 24[8]:73-79, August, [On-line], URL: http:// www.apologeticspress.org/articles/2553.

Hazen, Robert (2005), *Origins of Life* (Chantilly, VA: The Teaching Company).

Hitchens, Christopher (2007), *god Is Not Great: How Religion Poisons Everything* (New York: Twelve).

Huxley, Aldous (1937), *Ends and Means* (London: Chatto & Windus).

Huxley, Thomas (1865), "Emancipation—Black and White," [On-line], URL: http://aleph0.clarku.edu/huxley/CE3/B&W.html.

"In the Image and Likeness of God" (2001), [On-line]: URL: http://www.apologeticspress.org/pdfs/courses_pdf/hsc0203.pdf.

Jamieson, Robert, et al. (1997), *Jamieson, Fausset, Brown Bible Commentary* (Electronic Database: Biblesoft).

Jenni, Ernst and Claus Westerman (1997), *Theological Lexicon of the Old Testament* (Peabody, MA: Hendrickson).

Keil, C.F. (1996 reprint), *Commentary on the Old Testament—The Pentateuch* (Peabody, MA: Hendrickson).

Keil, C.F. and Franz Delitzsch (1981 reprint), *Biblical Commentaries on the Old Testament: The Pentateuch* (Grand Rapids, MI: Eerdmans).

Keller, Timothy (2008), *The Reason for God* (New York: Dutton).

Layton, Bentley (1987), *The Gnostic Scriptures* (Canterbury: SCM Press).

Lenksi, Richard C. H. (1943), *The Interpretation of St. Matthew's Gospel* (Minneapolis, MN: Augsburg).

Leupold, H.C. (1959), *Exposition of the Psalms* (Grand Rapids, MI: Baker).

Lewis, C.S. (1952), *Mere Christianity* (New York: Simon and Schuster).

Lockyer, Herbert (1969), *All the Trades and Occupations of the Bible* (Grand Rapids, MI: Zondervan).

Lyons, Eric (2002), "Ancient Nitwits or Knowledgeable Ancestors?" [On-line], URL: http://www.apologeticspress.org/articles/1798.

Lyons, Eric (2003), *The Anvil Rings: Volume 1* (Montgomery, AL: Apologetics Press).

Lyons, Eric (2005), *The Anvil Rings: Volume 2* (Montgomery, AL: Apologetics Press).

Lyons, Eric (2009), "Does God Really Know Everything?", [On-line], URL: http://www.apologeticspress.org/articles/607.

Lyons, Eric and Bert Thompson (2002), "In the Image and Likeness of God: Part 1," *Reason & Revelation*, 22[3]:17-23, [On-line]: URL: http://www.apologeticspress.org/articles/123.

Lyons, Eric and Kyle Butt (no date), *Receiving the Gift of Salvation*, [On-line], URL: http://www.apologeticspress.org/pdfs/e-books_pdf/Receiving%20the%20Gift%20of%20Salvation.pdf.

Lyons, Eric and Kyle Butt (2005), "The Eternality of Hell: Part 2," *Reason & Revelation*, 25[2]:9-15, February.

Mackie, J.L. (1982), *The Miracle of Theism: Arguments For and Against the Existence of God* (Oxford: Clarendon Press).

"Major Religions of the World Ranked by Number of Adherents" (2007), [On-line]: URL: http://www.adherents.com/Religions_By_Adherents.html#Nonreligious.

Matzke, Nick (2006), "Forrest Mims: 'Crazy Kook,' says Pianka," [On-line], URL: http://www.pandasthumb.org/archives/2006/04/forrest_mims_cr.html.

McCabe, Joseph (1935), *The Social Record of Christianity* (London: Watts and Co.).

Merriam-Webster Online Dictionary (2009), [On-line], URL: http://www.merriam-webster.com/dictionary.

Miller, Dave (2002), "Capital Punishment and the Bible," [On-line], URL: http://www.apologeticspress.org/articles/1974.

Miller, Dave (2003), "Jephthah's Daughter," [On-line], URL: http://www.apologeticspress.org/articles/2320.

Mills, David (2006), *Atheist Universe* (Berkeley, CA: Ulysses Press).

Mims, Forrest (2006), "Meeting Doctor Doom," *The Citizen Scientist*, [On-line], URL: http://www.sas.org/tcs/weeklyIssues_2006/2006-04-07/feature1p/index.html.

Morris, Henry M. (1976), *The Genesis Record* (Grand Rapids, MI: Baker).

"The National Day to Prevent Teen Pregnancy" (2008), [On-line], URL: http://www.thenationalcampaign.org/national/default.aspx.

The New York Times Everyday Reader's Dictionary of Misunderstood, Misused, Mispronounced Words (1972), ed. Laurence Urdang (New York: Weathervane Books).

Nietzsche, Friedrich (2007 reprint), *Beyond Good and Evil* (Raleigh, NC: Hayes Barton Press), [On-line], URL: http://books.google.com/books?id=C7sRYOPWke0C&pg=PA1&source=gbs_selected_pages&cad=0_1#PPP1,M1.

Phillips, Stone (1994), *Interview with Jeffrey and Lionel Dahmer*, [On-line], URL: http://www.youtube.com/watch?v=IjW7bezdddE.

Provine, William (1998), "Evolution: Free Will and Punishment and Meaning in Life," [On-line], URL: http://eeb.bio.utk.edu/darwin/DarwinDayProvineAddress.htm.

Rachels, James (1990), *Created from Animals: The Moral Implications of Darwinism* (New York: Oxford University Press).

"Revisiting the Pianka/Ebola Flap" (2006), [On-line], URL: http://tim.2wgroup.com/blog/archives/001280.html.

Rodgers, Joann (2001), *Sex: A Natural History* (New York: Henry Holt).

Rogers, Jay (1990), "The Documented Effects of Pornography," *The Forerunner*, [On-line], URL: http://forerunner.com/forerunner/X0388_Effects_of_Pornograp.html.

Russell, Bertrand (1957), *Why I am not a Christian* (New York: Simon & Schuster).

Sartre, Jean Paul, (1961), "Existentialism and Humanism," *French Philosophers from Descartes to Sartre*, ed. Leonard M. Marsak (New York: Meridian).

Schippers, R. (1971), "*Telos*," *The New International Dictionary of New Testament Theology*, ed. Colin Brown (Grand Rapids, MI: Zondervan).

Silcox, Preston (no date), "The Church Promised and Prophesied," [On-line], URL: http://www.gospelpreceptor.com/SilcoxP5.htm.

Singer, Peter (1983), "Sanctity of Life, Quality of Life," *Pediatrics*, 72[1]:128-129.

Singer, Peter (2000), *Writings on an Ethical Life* (New York: Harper Collins).

Smith, Morton and R. Joseph Hoffman, eds. (1989), *What the Bible Really Says* (Buffalo, NY: Prometheus).

Spence, H.D.M. and J.S. Exell, eds. (no date), *The Pulpit Commentary: Genesis/Exodus* (Grand Rapids, MI: Eerdmans).

"Sticks and Stones, or, Jesus the Son of God Thumbs His Nose at God the Father" (no date), *Agnostic Review of Christianity*, [On-Line], URL: http://members.fortunecity.com/brad1/stick_stone.html.

Strobel, Lee (2000), *The Case for Faith* (Grand Rapids, MI: Zondervan).

Summy, Kenneth R. (2006), "Letter Addressed to President and Board of Directors of the Texas Academy of Science," [On-line], URL: http://www.geocities.com/tetrahedronomega/kenneth-summy- letter.html.

"Teen Dead Who Opened Fire on Finnish Classmates, Police Say" (2007), *CNN*, [On-line], URL: http://www.cnn.com/2007/WORLD/europe/11/07/school.shooting/ index.html.

"Teen Discussion Guide" (2008), [On-line], URL: http://www.stayteen.org/quiz/assets/2008_ND_teen_guide.pdf.

"Teenage and 60-Year-Old Mums are Consequences of Evolution" (2006), *European Society of Human Reproduction & Embryology*, [On-line], URL: http://www.eshre.com/emc.asp?pageId=795.

Templeton, Charles (1996), *Farewell to God* (Ontario, Canada: McClelland & Stewart).

Thompson, Bert and Brad Harrub (2004), "The Origin of Consciousness—Parts 1 & 2," [On-line], URL: http://www.apologeticspress.org/articles/498.

Thorn, Anton (2000), "An Unchanging God?," [On-line], URL: http://www.geocities.com/Athens/Sparta/1019/Unchanging_God.htm.

Thornhill, Randy and Craig T. Palmer (2000), *A Natural History of Rape* (Cambridge, MA: MIT Press).

Vander Lugt, Dan (2001), "Why Does the Bible Seem to Tolerate the Institution of Slavery?", [On-line], URL: http://www.gospelcom.net/rbc/questions/answer.php?catagory=bible&folde r=slavery&topic=Sla very&file=slavery.xml.

Vander Lugt, Herb (1999), *What Does the Bible Really Say about Slavery?* (Grand Rapids, MI: RBC Ministries).

Vine, W.E. (1940), *An Expository Dictionary of New Testament Words* (Westwood, NJ: Revell).

Warren, Thomas B. (1972), *Have Atheists Proved There Is No God?* (Ramer, TN: National Christian Press).

Warren, Thomas B. and Antony G.N. Flew (1977), *The Warren-Flew Debate* (Jonesboro, AR: National Christian Press).

Webster's Third New International Dictionary (1993), (Springfield, MA: Merriam-Webster).

Wells, Steve (2003), *Skeptic's Annotated Bible* [On-linc], URL: http://www.skepticsannotatedbible.com/1cor/index.html.

Wenham, G.J. (1979), *New International Commentary on the Old Testament: The Book of Leviticus* (Grand Rapids, MI: Eerdmans).

Wright, Christopher (1983), *An Eye for An Eye: The Place of Old Testament Ethics Today* (Downers Grove: IL: InterVarsity Press).